SCHOOL OF ORIENTAL AND AFRICAN STUDIES

UNIVERSITY OF LONDON

Jordan Lectures in Comparative Religion

XII

The Louis H. Jordan Bequest

The will of the Rev. Louis H. Jordan provided that the greater part of his estate should be paid over to the School of Oriental and African Studies to be employed for the furtherance of Studies in Comparative Religion, to which his life had been devoted. Part of the funds which thus became available was to be used for the endowment of a Louis H. Jordan Lectureship in Comparative Religion. The lecturer is required to deliver a course of six or eight lectures for subsequent publication. The first series of lectures was delivered in 1951.

JORDAN LECTURES 1976

The Encounter with the Divine in Mesopotamia and Israel

by

H. W. F. SAGGS

Professor of Semitic Languages, University College, Cardiff

UNIVERSITY OF LONDON

THE ATHLONE PRESS

1978

Published by
THE ATHLONE PRESS
UNIVERSITY OF LONDON
at 4 *Gower Street London* WCI
Distributed by Tiptree Book Services Ltd
Tiptree, Essex

USA and Canada
Humanities Press Inc
New Jersey

© *H.W. F. Saggs* 1978

0 485 17412 X

Printed in Great Britain by
WESTERN PRINTING SERVICES LTD
BRISTOL

In piam memoriam

W. G. S. 1864–1950
E. S. 1874–1959
H. W. S. 1894–1968
A. R. S. 1924–45

PREFACE

The religion of an obscure ancient Near Eastern people, the Israelites, continues to exercise a major influence upon the culture of much of the most developed parts of the world several millennia later. By contrast, religions associated with far more prominent contemporaries of the Israelites have vanished, if not wholly without a trace, at least to such an extent that vestigial survivals are recognizable only by the antiquarian scholar. These are plain facts. The explanation of the facts is a matter of theory, and theories there have been a-plenty. One theory, which certainly should not be ignored although it is not susceptible of investigation by scientific method, is that the one religion was true and the others false. There are a number of other theories that do not explicitly make this value judgement but assert that there are discernible some particular differences of approach, which serve to set Israelite religion on one side as unique; this book is principally concerned with looking comparatively at the data on Israelite and Mesopotamian religion to test the validity of some theories of this kind.

The chapters of this book represent substantially the text of the six Jordan Lectures which I had the honour to deliver at the School of Oriental and African Studies in summer 1975. To those in the School responsible for the invitation to give the lectures, and to those who showed their loyalty, or stamina, in attending the lectures, I record my sincere thanks. I also wish to thank all other members of the School and of the University of London who helped to make my return there such a pleasant occasion.

Advent 1975   H. W. F. S.

CONTENTS

ABBREVIATIONS

An author's name given alone, or with only key words from the book title, refers to an entry under that author in the Bibliography.

ABL	HARPER, R. F.
ABRT	CRAIG, J. A.
Acc. and Heb. Ps.	WIDENGREN, G.
AfO	*Archiv für Orientforschung*
AHw	SODEN, W. VON, *Handwörterbuch*
AKA	BUDGE, E. A. W. and KING, L. W.
AM	OPPENHEIM, A. L., *Ancient Mesopotamia*
AnBi	*Analecta Biblica*
Ancient Fragments	CORY, I. P.
ANET³	PRITCHARD, J. B.
AnSt	*Anatolian Studies*
ARM	*Archives Royales de Mari*
AS	*Assyriological Studies* (Oriental Institute of the University of Chicago)
Asarhaddon	BORGER, R.
Assurbanipal	STRECK, M., II. Teil
Atrahasis	LAMBERT, W. G. and MILLARD, A. R.
BA	*The Biblical Archaeologist*
BASOR	*Bulletin of the American Schools of Oriental Research*
BDB	BROWN, F. *et al.*
Berossos	SCHNABEL, P.
BG	HEIDEL, A., *Babylonian Genesis*
BHT	SMITH, SIDNEY
Bib	*Biblica*
Biblical Motifs	ALTMANN, A.
BIN	*Babylonian Inscriptions in the Collection of J. B. Nies*

BMS	KING, L. W., *Babylonian magic*
BWANT	*Beiträge zur Wissenschaft vom Alten und Neuen Testament*
BWL	LAMBERT, W. G.
BZAW	*Beiheft zur Zeitschrift für die alttestamentliche Wissenschaft*
CAD	OPPENHEIM, A. L. *et al.*, *Assyrian Dictionary*
CBQ	*Catholic Biblical Quarterly*
CCK	WISEMAN, D. J.
CH	Code of Hammurabi, as edited in DRIVER, G. R. and MILES, J. C.
Chron.	Book of Chronicles
CMHE	CROSS, F. M.
CT	Cuneiform Texts from Babylonian Tablets in the British Museum
*Cultic Prophet*²	JOHNSON, A. R., *Cultic Prophet*
DES	THOMPSON, R. C., *Devils*
Deut.	Book of Deuteronomy
Divination	RENCONTRE ASSYRIOLOGIQUE INTERNATIONALE
DJ	VOLZ, P.
Dreams	OPPENHEIM, A. L., *Interpretation of dreams*
En. El.	*Enūma Eliš*, as edited in LABAT, R.
Enki	BENITO, C.
Exod.	Book of Exodus
Ezek.	Book of Ezekiel
GAG	SODEN, W. VON, *Grundriss*
GAL	WRIGHT, W.
Gebete	KNUDTZON, J. A., *Assyrische Gebete*
Gen.	Book of Genesis
Genesis Comm.	RAD, G. VON, *Genesis*
Gilg.	Epic of Gilgamesh, as edited in THOMPSON, R. C., *Epic*

God of the Fathers	3–77 in ALT, A.
Götterepitheta	TALLQVIST, K.
Hab.	Book of Habakkuk
HAI	VAUX, R. DE
Handerhebung	EBELING, E., *Akkadische Gebetsserie*
Haupttypen	FALKENSTEIN, A.
HebCW	STADELMANN, L. I. J.
HG	ALBREKTSON, B.
HI	BRIGHT, J.
HIR	FOHRER, G.
Hos.	Book of Hosea
HR	*History of Religions* (Chicago)
HTR	*Harvard Theological Review*
HUCA	*Hebrew Union College Annual* (Cincinnati)
IAK	EBELING, E. *et al., Inschriften . . . Könige*
IEJ	*Israel Exploration Journal*
Inanna und Enki	FARBER-FLÜGGE, G.
IR	RINGGREN, H.
Isa.	Book of Isaiah
J	'Jahwist' source in Pentateuch
JAOS	*Journal of the American Oriental Society*
JBL	*Journal of Biblical Literature*
JCS	*Journal of Cuneiform Studies*
JEOL	*Jaarbericht van het Vooraziatisch-Egyptisch Genootschap 'Ex Oriente Lux'*
Jer.	Book of Jeremiah
JNES	*Journal of Near Eastern Studies*
Joh.	Gospel according to St. John
Josh.	Book of Joshua
JQR	*Jewish Quarterly Review*
JSS	*Journal of Semitic Studies*
JTS	*Journal of Theological Studies*
Jud.	Book of Judges

KAH	MESSERSCHMIDT, L., *Keilschrifttexte aus Assur historischen Inhalts.* 2 Hefte. (Hinrichs, Leipzig, 1911, 1922)
KAR	EBELING, E., *Keilschrifttexte*
KB	*Keilinschriftliche Bibliothek*
Kgs.	Book of Kings
KS	WINCKLER, H.
KSB	*Keilschriftbibliographie* (in, or as separatum from, OrNS)
Lev.	Book of Leviticus
LSS	*Leipziger semitistische Studien*
Lugale	GELLER, S.
MAD, No. 2	*Materials for the Assyrian Dictionary,* No. 2, = GELB, I. J., *Old Akkadian writing and grammar* (University of Chicago Press, second edition, 1961)
MAOG	*Mitteilungen der Altorientalischen Gesellschaft*
Maqlû	MEIER, G.
Mat.	Gospel according to St. Matthew
MAW	KRAMER, S. N. (ed.), *Mythologies*
MDOG	*Mitteilungen der Deutschen Orient-Gesellschaft*
MDP	*Mémoires de la Délégation en Perse.* (Paris, 1900–)
Mic.	Book of Micah
MIOF	*Mitteilungen des Instituts für Orientforschung* (Berlin)
MN	BOTTA, P.-E. *et al.*
MSL	*Materialien zum sumerischen Lexikon.* In progress. (Pontifical Biblical Institute, Rome, 1937–)
MT	Masoretic Text of Hebrew Bible
MVAG	*Mitteilungen der Vorderasiatisch-Ägyptischen Gesellschaft*

n.	footnote
Nah.	Book of Nahum
Namengebung	STAMM, J. J.
NBBU	EBELING, E., *Neubabylonische Briefe*
ND (plus number)	excavation number of cuneiform tablet from Nimrud
NEB	*The New English Bible* translation
Nergal	WEIHER, E. VON
Num.	Book of Numbers
OIP, II	LUCKENBILL, D. D., *Sennacherib*
OrAF	*Orientalia*, old series
OrNS	*Orientalia*, new series
OTI	EISSFELDT, O.
OTS	*Oudtestamentische Studiën*
OTT	RAD, G. VON, *Old Testament Theology*
Pantheon	DEIMEL, A., *Pantheon Babylonicum*
Patterns	ELIADE, M., *Patterns*
Priesthood	SABOURIN, L.
Prophecy	LINDBLOM, J.
Prophetic Conflict	CRENSHAW, J. L.
Ps.	Book of Psalms
Psalms	MOWINCKEL, S.
R	RAWLINSON, H. C., *The cuneiform inscriptions of Western Asia* (London, 1861–1909). IV R^2 = vol. 4, revised edition, 1891. V R = vol. 5, 1909
RA	*Revue d'assyriologie et d'archéologie orientale*
RAI	*Rencontre Assyriologique Internationale*, comptes rendus
Religion	LEEUW, G. VAN DER
RHR	*Revue de l'histoire des religions* (Paris)
Rit. Acc.	THUREAU-DANGIN, F., *Rituels accadiens*
RLA	EBELING, E. *et al.*, *Reallexikon*
RSO	*Rivista degli Studi Orientali*

RSV	The Bible in *Revised Standard Version*
SAHG	FALKENSTEIN, A. and SODEN, W. VON
Sam.	Book of Samuel
Sargon	LIE, A. G.
Satan	KLUGER, R. S.
Schöpfung	GUNKEL, H.
SKL	JACOBSEN, TH., *Sumerian King List*
ŠL	DEIMEL, A., *Šumerisches Lexikon*
SM	KRAMER, S. N., *Sumerian mythology*
Ssabier	CHWOLSOHN, D.
Sumerians	KRAMER, S. N., *The Sumerians*
Sup	supplement (to periodical series)
Šurpu	REINER, E.
Tammuz	JACOBSEN, Th., *Towards . . . image of Tammuz*
TAPS	*Transactions of the American Philosophical Society* (Philadelphia)
TCL, III	THUREAU-DANGIN, F., *Huitième campagne de Sargon*
ThOrAr	*Theologische und orientalistische Arbeiten*
TuL	EBELING, E., *Tod und Leben*
Türen	SALONEN, A., *Die Türen des alten Mesopotamien* (= Annales Academiae Scientiarum Fennicae, ser. B, tom. 124; Helsinki, 1961)
Untersuchungen	HIRSCH, H.
VAB	*Vorderasiatische Bibliothek*
Vom mesop. Menschen	KRAUS, F. R.
VT	*Vetus Testamentum*
WdM	HAUSSIG, H. W. (ed.)
Wisd.	Book of Wisdom of Solomon (in Apocrypha)
WO	*Die Welt des Orients*

WUS	AISTLEITNER, J.
WZJ	*Wissenschaftliche Zeitschrift der Friedrich-Schiller-Universität Jena*
YOS, 10	GOETZE, A.
ZA	*Zeitschrift für Assyriologie*
ZAW	*Zeitschrift für die alttestamentliche Wissenschaft*
Zech.	Book of Zechariah
Zeph.	Book of Zephaniah

CONVENTIONS

In biblical references, chapter and verse are given in the form 2:3. For consistency this has also been applied in quotations from other authors using a different system.

Unless otherwise stated, biblical quotations follow the NEB translation, except that 'the Lord' is not substituted where the original text has the divine name 'Yahweh'.

'Yahweh' is always so spelt, even in quotations from books which favour the hybrid German-English 'Jahweh'.

š and ḫ/ḥ are transcribed as sh and h, and ' and ' omitted, in words treated in the text as proper names, but these symbols are employed in words discussed as technical terms.

A Matter of Method

'There are basically two types of religion—our own, and the religions of other peoples.' This is an implicit premiss not unknown in the study of ancient Near Eastern religions. Not infrequently a 'we'–'they' dichotomy manifests itself in such studies, with Israelite religion, accepted as an element in the western cultural tradition, regarded as standing with us on one side of a dividing line; beyond that line stand those religions which are both strange and false. There is often an underlying attitude that scholars studying Israelite religion are investigating religious truths, whilst those studying Mesopotamian or other ancient Near Eastern religions are merely examining religious data. This well exemplifies the second alternative of a dictum by Radcliffe-Brown, that 'the usual way of looking at religions is to regard all of them, or all except one, as bodies of erroneous beliefs and illusory practices'.[1]

This attitude is exemplified in various ways. Sometimes it is explicit and related to theological judgements. Typically the Old Testament theologian claims that the events recorded in the Old Testament are moving between a revelation and a goal, and that he knows both the one and the other. A. B. Davidson, for example, defined Biblical Theology as 'the knowledge of God's great operation in introducing His kingdom among men, presented to our view exactly as it lies . . . in the Bible'.[2] Procksch holds that the full spiritual meaning of the Old Testament is only accessible to Christian faith, thereby specifically denying not only the validity but even the possibility of an objective approach.[3] For Sellin, 'Old Testament theology is only interested in the line which was fulfilled in the Gospel'.[4] But the theological claim for a division of religions into one (our own) true and the rest false is perhaps stated in its bluntest and most uncompromising form by G. E. Wright: 'The world is full of sacred literatures and it is full of gods. But in the vast confusion the one source which can be relied upon for the truth is the Bible.'[5]

All this is legitimate, provided the theological value judgements are recognized as such, and not passed off as religio-historical judgements. However, cases are not infrequent in which even the most distinguished scholars are guilty of blurring this distinction. Examples may be given from John Bright's *A history of Israel*, a widely used and in most respects excellent study of the subject. Dealing with the Patriarchs, after a valuable examination of their possible place within the historical framework of the Near East in the first half of the second millennium, the author concludes: 'Enough has been said to establish confidence that the Bible's picture of the patriarchs is deeply rooted in history. Abraham, Isaac, and Jacob stand in the truest sense at the beginning of Israel's history and faith.'[6] So far Professor Bright is making historical and religio-historical judgements. But then he proceeds: 'With them . . . there began that restless search for the fulfilment of promise which, though realized in the giving of land and seed, could never be satisfied with that gift, but, like a pointing finger through all the Old Testament, must guide to a city "whose builder and maker is God" (Heb. 11:10).'[6] The whole of this latter sentence is a theological value judgement, in no way derivable from the historical and religio-historical evidence just adduced.

An instance of the 'we'–'they' dichotomy in the same author's manner of presentation of data is seen in his discussion of law. Speaking of ancient Mesopotamia he says: 'The Sumerian had a developed sense of right and wrong; earthly laws were supposed to be a reflection of the laws of the god. . . Yet it must be said that, as is the case in all paganisms' [here we have the dichotomy explicitly stated] 'the Sumerian drew little distinction between moral and purely ritual offenses.'[7] Elsewhere Professor Bright deals with law in Israel, but here the data are summarized from a different point of view. He says: 'covenant law was a central factor in Israel's life from the beginning. . . Integral to the covenant form. . . were the stipulations that the divine Overlord laid upon his subjects. . . They defined the policy by which members of the community must regulate their actions both toward their God and toward one another.'[8]

The difference of presentation in the two cases is clear, and significant. In the case of the Sumerians, the author starts from the human sense of right and wrong. In the case of the Israelites, he inverts his approach. Although in the latter the basis of his argument is the purely human institution of the vassal treaty, he states the situation in a form which sees the reality as the divine covenant, with this as the source which gave rise to the human law and the Israelites' sense of right and wrong. As Professor Bright represents it, the Sumerians had a sense of right and wrong which ultimately gave rise to supposed divine laws; the Israelites, contrariwise, had divine laws, which ultimately gave rise to the Israelites' sense of right and wrong. This distinction is not founded on religio-historical judgement, but on the implicit theological premiss that Israelite religion was true and Sumerian religion false.[9]

Not infrequently one finds *ad hoc* general comparisons made between Israelite religion and other religions on the basis of prejudiced value judgements—prejudiced meaning not that the value judgements are necessarily wrong but that the decision precedes adequate consideration of all available evidence on both sides. Thus we find G. E. Wright writing: 'In the faith of Israel, even in the earliest preserved literature, there is a radical and complete difference [from ancient Near Eastern polytheism] at every significant point... It is impossible on any empirical grounds to understand how the God of Israel could have evolved out of polytheism.'[10] As will be shown later, by selective treatment of material it would be quite possible to arrive at the opposite and equally prejudiced value judgement, that Babylonian religion was more spiritual and noble than Israelite religion.[11]

Even where it is not claimed or assumed that Israelite religion is true and others false, in comparisons between Israelite and other religions it is an almost invariable procedure to begin by stating or assuming (as in the passage just quoted) that Israel was in religious matters distinctive (in the sense of unique) in its ancient Near Eastern context,[12] and then to seek for the particular details which

establish this postulated distinctiveness. As one scholar, who himself takes this approach, points out: 'it is practically impossible to
offer any clearly defined grounds for this view [of the distinctiveness of Israel] without raising a retort from some quarter that
other nations shared in the aspect claimed as distinctive'.[13] This
fact requires us to examine whether or not clear specific points of
distinctiveness did indeed exist. Part of the reason for so easily
arriving at the conclusion that Israelite religion was in a different
category from that of Mesopotamia may be that quite different
questions are put to the evidence. It would be methodologically
sounder, and might be more productive, not to assume any
difference between the religious culture of Israel and that of its
contemporaries beyond what can be proved, and to ask not 'how
was Israel distinctive?', but 'was Israel distinctive?'[14] Clearly,
Israelites themselves thought that their religion was uniquely true,
but this is equally the case with all minority religions: the adherents
of a minority religion who do not think it is unique have no
adequate cohesive force to overcome the powerful pressures
making for their assimilation into the surrounding majority
religion. Mandaeans, Yezidis, Shebeks and Samaritans in the
midst of Islam, Fundamentalist or Pentecostal Christian sects or
Mormons or followers of witchcraft cults in Europe and America,
all feel that they have a unique knowledge of religious truth. The
subjective feeling of possessing the one true revelation is not proof
of distinctiveness: thus, E. T. Clark, in his *The small sects in
America*, is able to group together, as basically similar, sects whose
members would face death rather than identify themselves with
other sects falling under the same classification.[15]

It might be argued that the distinctiveness of Israelite religion is
sufficiently established by the fact that it gave birth to, or assisted
in the birth of, three great monotheistic religions. This generative
or obstetric function does not in itself prove that Israelite religion
was distinctive in the sense of being unique. Hinduism has given
birth to, or assisted in the birth of, a number of other religions,
whilst the old Iranian religion gave birth to Zoroastrianism. It
would be difficult to maintain that primitive Hinduism or the old

Iranian religion was because of these facts distinctive in the sense in which scholars like to use this term of Israelite religion, implying uniquely true.

A proposal to compare aspects of two religions necessarily involves the premiss that it is possible, as an antecedent, to arrive at a significant understanding of each of them individually. In the case of Mesopotamian religion this premiss has been explicitly denied, both in general on epistemological principles, and in particular on the grounds of our inadequate knowledge of Mesopotamian religious literature at the present stage.

The general denial in principle is due to A. L. Oppenheim, an Assyriologist whose work has substantially contributed to the understanding of Assyro-Babylonian religion. His approach to this question, which is sociological and psychological rather than theological, shows an interesting modification of the 'we'–'they' dichotomy applied to the study of Mesopotamian religion. Oppenheim claims that there is such a conceptual gulf between modern man and the civilization of ancient Mesopotamia that it is impossible to attain sufficient empathy to achieve any significant penetration into the essentials of Mesopotamian religion. He specifically states his conviction that 'a systematic presentation of Mesopotamian religion cannot and should not be written'.[16]

Oppenheim justifies his view by an examination of particular difficulties in understanding Mesopotamian religion. The difficulties that he mentions are real ones, but they do not necessarily involve Oppenheim's agnostic conclusions. Although some of the difficulties he refers to would appear to be equally relevant to Israelite religion, he himself appears to find no conceptual barrier to the understanding of the essence of Israelite religion. Clearly, for Oppenheim Israelite religion stands on the 'we' side, and Mesopotamian religion on the 'they' side, of a dividing line.

Oppenheim's different attitudes to Mesopotamian and Israelite religion are related to his view of Mesopotamian civilization as a whole. His view of the latter is implicit in the sub-title of his important (and, in many ways, masterly) book *Ancient Meso-potamia*; this sub-title reads *Portrait of a dead civilization*. This succinctly summarizes the view that there is no continuum between Mesopotamian culture (including its religion) and any living culture; that—as Oppenheim puts it—the concepts of ancient Oriental religion are 'removed from us as if pertaining to another dimension'.[17] Oppenheim does not make it clear in what respects he considers the understanding of Mesopotamian religion to constitute a problem of a different kind from the understanding of any other religion—such as Greek, Roman, or Nordic—which has left no major living descendant; and, as already mentioned, his writings implicitly assume that we are positively equipped to understand the essence of Israelite religion.

Historically, it is difficult to accept a total absence of continuum in conceptual links between ancient Mesopotamia and the present. Leaving aside the very disputable ground of whether or not the concepts of Mesopotamian religion are in any respects preserved in such minority religions as those of the Mandaeans[18] and Yezidis, it is possible to argue that Israelite religion itself serves as a conceptual link.

It is not reasonable to maintain that there was a total conceptual barrier between Yahwism and the religions of contemporary non-Israelite peoples. The whole history of the struggle of the Israelite prophets with syncretism shows that to the ordinary Israelite there was no fixed boundary between Yahwism and those cults of his contemporaries which we refer to as pagan, and that other cults and religious practices and concepts could easily be accepted into the framework of Yahwism. This indicates that in the monarchy period in Israel there was a horizontal (or, if one prefers the term, synchronic) continuum from Israelite Yahwism into the religions of the Canaanites and of Assyria and Babylonia.

Apart from this general consideration, some particular points may be taken into account. Significant here is an instance of a Yahwist pretending to be a Baalist. The usurping king Jehu, a fanatical Yahwist, on pretence of taking part in a Baal ritual summoned all the Baal cult functionaries to a temple where he intended to butcher them in cold blood, and was able to go through all the preliminary motions of preparing for a Baal ritual without arousing any suspicion, in any of the hundreds of experts in Baalist cult practices assembled there, that he was an impostor.[19] This deception could only have been carried through if there was no marked difference in the ordinary way of life to indicate at once whether a man was a Yahwist or a Baalist, and no significant cultic differences such that a man might betray himself as a Yahwist by ignorance of some detail of Baalist cult practice.

There is other specific biblical evidence of a conceptual continuum between Yahwism and other contemporary religions. The religion of senior Assyrian officials at the time of Hezekiah was certainly not 'removed from [that of Judah] as if pertaining to another dimension'.[20] This is clear from part of the proclamation attributed in 2 Kgs. 18:22-5 to the Assyrian General, speaking outside Jerusalem at its siege in 701 B.C. The proclamation credits the Assyrian official not only with knowledge of the recent cultic reforms in Judah, but also with insights of the conclusions which might well have been drawn from these by many of the Judaean population.[21] Undoubtedly, in terms of value judgement, the editor of the Books of Kings regarded his own religion as true and that of the Assyrian General as false; but equally, it is clear that he accepted that sufficient common ground existed between the religious concepts of the Assyrians and those of the Judaeans for effective communication of ideas to be possible in this sphere.

Further examples can be offered. The post-exilic Book of Jonah presupposes that the religion of Nineveh, though false and different from that of Israel, was not different in a way that would justify a prophet in seeing a conceptual barrier. Deutero-Isaiah, despite his damning condemnation of Babylonian idolatry, which was a matter of value judgement, gives no indication of supposing that non-Israelites thought on religious matters in a dimension essentially different from that of Israelites; positive proof that he did not so regard non-Israelites is made clear by the affinity he recognized with Cyrus, although he specifically mentions that Cyrus did not know Yahweh,[22] and although Cyrus himself had sufficient empathy with Babylonian cults to extend the same tolerance to them that he did to Yahwism.[23]

There was thus demonstrably a horizontal continuum between the religious concepts of Israel and those of Assyria and Babylonia. It follows, therefore, in view of the indisputable vertical continuum between Israelite religion and modern Judaism and Christianity (and, less markedly, Islam), that the conceptual barrier between ancient Mesopotamian and modern religious thought need not be as absolute as Oppenheim supposed.

St. Paul, and later Christian theologians also, saw pre-Christian paganism as foreshadowing Christian truth and thus as not different in category. It is true that the particular evidence for St. Paul relates to Greece, but this was at a time when Greek religion had been much exposed to oriental influences, and there is no reason to think that Greek religion at the time of St. Paul was different in category from the religions of Asia Minor, Anatolia, Syria and Mesopotamia. A point St. Paul made to the Athenians was this:

As I was going round looking at the objects of your worship, I noticed among other things an altar bearing the inscription 'To an Unknown God'. What you worship but do not know—this is what I now proclaim. (Acts 17:23.)

Removing the value judgement from this, it leaves the view that the phenomena of pre-Christian paganism are of the same category as those of early Christianity. St. Paul was followed in this attitude by Clement of Alexandria, who accepted that pre-Christian philosophies and religions, including the worship of celestial bodies, were preparations for the fuller revelation. 'There is one river of Truth, but many streams fall into it on this side and on that.'[24] In the view of St. Paul and Clement the concepts of ancient Near Eastern religions, of which Mesopotamian religion was a part, are not (in Oppenheim's phrase) 'removed from us as if pertaining to another dimension'.

It is also relevant to this question that there were both overlaps and direct contacts between early Christianity and late survivals of Mesopotamian-influenced paganism in Syria. Thus, the worship of specifically Assyrian deities with festivals at the same dates as in the New Assyrian period continued at least until the beginning of

the third century A.D.[25] This does not of course in itself prove that
the old Assyrian ideas were understood by Christians; but since
the old and the new existed contemporaneously within the same
general society, it does point to the probability that there was not
a total discontinuity between the two complexes of religious
concepts. This point is put beyond doubt by the fact that many
converts to Christianity came from pagan backgrounds, and some
of them from areas of paganism where beliefs and practices of
the old Mesopotamian religion survived, so that they would certainly have been familiar with both groups of concepts. Gregory
Thaumaturgus, speaking of the education he received under
Origen at Caesarea, is quite specific about Christian knowledge of
non-Christian religious ideas. He attests: 'No subject was forbidden us. . . We were allowed to become acquainted with every
doctrine, barbarian or Greek.'[26] Isaac of Antioch in the fifth
century knew of the continuing practice of a Tammuz cult and
the worship of the stars,[27] and corresponding evidence is found in
not a few other patristic authors. References of this kind indicate
that though the pagan survivals were rejected as false, they were
not felt by early Christians to be conceptually incomprehensible
and in a different dimension.

One sometimes finds in writers of the early Christian centuries
quite detailed data about Mesopotamian religion. Thus the
Neoplatonist Damascius, of the fifth and sixth centuries A.D., gives
a quite accurate account, with comments, of the theogony found
in the Babylonian creation myth *Enūma Eliš*. He writes:

The Babylonians, like the rest of the barbarians, pass over in silence the
One principle of the universe, and they constitute two, Tauthe and
Apason; making Apason the husband of Tauthe, and denominating her
the mother of the gods. And from these proceeds an only-begotten son,
Moymis, which I conceive is no other than the intelligible world
proceeding from the two principles. From them, also another progeny
is derived, Lache and Lachus;[28] and, again, a third, Kissare and Assorus,
from which last three others proceed—Anus, Illinus and Aus. And of
Aus and Dauce is born a son called Belus, who, they say, is the fabricator
of the world, the Demiurge.[29]

Here there is not only a statement of the mythological tradition, but also an interpretation of it. It could be argued that our evaluation of the interpretation of the myth rests upon the assumption that we ourselves have more than a superficial understanding of it, and this point would be valid; it is, however, significant that Damascius gives no indication of finding a conceptual barrier in his examination of Babylonian religion of a different order from that found when examining Orphism or the theogonies in Homer and Hesiod, which are discussed in adjoining sections.

Such considerations admit the possibility that modern scholars may be able not only to learn the superficial details of Meso-potamian myths and rituals, which is virtually all that Oppenheim would grant, but also to enter to some significant extent into an effective understanding of the underlying religious concepts. Indeed, were this not a possibility, much of the earlier research of Oppenheim himself on Assyro-Babylonian religion would have to be dismissed as no more than inspired speculation.

A second and distinct type of objection has been raised against offering any synthesis of Mesopotamian religion at the present time. This objection rests on the alleged impropriety of employing the abundant textual evidence available upon Mesopotamian religion without a detailed form-critical study of the sources, which, with minor exceptions, has not yet been undertaken. Any attempt to view a Mesopotamian religious text within a wider setting than its own immediate context tends, whatever its other merits, to be condemned for such deficiencies. Thus, a number of attempts have been made to compare biblical Psalms and Sumero-Akkadian texts, and the scholars concerned have been severely criticized for this on the ground that 'they tend to exempt the Mesopotamian material from the very *Gattungsforschung* [form criticism] which, following Gunkel, they accept as axiomatic for Hebrew psalmody'.[30]

However, important as form criticism (and, indeed, traditio-historical method) undoubtedly is in any research on ancient literary material, in relative importance it can in frequent instances be less significant in connection with Mesopotamian than with Israelite textual material. There is an important difference in the form in which the literary material reaches us from the two sides. The Old Testament material all comes to us from the same chronological point of transmission, and it is only from internal evidence that we can date the period and circumstances of origin of particular texts: a vital technique (though not the only technique) for this purpose is form criticism. With the Mesopotamian material the situation can in a number of respects be quite different. Very often a religious text is accurately dated (at least as to *terminus ante quem*, less commonly as to original date of composition) by stratification or colophon or epigraphic considerations or all three. The discovery of earlier and later editions of a text, which is not infrequent, can give direct information upon its literary history. Association of, for example, a prayer with a ritual, will explicitly give the *Sitz im Leben* of a religious composition. Thus, in the Mesopotamian situation it can happen that we are directly given the data which might otherwise only have been obtainable by form criticism.

Even apart from the foregoing consideration, it is not self-evident that Gunkel's *Gattungsforschung* method and its traditio-historical developments are prerequisites for every aspect of research into either Israelite or Mesopotamian religion. The basic object of form criticism, as applied to the study of Old Testament religion, is to discover the *Sitz im Leben* of compositions used in the cult. It is evident that the information this provides can tell us a great deal about the history of the use of a text at particular times and in a particular form. What is not evident is that nothing of value for the study of religion can be learnt from the text without such information. As a familiar example, one may consider the Decalogue. A great deal of form-critical analysis has been undertaken in relation to its own form and the form of its framework, and certainly a number of form-critical (as well as other) problems arise. Thus: is the Decalogue set within a vassal-treaty *Gattung*, and if so, of what period? Is it related to the Theophany *Gattung*? But when all this has been considered, the fact still remains that the

Ten Commandments give us information about Israelite religious concepts irrespective of the text-category in which they are set. The Ten Commandments comprise prescriptions about the activity of man in relation to God and fellow-man, whether these were of divine or human origin being irrelevant for the immediate point. To be committed to writing they had to be put into a particular text-category; but whilst the category chosen may well give us information about the social and historical context in which the formulation was fixed, the religious significance of the prescriptions may be substantially grasped without this knowledge.

Old Testament form critics, from Gunkel himself to the present time, have made quite considerable use, in the study of Israelite religious literature, of Assyro-Babylonian and other ancient Near Eastern material, without prior form-critical study of these sources.[31] There would appear to be an inconsistency in making the implicit assumption that knowledge of the Assyro-Babylonian (or other ancient Near Eastern) material is adequate to allow it to be used comparatively as a basis for Old Testament form-critical research, whilst asserting that it is not adequate for it to be studied in relation to its own contents, without prior fulfilment of the impossible condition of a form-critical study of all its texts. Whilst, as an ideal, it might be desirable, in the study of any aspect of Mesopotamian or Israelite religion, to have available a full form-critical treatment of all texts in any way related to the problem, this provides no justification for neglecting what can be done by phenomenological method with textual material already available.[32]

There is another consideration bearing upon the use of form criticism in the study of religion. The objective of the form-critical method is the analysis of religious literature and the understanding of its function in particular settings. Whilst this may, and does, produce useful data for the study of religion, it is not in itself directly concerned with religion, but with the significantly different subject religious literature. The conclusion one draws from this distinction will depend upon one's understanding of the nature of religion, and the relative importance one attaches to its main elements—beliefs, cultic practices, personal behaviour and social patterns. In the study of religion, the ultimate desideratum (whether or not it is actually achievable) is not merely to get back to the setting of the religious literature in the cult, but to get behind the religious literature to the attitudes and concepts to which it originally gave expression. The quest for the original sense of a passage has been derided as purely subjective,[33] but this judgement is itself subjective, and based on the unproved assumption that texts which exist in the cult reflect nothing but the cult. Yet unless one regards cultic practices alone as primary and the other elements of religion as derived, there is no reason to deny *prima facie* that some parts of religious literature now found in the cult may have grown out of other elements and not have originated in the cult, even though they have since come to be expressed in a particular way within that framework. There are no irrefutable grounds for denying the possibility that some passages now in cultic texts might have had *Sitze im Leben* in a personal situation before their *Sitze im Leben* in the cultic or literary situation in which they are finally found. Any manifestation of religion in the form of a religious text must have come in the first place (to use the terminology of Paul Radin) in answer to a psychical crisis within a religious man.[34] That this was subsequently shared by what Radin calls 'the indifferently religious' in a community group-setting (that is, in a cultic setting or eventually in a literary setting) does not invalidate the possibility that it may originally have expressed a religious attitude or belief independently of the cult. The reason that certain texts were incorporated into and lived on in the cult is that they gave coherent expression to the deepest religious emotions of the religiously inarticulate masses.

This has a bearing on Oppenheim's use of the form-critical argument in relation to the evidential value of Mesopotamian prayers for the study of Mesopotamian religion. Oppenheim pointed out that such prayers 'are always linked to concomitant rituals' and argued that 'to interpret the prayers without regard to the rituals in order to obtain insight into the religious concepts they may reflect distorts the testimony'.[35] He went on to say that 'the wording of the prayer exhibits a limited number of invocations, demands and complaints, and expressions of thanksgiving', but 'such material . . . does not contain much information for our area of inquiry'.

What is given inadequate consideration by Oppenheim (and by Mowinckel in a corresponding argument for Hebrew Psalms[36]) is that even the most conventional phrases of Akkadian prayers and Hebrew Psalms themselves represent concepts that were either currently accepted or—allowing for changes in concept alongside conservatism in form—had been generally accepted at a rather earlier period. Even the most stereotyped phrase was not in origin meaningless, and its form, or its place in a particular *Gattung*, does not make its testimony irrelevant for the original occurrence of the concept, whatever usage that phrase may have come to have in the *Gattung* or however emptied it may have become of meaning. A simple illustration of this may be given from English. There is a phrase 'suffered under Pontius Pilate', which is never heard other than in the Creed *Gattung*, and there is another—the expletive 'Zounds!', elliptical for 'by God's wounds!'—which occurs only as a conscious archaism in historical novels. Both phrases, however, contain testimony to an aspect of Christian belief—the passion of the incarnate God in Jesus Christ. The form in which the words are preserved depends upon the particular text-categories, but the ideas the words convey (or once conveyed), and their testimony for Christian belief, are in no way dependent upon nor related to the text-category. The place of a document in a cultic or other text is not necessarily the indispensable key to the meaning of that text to the worshipper. The *Gattung* is the framework in which the idea is preserved, not necessarily the setting in which it was created.

Comparisons between Israelite and Mesopotamian religion have a long history, though the purpose of the earlier instances was purely polemic. The first attested comparison was by the anonymous prophet whom we know as Deutero-Isaiah. For him, on one hand stood a religion worshipping the true God who 'sits throned on the vaulted roof of the earth', who had 'weighed the mountains on a balance, and the hills on a pair of scales', and to whom 'nations are but drops from a bucket', and on the other a religion centred on idols cut out of trees—and not even sacred trees at that, but trees of which the part left over from making a god might be used as fuel to cook a meal.[37] Deutero-Isaiah's invective was splendid but his comparison was methodologically unsound. He was highly selective in his evidence; he presented the data in a manner which made him guilty of conscious distortion;[38] and he placed a phenomenological description of Mesopotamian religion alongside a theological description of Yahwism. A Babylonian could, by using corresponding methodology, without any distortion of data, have turned the tables on Deutero-Isaiah.[39] The Babylonian might have pointed out that for several centuries Yahweh, after emerging from the obscurity of a remote desert, had lived inside, or at the least in close association with, a decorated chest made of acacia wood.[40] He was of rather uncertain temper, but in the main could be kept good-humoured by regular offerings of the smoke of burnt beef fat, of which he was inordinately fond. In contrast, Marduk was a spiritual being, creator of heaven and earth, and so transcendent that it was impossible to see or to comprehend him.[41] He was indeed so vast that he filled the universe, so that the Babylonian in his prayer to the god could say: 'The underworld is your basin, the sky of Anu your censer.'[42] Of another Babylonian god it was said: 'He wears the heavens on his head like a turban; he is shod with the underworld as with sandals.'[43]

Deutero-Isaiah's representation of the religions of other peoples in terms solely of the worship of anthropomorphic idols was indeed a travesty. It would have been recognized as such by earlier Israelites, who well knew that the non-Israelite concept of deity was neither limited to images, nor essentially anthropomorphic. This is clear from Deut. 4:19, where it is specifically stated that the objects of worship allotted by Yahweh to other peoples included the sun, moon and stars; not only were these not anthropomorphic in themselves, but in this context, where the Israelite is warned against lifting his eyes to heaven and being drawn away to the worship of these objects, they were not even thought of as worshipped through the medium of an anthropomorphic representation.

Deutero-Isaiah's approach is reflected in later Jewish writings, for example, in the apocryphal Letter of Jeremiah, which deals with the Babylonian cultus with equal hostility and more detail. It gives indications of being the work of a writer with some personal knowledge of the cultus as well as of some of the scandals alleged against the Babylonian hieratic personnel.[44]

The author of the Wisdom of Solomon, though not specifically dealing with Mesopotamian religion, took up and elaborated Deutero-Isaiah's satire on idolatry.[45] He went beyond Deutero-Isaiah, however, in offering an interesting suggestion about the origin of idol-worship. His hypothesis involved a form of euhemerism, in which the concept of the god developed from the grief of a bereaved father over a lost child.[46]

In the literature of the early centuries of the Christian era there occur, in classical and Patristic writers and their Jewish, Neoplatonist and Gnostic contemporaries, occasional comments on or allusions to ancient Mesopotamian beliefs and practices, sometimes in the form of a comparison with Jewish and Christian ideas. Aristides, for example, made an enquiry into the religious beliefs of idolaters, Jews and Christians, dividing the idolaters into Chaldaeans—that is, representatives of ancient Mesopotamian religion—Greeks and Egyptians.[47] Comparisons of this kind were, however, predominantly with polemic intent.[48]

Data from ancient paganism, including classical reports on Mesopotamian religion, were still being adduced comparatively by Protestant writers in the early post-Reformation period, now largely with the polemic purpose of equating Roman Catholicism with ancient pagan practices.[49] The scientific comparative study of ancient religions cannot be considered to have been initiated until the appearance of G. Meiners' *Allgemeine kritische Geschichte der Religionen*, published at Hanover in 1806. At that time Meiners had, of course, no data on Mesopotamian religion other than what could be gleaned from biblical and classical sources. Of particular and continuing importance in his work is an observation made on the first page:

All religions may have as many particularities as they wish; none the less, it is quite certain that any religion is similar to other religions in many more features than those in which it differs from them.

Significant new information about ancient Mesopotamian civilization, and ancient Mesopotamian religion as an aspect of it, began to appear with Assyrian excavations in the 1840s, particularly those of Austen Henry Layard, in which the recovery of Assyrian bas-reliefs and sculptures was prominent. At first the religious interest in these was not for their bearing on ancient Mesopotamian religion itself but for the light the new discoveries would throw on the Bible. A cynical friend of Layard wrote to him to say:

The interest about your stones is very great, I hear—and if you can as I before said attach a Biblical importance to your discoveries you will come the complete dodge over this world of fools and dreamers: you can get some religious fellow to inspire you with the necessary cant, for which I won't think a bit the worse of you.[50]

The subsequent history of the comparative study of Israelite and ancient Near Eastern religion has been well summarized by Vriezen,[51] and need not be repeated here. It may, however, additionally be noted that far more has been written to explain Mesopotamian religion through the Old Testament, or the Old Testament through Mesopotamian religion, than in comparison of them as two partly contemporary religious systems of the ancient Near East.[52]

The evidence available on the nature of ancient religion differs significantly between Mesopotamia and Israel; the difference involves not only the content of the evidence but also the factors underlying the very existence of the evidence. For Israelite religion, it is generally recognized that the biblical evidence—which is by far the major part of the evidence available to us—is neither a complete collection of all Israelite religious literature nor a random miscellany. It is on the one hand incomplete, and on the other selective and tendentious. As Eissfeldt put it, the corpus of the Old Testament is 'an entity which has come into being within the development of a particular political and religious history'.[53] To at least some degree it has been subject to conscious religious censorship. Much of it has been edited, and all of it scrutinized to decide what should be canonical, by men who were more interested in prescribing what Israelite religion should have been than in describing what it was, although details of the rejected reality are often reported for their bearing upon the unachieved ideal.

For Mesopotamian religion, the vast quantity of relevant cuneiform textual material has been subject to the accidents of archaeological discovery in a way that the Israelite evidence has not. It is self-evident that the random nature of archaeological discovery may result in gaps in the evidence and false emphases, but it might be supposed that in compensation this circumstance would ensure that the sources which actually become available to us would be free from deliberate distortion and suppression. The latter is not, however, wholly the case. There are many series of texts which have been edited into a standard form, which was clearly regarded as authoritative, so that the term 'canonical' may properly be applied to it.[54] In a number of cases archaeology has recovered for us earlier discarded forms of texts, which, when compared with their 'canonical' successors, enable us to recognize that certain concepts had in the course of time been suppressed, added, or modified. Clearly deliberate changes had been made, and some of these changes can be seen either to reflect modifications of religious concepts or to conceal older concepts later felt to be offensive. There is traceable, in fact, the same process which produced the canonical form of the Old Testament. However, whereas in the Old Testament material the editing process has left relatively few relics (though many indications) of older rejected stages, in the Mesopotamian material we possess in a number of cases, by the accident of random archaeological discovery, documentation for successive stages in the changes in concepts and emphasis. Thus, for example, it has been shown that after 1000 B.C. the god Ashur played a markedly less prominent part in Assyrian religion, outside the official state cult, than earlier.[55] Ishtar, earlier venerated as goddess connected with sexuality, was in the first-millennium recension of the *Gilgamesh Epic* grossly mocked for her libertine behaviour.[56] A very clear example of change of emphasis has been pointed out by Oppenheim in the ritual for covering with a bull's hide a kettledrum which was important in the cult; in an earlier form of the ritual the slain bull was treated as if it was a god and its killing sacrilegious; in a later form of the ritual, this tension concerning the bull had disappeared.[57]

It is commonly recognized that some biblical texts are tendentious and that their statements need to be interpreted in a certain historical, political, social or religious context. As obvious examples, one may instance certain traditions relating to Bethel, or to Aaron.[58] It is necessary to recognize that factors of a corresponding kind may have underlain the form of some Mesopotamian texts. A notable instance is a text of the time of Sennacherib which describes the trial and condemnation of Marduk; here Babylonian mythological concepts were being deliberately distorted for political ends.[59] Much earlier, in the twenty-fourth century B.C., there had been a deliberate creation of syncretism between Ishtar and the Sumerian goddess Inanna for the purpose of allowing the Semitic Sargon of Agade to claim dominion over Sumerian city states.[60]

The occurrence of conscious religious censorship within the Mesopotamian literary tradition is suggested by the fact that some major concepts found in early texts have no reflection in later ones: a striking case in point is adduced by E. Reiner, who in the conclusion to an interesting study on 'The etiological myth of the "Seven Sages"' (the latter being primeval culture-heroes), suggests that 'the scribes deliberately suppressed a cycle dealing with those human beings who, at one time or other of history . . . revolted against the gods'.[61] Again, Oppenheim adduces evidence which leads him to postulate 'the existence of . . . cult organizations in Mesopotamia . . . based on secret teachings . . .';[62] the evidence offered is both scattered and scanty, but if Oppenheim's insight is sound here, the absence of more detailed and extensive data on these must be due either to the secrecy of the members of such esoteric organizations, or to suppression at the hands of scribes concerned with the official cultus. In either case, the consequence is that the data at our disposal about the totality of Mesopotamian religion have in this area been subject to censorship.

An attitude of religious authoritarianism is also found in some circumstances in Mesopotamia. This, which might well have lent itself in literary aspects to religious censorship, is shown by reports, from the side of what might be called the religious establishment, of successfully contained attempts to introduce changes into the cultus; the most notable instance is the vigorous opposition to the attempted reforms of Nabonidus, reported in the 'Verse Account of Nabonidus'.[63]

Nabonidus, in the middle of the sixth century B.C., had attempted to introduce into Babylon a new cult based on the worship of the Moon-god, described by his opponents in these terms:

. . . he formed a phantom;
He formed the image of a god that no one had ever seen in the land;
He set it on a dais within the temple;
. . . he called its name 'Moon-god'.

The form of this novel god, said the religious establishment, was wholly unprecedented, and by that fact, wrong:

> The god Ea-Mummu could not have fashioned it;
> Not even the sage Adapa knew the name of that thing.

The establishment therefore welcomed the Persian conqueror Cyrus, who defeated Nabonidus and restored the old order:

The images of Babylon, male and female, Cyrus brought back to their shrines;
. . .

Whatever Nabonidus had created, Cyrus made the fire consume.

The Nabonidus incident does not stand alone. There are, for

example, hints in an inscription of Sargon II of Assyria, over a century and a half earlier, that his immediate predecessor Shalmaneser V had attempted to introduce cult changes in the city of Ashur, which had encountered violent and successful opposition.[64] Such evidence shows, on the one hand, that there were religious views current differing from those of the ancient establishment, and on the other, that there were limits to the tolerance commonly ascribed to ancient polytheistic systems. On the latter point, it is to be noted that, at Sennacherib's rape of Babylon, we have reference to his troops bringing out the gods of the city and smashing them,[65] whilst in the middle of the seventh century Ashurbanipal deliberately desecrated Elamite holy places.[66]

Not only does the nature of the evidence differ as between Mesopotamia and Israel, but also there is sometimes seen a tendentiously selective treatment of the evidence from the two areas.

In any study involving examination of the nature of Israelite religion, there is the danger, because so many scholars (including the present writer) accept it as the living root of their own religion, of making a deliberate selection of evidence from the total evidence, treating that part of the evidence which meets with approval as alone representing 'true' Yahwism[67] and the features found objectionable as false or corrupt Yahwism or contamination imported from something which was never any part of Yahwism at all. The justification claimed, or tacitly assumed, when this is done is that authoritative biblical writers themselves rejected certain elements of popular Israelite worship as not true Yahwism. But it was not, with rare exceptions, the purpose of such writers to offer historical judgements as to whether or not such elements had ever been found inside Yahwism; their objective was prescriptive, not descriptive. They were explicitly offering theological value judgements as to whether certain rejected features ought to be present within Yahwism, and in most instances their criticisms make it clear that as an historical fact the element in question either was, or had been, present there. To give a notorious example, though cult prostitution was not a part of what the

Deuteronomist school regarded as normative Yahwism, it was certainly—on the testimony of that school itself—a part of the cultus at the principal Yahwist shrine until the reign of Josiah.[68] To obtain a valid picture for comparison, it is Yahwism as it was (the Yahwism of historical fact), not Yahwism as it should have been (the Yahwism of theological judgement), nor Yahwism as it ultimately became in consequence of the repression of certain features, that we must consider.

The elitist Deuteronomist writers had a clear picture of what they felt Yahwism should be, and this is sometimes projected on to the evidence to give a false—or at least incomplete—picture of what Yahwism in practice really was. Against the centralization advocated by the Deuteronomist school, it is clear that (at least until the action taken by Hezekiah or Josiah) there were many local shrines where burnt offerings and a cult were directed not to Baal but to Yahweh.[69] Despite the prohibition of images, not only is it accepted that there were golden calves installed at Bethel and Dan by Jeroboam I, but also it is clear that acceptance of them was not restricted to those kings wholeheartedly condemned by the Deuteronomists. The fanatical Yahwist Jehu, with the dour Rechabite Jehonadab as his ally, accepted the golden calves in the cultus at Bethel and Dan.[70] They must also have accepted an Asherah (a sacred object associated with a goddess and implying a polytheistic background) in Samaria, since one existed there in the reign of Jehu's son Jehoahaz, and the manner in which it is mentioned is against any suggestion that Jehoahaz was an innovator in this respect.[71] Similarly Joash of Israel, in the last third of the ninth century, was not only supported by the prophet Elisha,[72] but also regarded as a good king in Deuteronomist tradition;[73] there is no implication that the golden calves which Joash allowed to remain at Bethel and Dan offended the good Yahwist Elisha. Whilst the prevailing view in current biblical scholarship is that the golden calves were not representations of a deity, but rather thrones for an invisible deity, there must be taken into consideration not only the biblical accusation that the people of the northern kingdom 'feared other gods' (2 Kgs. 17:7) and 'went after false gods' (2 Kgs. 17:15), but also some extra-biblical data bearing on the matter. Amongst the booty listed as taken from Samaria in 721 B.C., Sargon II of Assyria included 'the gods in whom they trusted'.[74] Whatever tendentious elements there may have been in statements made by biblical writers about the cultus in Samaria, it is unlikely that the Assyrians, who possessed not only representations of their gods but also such subsidiary images as *kuribu* ('cherubim') and winged bulls and lions, would have mistaken mere specimens of these latter classes for gods, particularly as their own gods were predominantly anthropomorphic and not theriomorphic.

Even in the Temple at Jerusalem there stood, uncontested until the end of the eighth century, both an Asherah (not attributed nor attributable to Ahaz)[75] and a bronze snake-image,[76] the latter of such thorough-going acceptance by Yahwists until the time of Hezekiah that it was attributed to Moses himself. In the northern kingdom there were, quite apart from the golden calves at Bethel and Dan, images at Yahweh's local shrines:[77] the Yahwism-as-it-should-have-been school attributes these to Baalism, but the whole weight of the biblical evidence makes it clear that these were regarded by the worshippers as part of the cult of Yahweh, not of a separate deity Baal, who had his own distinct temples and shrines.[78] Moreover, it cannot be claimed that images were limited to the northern kingdom, for there is a specific statement that they existed in Judah at the time of Josiah; they are mentioned along with teraphim, with nothing to support the common assumption that they had been introduced by Manasseh and belonged to a cult other than that of Yahweh.[79] Even human sacrifice was practised in Jerusalem, presumably—in the eyes of the devotees—to Yahweh, since Jeremiah found it necessary to deny that this had been commanded by Yahweh.[80]

A different aspect of selectivity in comparisons between Israelite and Mesopotamian data may occur in relation to texts which in the course of time had been subject to a change of interpretation, without any significant modification in the wording. There is a tendency for such changes of interpretation to be insisted upon in relation to the Old Testament, but disregarded for the assyriological evidence. This has the consequence of making it easy to present a specious contrast between the supposedly backward and earthy Mesopotamian religion and the pure and spiritual religion of Israel. An example may be seen in relation to food-offerings to deities. In the Old Testament the regular description applied to a burnt-offering was 'a whole-offering, a food-offering of soothing odour to Yahweh' (Lev. 1:9 et passim). The Oxford Annotated RSV hastens to preclude any objectionable conclusions from the literal sense of the term 'soothing odour' (or, as RSV renders it, 'pleasing odour'), by a note explaining the phrase as 'a traditional expression for an offering acceptable to God'. This is accurate, if one is thinking of Israelite religion at the time of the canonical prophets, since by that period the phrase had certainly become (at least in elitist circles) emptied of physical connotations. But equally certainly, the phrase had at an earlier period in Israel borne the literal sense. Num. 28:2 makes Yahweh call the fire-offering *laḥmi* 'my food' (although in NEB this is arbitrarily emended out of existence), whilst in four places in Lev. 21 and 22 the offerings made by the priests are unequivocally called 'the food of their God' (Lev. 21:6, 8, 17; 22:25).

Distortion arises when synchronous comparisons are made between Mesopotamian religion and Israelite religion, taking the Mesopotamian terminology literally but the Israelite as emptied of literal content, without recognition of the fact that similar processes to eliminate the more grossly physical concepts of deity were at work in both religions. Thus, conclusions have at times been drawn about the primitiveness of Mesopotamian religion from the incident, at the end of the Flood story in the *Gilgamesh Epic*, in which the gods, smelling the sweet savour of the sacrifice provided by the surviving hero, clustered round him like flies.[81] In fact, it is likely that, at the period of the recension containing this phrase, the passage was not a reflection of crude physical imagery at all, but on the contrary a sophisticated 'secularizing', mocking at earlier crude ideas.[82]

Another possible distorting factor in the examination of ancient religions, particularly Israelite religion, needs to be taken into account. Radcliffe-Brown has pointed out that 'in European countries, and more particularly since the Reformation, religion has come to be considered as primarily a matter of belief'; he criticizes such an approach on the ground that 'the rites and the justifying or rationalizing beliefs develop together as parts of a coherent whole'.[83] The approach criticized is not uncommon in the study of Israelite religion, and the influential Lutheran theologian G. von Rad goes even beyond this in treating Israelite religion not even as a matter of religio-historical beliefs but wholly as a system of doctrines; he defines 'the religion of the people of Israel' as 'the special features in her conception of God, . . . the way in which Israel thought of God's relationship to the world, to the other nations and, not least, to herself; . . . the distinctiveness of what she said about sin and had to say about atonement and the salvation which comes from God'.[84] In fact, just as the Christian religion is not simply a creed but includes such rites as Baptism and the Mass, so Israelite religion was not merely a system of doctrines but included such things as rituals in the home, at High Places and the Temple, the scapegoat ritual, and (as already mentioned) at some periods and places cult prostitution. To attempt a comparison in which Israelite religion is treated primarily as a system of beliefs is to distort.

The risk of producing distortion by selectiveness in the evidence adduced is not, of course, peculiar to the examination of Israelite religion. Eliade has pointed out that any religion may be exemplified by the beliefs and practices of either a small religious elite or of the uneducated masses, and that both represent equally valid (if incomplete) evidence.[85] They are indeed complementary.[86] But they are not equatable, and in any comparison of two religions it is essential that as far as possible the evidence compared shall be on the same level. This criterion has not always been observed; in the comparative examination of Mesopotamian and Israelite religion, the tendency has been to treat as the 'true' Israelite religion that of the prophetic-priestly elite of the late eighth to sixth centuries B.C., to be compared (as indeed it was by

Deutero-Isaiah) with Mesopotamian religion at a crude popular level. It may be noted, as an historical curiosity of no enduring importance, that the Panbabylonian school tended to operate the reverse of this procedure.

Finally, one further problem of method may be referred to. There frequently arises in the discussion of Assyro-Babylonian religion the question whether or not it was Semitic. The most recent reference to this question was by a scholar who speaks in terms of decomposing Mesopotamian religion into its component elements, which he claims as 'essential if Semitists ever hope to produce an adequate treatment of the history of Semitic religion'.[87]

It is probably true that in certain instances one may be able to connect a new religious concept with a new immigrant group. One example of this has already been adduced, in the third-millennium syncretism between Ishtar and Inanna. One might even take seriously the possibility that the characteristics of a particular language may direct attention in particular ways, and so produce a particular way of looking at things, and make explicit a new approach on a religious matter.[88] But against this it must be pointed out that a religion cannot exist or be studied *in vacuo*. The religion is part of the total society. The old dispute about whether the religion of ancient Mesopotamia was 'Semitic' or 'Sumerian' is therefore a quest of a chimaera, and no more meaningful than the question of, for example, whether the beer drunk in Babylon at the time of Hammurabi was Semitic or Sumerian beer. The tracing of origins proves nothing about the nature of the living religion of ancient Mesopotamia. Even where a concept, symbol or practice can be shown to have been brought into a society by a particular group,[89] the subsequent significance and development of that concept, symbol or practice, from the moment of introduction onwards, is conditioned by the total society into which it was introduced, not by the society from which it came. Mesopotamian religion was the religion of a particular society, which developed where immigrating Semitic-speaking and Sumerian-speaking groups (and possibly members of other groups, whose original presence is suggested by place names which are neither Semitic nor Sumerian in form)[90] came into contact in an area of large-scale irrigation economy. One need not commit oneself to cultural determinism to reject the implication that the type of a religion can be a matter of genetics. The elements in the religion of Mesopotamia as we find it from the second millennium onwards are not 'Semitic' and 'Sumerian' elements, but elements produced by the action upon, and reaction to, features of a settled irrigation society by nomads from the desert who happened to speak a Semitic language. The fact that a particular group spoke a particular Semitic language tells us something about their cultural antecedents; it is not diagnostic for certain attitudes towards religion. And the fact that a deity, or a concept, can be traced back to an earlier pre-Mesopotamian stage tells us nothing of the function of that deity or concept in Mesopotamia at a later time, where it can only be understood as part of the total society.

In selecting a subject for comparative treatment, when honoured by the invitation to deliver the Jordan Lectures, whilst I had no doubts as to which two religions to compare, I was in a dilemma as to the treatment. My alternatives were to select some single limited problem for minute and exhaustive treatment, or to offer an impressionistic and necessarily incomplete examination of a wider major area. The former, for which a large number of possibilities suggested themselves, I rejected on two grounds. One ground was the general inappropriateness of making the minutiae of one strictly limited point in comparative religion, which (except by a very few specialists) could only be evaluated after subsequent access to documentary sources, the whole subject matter of a series of public lectures. The other ground was more strictly academic. The more limited the area and the more detailed the treatment, the more readily differences are seen. Yet differences of detail may have little bearing upon basic differences of principle. But with only a very small area under consideration, the significance of differences of detail is likely to appear much greater than if the data were being considered within a wider framework, giving the risk of arriving at yet another specious claim for having identified the basic element which distinguished Israelite religion from all other religions.

I therefore opted to attempt an impressionistic (and necessarily incomplete) examination of a wide area, namely, the view taken of the divine in various aspects. The objections to this approach are very obvious. One objection represents the converse of the criticism made of the over-detailed approach: an approach on an over-wide basis may be too superficial to do more than pick out general similarities whilst failing to identify significant underlying differences.

A second objection is related to the undoubted fact (stressed in particular by Oppenheim) that Mesopotamian religion was multi-layered and complex, for which reason it has been urged that it should not be considered as one religion but as a group of religions. However, it must be noted that, allowing for the smaller spread in space and time, a similar situation applies in principle for Israelite religion. The religion of the priest Samuel, who sacrificed at a High Place, was certainly not identical with the religion of Ezra; whilst even contemporaneously there existed, during the Monarchy, such differences between the Yahwism of Samaria or Bethel and that of Jerusalem as to permit some devotees of the Yahwism of the southern kingdom to think of northern Yahwism as idolatrous or pagan.[91] Yet, in both Israel and Mesopotamia, there was, despite the unquestioned differences of emphasis and detail with time, region, and social stratum, a continuum which justifies the treating of each group as a single complex. Oppenheim writes disapprovingly of such an approach as 'projecting all data [of different periods, regions, social strata] . . . upon one plane'.[92] In fact, to use data from different periods, regions and strata is not necessarily to put them all on one plane; one can use a piece of evidence from one situation to illuminate evidence from another without necessarily treating all data as equally relevant in all situations and at all times. Whilst few would wish to dispute that there were considerable and significant differences in Mesopotamia between popular and state religion, I would reject the extreme statement of the situation offered by Oppenheim, who, speaking of 'the religion of the Common Man without cult, priests or temples' as sharply contrasted with 'the Royal Religion with one adherent, the King',[93] implies that they were virtually separate religions. I would similarly reject any approach to Israelite religion seeking to suggest that its sacral kingship aspects can be entirely divorced from the religion of the common man. In both Israel and Mesopotamia the attitudes found in the religion of the king and of the common man mutually illuminate each other.

But the main objection to attempting a widely-based comparison of Israelite and Mesopotamian religion is the sheer quantity of material available; every one of the sub-sections included in the following treatment has engendered several books and a steady stream—in some cases, a raging torrent—of articles. Yet, if ancient Near Eastern religion is to be seen as a significant aspect of the human past, and not a mere mine in which to dig for Ph.D.s, scholars must attempt, however inadequately, to draw the threads of thought together and to attempt to weave an overall pattern, if not of the material as a whole, at least of major areas of the material. That any attempt is certain to be incomplete is irrelevant.

I have therefore ventured upon the attempt to look at the way in which the ancient Israelites and the people of Mesopotamia saw God or the gods. I have attempted to approach this through a number of aspects; in relation to creation, history, good and evil, communication between man and the divine, and personal religion and universalism. In relation to each of these aspects, I have concentrated in particular upon investigating the validity of certain proposals to find basic differences of approach between Israel and Mesopotamia which allegedly serve to define the distinctiveness of Israelite religion. In attempting this, I have had to be severely selective. Since the basis of selection necessarily in places involves my own subjective view of the nature of ancient religion in general, it is perhaps proper that I should confess that for both Israel and Mesopotamia I accept the possibility that in his claim for encounter with the divine, ancient man was speaking not of a phantasy of his own creation but of ultimate reality.

The Divine in Creation

Cosmic creation stands at the beginning of the Old Testament. In view of this, it might appear not unreasonable to conclude that cosmic creation was a central idea of Israelite religion. However, this conclusion is rejected by the theologian Gerhard von Rad and the traditio-historical school associated with him. For this school, the theological doctrine of creation in the Old Testament is not only late but also peripheral.[1]

This view is connected with von Rad's understanding of the Old Testament in general. For him, the Old Testament is primarily concerned with Salvation History. This is a concept which will be discussed in more detail later, but briefly it implies the view that the central concern of the Old Testament is not what Yahweh says but what he does for Israel in history. Von Rad is explicit in the view that 'the Old Testament writings confine themselves to representing Yahweh's relationship to Israel and the world in one aspect only, namely as a continuing divine activity in history'.[2] This is claimed as valid not only for the Hexateuch but also for the prophets, with the difference that in general the prophetic oracles stand not after but before Yahweh's divine acts in history to which they relate.[3]

Von Rad argues that the oldest representations of this doctrine of Salvation History are in certain cultic Credos, such as that of Deut. 26:5-9:

My father was a homeless Aramaean who went down to Egypt with a small company and lived there until they became a great, powerful, and numerous nation. But the Egyptians ill-treated us, humiliated us and imposed cruel slavery upon us. Then we cried to Yahweh the God of our fathers for help, and he listened to us and saw our humiliation, our hardship and distress: and so Yahweh brought us out of Egypt with a strong hand and outstretched arm. . . He brought us to this place and gave us this land, a land flowing with milk and honey.

Because there is nothing here about creation, von Rad argues that the theological doctrine of creation only developed when creation was seen in relationship to these events, which he treats as central. This development took place by stages, on von Rad's interpretation of the data. First, there was an incorporation of traditions taking the Salvation History back to Abraham. Then there was prefixed the primeval history from Adam onwards through Noah, stemming in the main from the Yahwist writer. Finally, the line of Salvation History was linked theologically with the creation, in the Priestly account at the beginning of Genesis. Von Rad emphasizes, however, that in his view the chapters on creation remain no more than a preface ancillary to the subsequent teaching about salvation and election: they are not 'a central subject of Old Testament faith'.[4]

The date at which von Rad places the beginning of a theological doctrine of creation is not earlier than the seventh century.[5] He does not deny that there were passages earlier than the seventh century which referred to Yahweh's creative activity, but he uses for these the description 'older beliefs' in distinction from 'a doctrine of creation'.[6] The basis for von Rad's distinction between a reference to God's creative activity which is a mere belief and one which represents a doctrine is not self-evident, but von Rad comes close to offering a definition of what he understands by the distinction, in the following passage:

Probably the sole reason for the lateness of the emergence of a doctrine of creation was that it took Israel a fairly long time to bring the older beliefs which she actually already possessed about it into proper theological relationship with the tradition which was her very own, that is, with what she believed about the saving acts done by Yahweh in history. In the old cultic Credo there was nothing about Creation... What had been opened up for [Israel] through Yahweh's revelation was the realm of history, and it was in the light of this as starting-point that the term creation had first to be defined.[7]

Here von Rad operates on the assumption that the only thing that could originally be thought of as embodying a theological doctrine was the 'old cultic Credo', and on the implicit definition that a theological doctrine was a belief that had become defined in terms of the associated Salvation History. His definition of the difference between a belief and a theological doctrine is thus based on the relationship of the group of ideas to Salvation History. Therefore, in saying that a doctrine of creation did not emerge from the old beliefs about creation until the latter had been brought 'into proper theological relationship' with Salvation History, von Rad is not (as he supposes) making an objective statement about developments within Israelite religion; he is merely re-stating the phenomena in terms of his own definition and terminology. What he purports to offer as a conclusion is merely an inevitable consequence of his understanding of what constituted a 'theological doctrine' in Israelite religion. So long as a concept is not related to Salvation History it is for von Rad only a belief and not a theological doctrine; as soon as the concept becomes related to Salvation History it is for von Rad *ipso facto* a theological doctrine.

In his discussion of the place in the Old Testament of ideas about creation, von Rad is in fact conflating two statements which are on different planes and need to be distinguished. The two statements in question are: (1) that beliefs about creation were only brought into relationship with Salvation History from the seventh century onwards, and (2) that only ideas which are in relationship with Salvation History are to be regarded as theological doctrines. The first statement is a conclusion from literary data, and may be accepted independently of the second, which is only a reflection of von Rad's definitions and terminology.

It is thus possible to accept with von Rad, on the one hand that belief in Israel that cosmic creation must be attributed to Yahweh went back well before the seventh century, and on the other that from the seventh century onwards these beliefs were given an extended emphasis, without accepting his view that the nature of the change in the seventh century and onwards was specifically that these beliefs became systematized into theological doctrines by being brought into relationship with what von Rad regards as the old cultic Credo.

Acceptance of the view that cosmic creation was attributed to

Yahweh well before the seventh century raises the question of the sense in which Yahweh may be regarded as a creator-deity, and whether cosmic creation was originally an essential aspect of Yahweh. In a polytheism, both cosmic creation and the creation of humans are normally the function of certain specific deities; it is not necessary for both creative operations to be the work of the same deity. With cosmic creation falling within the sphere of some deities and the creation of man being the responsibility of others, it is possible for there to be many deities who are in no sense creators.

In a monotheism, the problem is different. There, if doctrines of cosmic creation and of the creation of man are held, only two solutions are possible. One is that the creator was the Sole God himself, acting directly. The other is the Gnostic solution (of which no trace is found in the Old Testament) that the actual creator was a demiurge whom the Sole God had created, either directly or through a series of beings, of whom the first was created by the Sole God. Thus, in so far as a theological doctrine of creation came to be held in Israel, it had to be Yahweh who was the creator both of the cosmos and of man. There is thus the possibility that it was only secondarily that Yahweh became a creator-deity; that he was eventually regarded as a creator does not require that he was in essence originally a creator-god, nor does it require that a cosmogonic mythology was originally attached to him.

To discuss meaningfully the question of whether and in what sense Yahweh was a creator-deity, it is first necessary to determine what is understood by the term 'Yahweh'. This is a point at which the multilayered nature of an ancient religion, which Oppenheim stresses in the case of Mesopotamia, becomes highly relevant for Israel. The term 'Yahweh' clearly connoted a different concept of God in different strands of the Old Testament traditions. The characteristics of Yahweh of the claimed revelation associated with Moses are not necessarily identical with those of the Yahweh of Deutero-Isaiah, nor again with those of the God of Abraham. Whilst it is difficult or impossible to state definitely what the characteristics of the concept of deity of each of these religious strata are, it is possible to recognize certain differences between them. We may consider first the stratum of concepts traditionally attached to the oldest of these historical periods. The problem of the nature of the patriarchal god or gods is a very complicated one, discussion of which, set on a new course by Alt's *The God of the Fathers* in 1929, continues unabated.[8] Alt attempted to establish that each of the three major Patriarchs (whose kinship relationship was a secondary product of the tradition) received a revelation of a nameless god whose cult was continued by the descendants of that Patriarch under titles of the type 'the Dread[9] of Isaac', 'the Mighty One of Jacob'. These cults were subsequently syncretized with the cult of the deity or *'el* of local Canaanite sanctuaries in the regions in which the descendants of those Patriarchs settled, the separate deities concerned ultimately becoming identified with each other, and then with Yahweh of the Mosaic revelation. Subsequent scholars have modified or developed Alt's hypothesis in various details, the most significant correction being that which recognizes, on the basis of the Ugaritic evidence, that *'el* was not a common noun for 'deity', but the proper name of a specific deity. If this is accepted, it becomes clear that the terms *'el shaddai*, *'el 'elyon*, and so on, with which the patriarchal numina were syncretized, were not originally a number of distinct local deities, but rather were local aspects of one High God El.[10] Thus on almost all modifications of Alt's basic thesis it is now generally accepted that the God revealed in the Old Testament in relation to the time terminating in the Settlement in Palestine subsumed characteristics of at least three distinct manifestations of deity, or classes of deity, of which one, Yahweh, was in origin distinct from the other two. F. M. Cross has, indeed, attempted to avoid this conclusion by the argument that the name 'Yahweh' was originally a cult-name of the High God El 'as patron deity of the Midianite League in the south',[11] but this rests upon a chain of speculative arguments and assumptions.[12]

Each of the three manifestations of deity distinguished by Alt gives rise to a number of problems. The name 'Yahweh' itself remains enigmatic, but its immediate origin is undisputed. It is the proper name of the deity who brought Israel out of Egypt to Palestine; that is, his original association was with what von Rad regards as the circumstances of the central Credo of Salvation History. But the Old Testament in its final form restricts the activity of the God of Israel neither to that period nor to the deity under the name of Yahweh. None the less, it transmits the explicit claim that Yahweh was not known by name before this. The identification of Yahweh with the patriarchal God or gods, though subsequently of the highest significance, is generally recognized as not Mosaic.[13] From where, in human terms, Moses derived the name Yahweh remains disputable;[14] the original pre-Mosaic history of Yahweh is, however, less significant than the form Yahweh manifested after the Mosaic revelation.

The characteristics of the god originally named Yahweh appear particularly in the Book of Exodus. This is not to suggest that the narratives as they stand are being taken either as literal history or as in a literary form deriving from an historical period close to the time to which they purport to relate, which at many points is manifestly not the case. What is being assumed is that these stories have been linked to the Exodus tradition, because the concept of God that they reflect conforms to, or is consistent with, the characteristics of the deity originally associated with that tradition.

The following points about the original Yahweh emerge from the Exodus narratives. He was specifically a desert god: it was only there that sacrifices could be offered to him. He was visible in the form of a fiery cloud. He was a magician, and one of particular skill: any qualified Egyptian magician could turn a stick into a snake, but Yahweh's competence in this sphere was so surpassing that the snake he brought into being could eat up all the others. He controlled the weather, and he controlled plagues and diseases.[15] But with all this miracle-working there is no suggestion that he possessed cosmic power: the passage speaking of the thick darkness which Yahweh brought over Egypt gives no indication that a cosmic event is meant,[16] and there is nowhere any threat of shaking the earth and making the sun and moon cease to shine.

The whole group of plague stories could be taken to have the positive implication that Yahweh definitely did not possess cosmic power in that level of Israelite thought. The reason attributed to him for hardening Pharaoh's heart was to give him an excuse to assert his power, to compel the Egyptians to recognize him,[17] and any deity who had created the cosmos and now controlled it could have achieved this without resort to local thaumaturgy, in the manner threatened in the Book of Jeremiah:

> I saw the earth, and it was without form and void;
> the heavens, and their light was gone.
> I saw the mountains, and they reeled;
> all the hills rocked to and fro. (Jer. 4:23-4.)

Other aspects of the nature of Yahweh of the Exodus narratives are that he was the opposite of universal, making a deliberate and specific distinction between Israelites and other peoples; and that he was not omniscient, since he was unable to distinguish between dwellings occupied by Egyptians and those in which Israelites lived, except by marks on the doorway.[18]

There are many features in this picture of Yahweh of the tradition associated with the period of Moses which differ from those linked to the religion of the Patriarchs. The assumption is commonly made that Mosaic Yahwism represented an advance over patriarchal religion;[19] but, in so far as no attempt is made to substantiate this view by evidence, it appears to rest on no more than an evolutionary view of religious development. If one proposes to make value judgements about the matter, it is at least a theoretical possibility that the concept of deity attributed to the Mosaic period was a retrogression from that of the Patriarchs. As soon as Moses appears in the tradition, the concept of God is narrower, less tolerant and more naive. The religion transmitted through the clans that we are accustomed to subsume under the term 'the Patriarchs', though certainly not a philosophical mono-theism, was—whatever the status of the patriarchal numina at various stages of development—a cultus which at some period was able to accept and assume dependence upon a single High God

El, who was universal and cosmic. It may be observed that it is nowhere claimed in the Old Testament that the Mosaic revelation was an advance over the patriarchal concept of deity. Even in the actual account of the revelation to Moses at the burning bush there is no suggestion of this; the only new element claimed is the name of the deity.[20] The principal criticism which can be made of assessing the facts in this way is that it comes close to the unfashionably conservative view, expressed in the words of a distinguished Jewish scholar: 'Abraham and not Moses was the founder of Israel's monotheism.'[21]

Examination of the qualities originally ascribed to deity in the concepts linked to the Patriarchs is difficult, in view of the literary problem of determining what is an original part of the traditions and what is secondary. Alt has, of course, dealt in detail with some aspects of the patriarchal form of deity, but primarily from the point of view of typology of deity rather than in connection with the essential qualities of the deity. The question of what qualities attached to the patriarchal deities originally is not wholly solved by source analysis. It could be argued, for example, that if a tradition of a particular quality of a deity is strongly linked to a Patriarch, if there is no credible and likely explanation for the origin and linking of the concept at a later period, its connection with the tradition of the patriarchal concept of deity is not necessarily to be rejected, even if the source in which it occurs is (as a written document) demonstrably late.

Looking at the concept of deity as found in the patriarchal stories, with an eye particularly on contrasts with the picture of Yahweh in the Mosaic revelation, one may tentatively isolate the following points. God, although he chose Abraham, was not concerned only with one people: his ultimate concern was with 'all the families of the earth'.[22] There is specific indication of his care for other peoples, as well as for the Israelites; thus he protected Hagar and her son Ishmael and through them their descendants the Beduin.[23] When God took action against the current Pharaoh, it was not, as in the Exodus narratives, in order to show his power and prove his divinity but in order to punish sin.[24] The God of the

Abraham saga was altogether more forbearing than the God of the Exodus events: whereas the latter was prepared to destroy, because of the stubbornness of the Pharaoh, vast numbers of innocent people and animals, God as it was felt appropriate to represent him in the Abraham saga was ready to spare an evil city if there were as few as ten just men in it.[25] The story of God's testing Abraham in the requirement to sacrifice Isaac shows that tradition held that the God of the Patriarchs cared for the love and loyalty of the individual.[26] The point may be recapitulated that it is not a compelling objection against such conclusions that some of the stories about the Patriarchs are provably late in origin as literary units: the fact that they could be attached to the Patriarchs shows that the tradition about the nature of the patriarchal deity was such that these stories were felt to fit into the accepted concepts. It is significant that it was not possible to attach the same kind of stories to the Yahweh of the Moses tradition. For example, before the final plague of Egypt, the Egyptians as a whole, except Pharaoh himself, had become well disposed towards Moses and the Israelites;[27] this, however, did not exempt any of them from the culminating terror of the massacre of the first-born.

In tradition, therefore, the God of the Patriarchs had quite different qualities from those of the original Mosaic God Yahweh; a tincture of universalism as against ethnic exclusiveness; mercy and tolerance against intolerance and vindictiveness; a calm prosecution of a predetermined plan as against aggressive self-assertion and *ad hoc* reaction.

The original Yahweh of Mosaism shows no indication at all of having been regarded as cosmic creator, to judge by his actual activities in the texts. It has been, and continues to be, argued that the name 'Yahweh' itself implies that the god so named exercised creative activity, the argument being that it is a verbal form meaning 'he causes to exist'.[28] This grammatical analysis is, however, open to serious objection.[29] Furthermore, even if the name ever carried the meaning 'he causes to exist', it need not have implied cosmic creation.[30]

The evidence for the original patriarchal concept of deity

having involved the idea of cosmic creator is scarcely more. The only action attributed to the patriarchal God which might be regarded as impinging upon this area is that of raining down fire and brimstone from heaven upon the cities of the plain;[31] at the most, however, this could be taken to permit, but not to require, the idea that God was cosmic creator. The use of the terms 'God of heaven' and 'God of earth' is ascribed to Abraham,[32] but— irrespective of whether or not the use of these epithets was an original part of the Abraham tradition—this usage would not positively prove a belief in God as cosmic creator, though it would be consistent with such a belief.

The third main element subsumed under the final concept of God of Israel was designated by the term '*el*, which, as Alt showed, was associated with a manifestation of deity from which, despite early assimilation, the patriarchal form of deity was originally distinct. For Alt, '*el* by itself was the common noun meaning 'a god'; but, as already mentioned, evidence from other parts of the Near East in the second millennium B.C. and earlier, shows that it was in such usages not a common noun but a proper name.[33] This god El, where he occurs outside the Bible, is head of the pantheon; whilst both in Genesis and in extra-biblical texts he bears titles which describe him as, or at the least imply that he is, cosmic creator.[34]

The whole testimony of the occurrences of such terms for God as '*el 'olam*, '*el šaddai*, and the like is now generally accepted as indicating that the worship of God under the title and characteristics of El went back among the ancestors of Israel well before the revelation of Yahweh. This accords with explicit biblical statements, such as the title El-Elohe-Israel, 'El is the god of Israel', given to an altar of the pre-Mosaic period.[35] Moreover, the very name 'Israel', compounded with El, not with a form of Yahweh, would itself be sufficient to confirm that proto-Israelites worshipped the god El before they knew Yahweh.

Eissfeldt has demonstrated that the Old Testament shows clear traces of stages by which Yahweh was assimilated to El.[36] He has convincingly argued that the biblical usages of El as a proper name

for a god fall into three main groups. Firstly, there is a group
in which El is used as the equivalent of Yahweh without self-
consciousness, simply as an alternative name for the same god. A
number of examples could be given, such as, from a lament in a
pre-exilic psalm,

> Arise, O Yahweh; O El, lift up thy hand;
> forget not the afflicted. (Ps. 10:12 RSV.)

Or one might quote instances from the oracles of Baalam,
certainly not later than the eighth century B.C. in their final
form:

How can I denounce whom El has not denounced?
How can I execrate whom Yahweh has not execrated?[37] (Num. 23:8–9.)

Secondly, there are a number of Old Testament instances in
which the term El is used in such a way that it is not being taken
for granted as an alternative name for Yahweh, but rather is being
consciously claimed for him. This implies conscious recognition
that there was the concept of a god El with attributes which had
not always, or in all circles, been regarded as attributes of
Yahweh.[38] Now, in these passages, it is insisted that the attributes
of El are the attributes of Yahweh. The passages of particular
relevance for this are all in Deutero-Isaiah. Thus:

> I am Yahweh, I myself,
> and none but I can deliver.
>
> . . .
>
> I am El; from this very day I am He. (Isa. 43:11, 13.)

Or again:

> Look to me and be saved,
> you peoples from all corners of the earth;
> for I am El, there is no other. (Isa. 45:22.)

The final claim occurs again in another passage.[39]

There is yet a third group of usages, in which, according to
Eissfeldt, El represents an entity distinct from and indeed possibly
originally superior to Yahweh.[40] These, however, though of

considerable interest in themselves, are probably all earlier than the passages of the other two groups, and do not bear directly upon the conscious re-opening of the question of the identification of El and Yahweh in the sixth century.

There is an odd circumstance connected with the first two groups of passages. If they represented stages in the evolution of belief, one would have expected those passages which un-questioningly assume the identity of Yahweh and El to be later than those in which it is consciously claimed. But this is not the situation. Whilst there are certainly some passages assuming this identification which cannot be accurately dated and which may be late, there are undoubtedly some in this category which can con-fidently be dated to not later than the eighth century. On the other hand, with the possible exception of Gen. 14:22 (where, in addition to the problem of the date of the verse, there is also the problem of whether the occurrence of the name Yahweh, identified with El Elyon, is original in the text), all the passages which mention El as a deity with whom Yahweh is consciously being equated are from the late sixth century.

This evidence seems to indicate that the identification of Yahweh with El had at one time, within the closed Israelite religious system during the Monarchy period, been taken for granted, and that then, some two centuries later, the question was re-opened, or, at the least, circumstances arose requiring the identification to be consciously re-asserted.

Now the particular prophet by whom this question was re-opened was Deutero-Isaiah. It may therefore be significant that it was he who was the prophet most concerned to establish Yahweh's power of cosmic creation and to show the nullity of Babylonian gods; and that the place where the question was reopened was among the Jewish community in exile in Babylonia.

The question of Yahweh's power of cosmic creation and its political implications was already raised by Jeremiah. In a passage from the beginning of the sixth century, he gave a theological argument from Yahweh's status as creator, in connection with Nebuchadrezzar's imperial conquests:

These are the words of Yahweh of Hosts the God of Israel: . . . I made the earth with my great strength and with outstretched arm, I made man and beast on the face of the earth, and I give it to whom I see fit. I now give all these lands to my servant Nebuchadrezzar king of Babylon. (Jer. 27:4-6.)

Here was made, apparently for the first time as a theological argument, the explicit claim that Yahweh had power over all the kingdoms of the earth, and that the reason he had this power was that he was cosmic creator. Deutero-Isaiah used the same argument in connection with the rise of Cyrus the Persian:

> I alone, I made the earth
> and created man upon it;
> I, with my own hands, stretched out the heavens
> and caused all their host to shine.
> I alone have roused this man in righteousness,
> and I will smooth his path before him. (Isa. 45:12–13.)

Passages of this kind stress that Yahweh's power to control history stems from the fact that he created both the universe and man.

Despite the parallel between the Jeremiah passage concerning Nebuchadrezzar and the Deutero-Isaiah passage concerning Cyrus, there is a significant difference between them, which is disregarded by von Rad. Speaking of the Deutero-Isaiah passage, von Rad says:

The words are reminiscent of Jeremiah's thoughts about the dominion over the world which, at that time, Yahweh had given to Nebuchadnezzar. . . His day is past, and it is now Cyrus who, as master of the world, accomplishes the will of Yahweh. Yet again Israel is and remains the object of these world-wide historical designs of Yahweh: it is for her sake that Cyrus has been 'stirred up', and it is for her sake that he must be furnished with a world empire.[41]

By his 'yet again', von Rad makes the Jeremiah passage wholly parallel to the Deutero-Isaiah passage. But this is not legitimate. For the parallel to be complete it would be necessary to be able to say for the Jeremiah passage that 'it is for Israel's sake that Nebuchadrezzar has been "stirred up", and it is for her sake that he must be furnished with a world empire'. But such a statement would not only not accurately reflect the view of Jeremiah; it would run counter to it. Far from the rise of Nebuchadrezzar being intended for Israel's benefit, 'if any nation or kingdom'—including by implication Judah—'will not serve Nebuchadrezzar king of Babylon or submit to his yoke, I will punish them with sword, famine, and pestilence, says Yahweh, until I leave them entirely in his power'.[42] Thus Jeremiah's claim does not (contrary to the implication of von Rad's statement) relate Yahweh's creative activity primarily to Israel.

Jeremiah is now asserting, as a central part of the nature of Yahweh and one that defined his activities, something that was (as von Rad correctly says) no part of the Yahweh of traditional Mosaism. Far from bringing this into relation with the ideas surrounding what von Rad calls 'the old cultic Credo', Jeremiah, in viewing the activities of Yahweh in a context of world history, not in one which was Israel-centred, was implicitly rejecting the premisses of the doctrine of Salvation History. It remained to Deutero-Isaiah to show that the old and the new could be reconciled.

This new element, found in Jeremiah and developed in Deutero-Isaiah, makes two linked claims—that it is Yahweh who is cosmic creator and that it is because of this that he controls all world history. This gives no indication of being an evolutionary development internal to Israelite religion, and the fact that, as first presented by Jeremiah, it was in a form sharply conflicting with central concepts of traditional Mosaism, makes it improbable that it was. One may therefore posit that this new development is perhaps to be explained from factors external to the old closed religious system of Israel.

The specific theological claims of a god to control kingdoms and world history because he was cosmic creator, though new in Israel at the time of Jeremiah, was already known elsewhere in the ancient Near East, particularly in Babylonia. It may thus be suggested that Jeremiah was taking over for Yahweh claims he found already made for Marduk of Babylon.

Against such a conclusion, it could be pointed out that the reign of Nebuchadrezzar was not the first time Judah had come into contact with Mesopotamian cultural influence; there had already been contacts with Assyria since the time of Isaiah of Jerusalem, more than a century before. It might also be argued that there was nothing new or non-Israelite in the idea that Yahweh of Hosts governed the peoples of all lands, and that this had inherent in it the idea that God might give the government of the world to whom he would; the king of Assyria had already been regarded by Isaiah as God's agent, given power for a time 'to spoil and plunder at will'.[43]

There are, however, two major differences between the views of Isaiah of Jerusalem and Jeremiah about God's grant of power to foreign rulers. One difference is that Isaiah did not link God's control of history to his status of cosmic creator. The other difference is that Isaiah's view was still essentially Israel-orientated. God's power to control peoples other than Israel was indeed assumed, but the reason he chose to control them was because he wished to use them in connection with Israel's destiny. The Assyrians were being used specifically to punish Israel, and would themselves be punished in turn. Isaiah's argument was from God's power to use any instrument he would to shape Israel, not, like the argument of Jeremiah, from God's right to control the whole world because he had made it.[44]

Jeremiah was turning away from the old idea that Yahweh's concern was primarily with one particular land, the land of Palestine, and with the guidance of one particular people. The old Israelite idea, that Yahweh had chosen one people and granted a land to them, and that he would preserve it to them, was associated with the concept underlying what von Rad and others have called 'the holy war' of Yahweh. The latter concept can be traced over a long period. As von Rad points out, in the time of the Judges it was Yahweh 'who rose up to protect his people in . . . holy wars, and the action which was decisive was his—the men of Israel "came to help him" (Jud. 5:23)'.[45] That is, Yahweh himself was directly involved. Later on, Yahweh was directly concerned in the actual waging of war in the time of Elisha.[46] The Book of Deuteronomy still thinks of Yahweh himself as personally involved in warfare on behalf of Israel:

When you take the field against an enemy and are faced by horses and chariots and an army greater than yours, do not be afraid of them; for Yahweh your God, who brought you out of Egypt, will be with you. When you are about to join battle, the priest shall come forward and address the army in these words: 'Hear, O Israel, this day you are joining battle with the enemy; do not lose heart or be afraid, or give way to panic in face of them; for Yahweh your God will go with you to fight your enemy for you and give you the victory.' (Deut. 20:1–2.)[47]

Such passages show that, up to the time of Jeremiah, the usual basic Israelite assumption, in connection with Yahweh's grant of lands and kingdoms and his preservation of these to those to whom he had granted them, was that Yahweh was personally and immediately involved. Although it was accepted that God had a basic intention of ensuring possession of the holy land to Israel, the emphasis was upon *ad hoc* divine intervention rather than upon a self-fulfilling original divine plan. Knowledge of similar concepts was attributed to the Assyrian officer giving his speech of psychological warfare outside besieged Jerusalem in 701 B.C.:

Did the god of any of [the nations attacked by Assyria] save his land from the king of Assyria? (2 Kgs. 18:33.)

It is not surprising that the Assyrians should be familiar with such ideas, since they themselves frequently spoke of their own gods as immediately interested in, and sometimes personally involved in, battles. One certainly finds in Assyria traces of the idea that the gods had long-term plans for particular rulers, but much more common is the concept of immediate and sometimes *ad hoc* divine control of the outcome of particular battles, examples of which are liberally sprinkled throughout Assyrian royal inscriptions. One may quote a few examples chosen at random:

With the weapon of my lord Ashur I struck them down;[48]

The terrors of the weapon of my lord Ashur overpowered them and they bowed in submission to my feet:[49]

The people of Kummuh . . . whom my hands captured with the help of the great gods my lords . . . ;[50]

Peoples of the lands, conquest of my Lord Ashur, I settled;[51]

In my seventh campaign my lord Ashur gave me support and I went against Elam;[52]

I raised my hands in prayer to Ashur, Sin, Shamash, Bel, Nabu and Nergal, to Ishtar of Nineveh and Ishtar of Arbela, and they received my words with favour. In token of their sure approval they favoured me with a trustworthy oracle: 'Go, do not give up. We will go at your side, we will kill your enemies.'[53]

In Ashurbanipal's attack on Elam, Ishtar of Arbela even arranged a message in a dream for the benefit of the king's forces, saying: 'I will go before Ashurbanipal, the king whom my hands have formed.'[54]

The national Assyrian god Ashur is indeed sometimes given titles appropriate to cosmic creator, amongst other places in the introduction to some Assyrian royal inscriptions;[55] but this does not affect the fact that in the historical narrative portions of royal inscriptions there is no suggestion that his control of the fate of nations is operated as part of a cosmic plan (though indeed this idea is not unevidenced elsewhere); rather, the situation reflected in the royal inscriptions is that Ashur (and this sometimes applies to other deities) is on the immediate scene and—as for Israel's God up to the time of Deuteronomy—his control can be exercised on behalf of the nation because he is a god mighty in battle. This was a claim which Israel could understand and answer on its own grounds. The Assyrian imperial concept had presented no challenge to Israelite theology except the challenge to show—as the first Isaiah insisted was the case—that Yahweh could and would act effectively in the immediate case, in the protection of Jerusalem.

It would be hazardous in the present state of knowledge to make overbold statements about either Babylonian or Assyrian state theology. However, it is clear that differences existed between the state theology relating to the national god Marduk in Babylonia and that relating to Ashur in Assyria, and that during the first millennium, if not before, the functions attributed to Marduk were such that the Assyrians came to make new claims for Ashur. Thus, it is well known that *Enūma Eliš*, the Babylonian Myth of Creation, recited in Babylon for the exaltation of Marduk, was taken over in Assyria, and that there Ashur replaced Marduk throughout and was credited with all his properties and functions. Later, probably in the time of Sennacherib, an Assyrian text was composed with the deliberate object of denigrating Marduk.[56] This contains the significant line: 'It is said within *Enūma Eliš*, "When heaven and earth were not created, Anshar came into being.'[57] Originally, Anshar in *Enūma Eliš* was a primeval being existing before the great gods of the historical pantheon, but in late Assyrian times a writing in the form 'Anshar' came into use to represent the name of the god Ashur. Thus the line quoted is using this interpretation of the name Anshar in *Enūma Eliš* to establish that the Assyrian national god Ashur was in existence primevally, before the creation of heaven and earth.[58] That is, the deliberate claim is made, and a theological basis contrived for it, that it was Ashur who was the cosmic creator *par excellence*.

If the encounter of Assyria with Babylonian culture led to the need to re-define the position of the Assyrian god Ashur relative to cosmic creation, it is at least *prima facie* possible that a corresponding consequence ensued from the encounter between Judah and the Babylonians. That Jeremiah had interviews with prominent Babylonians is clear from the biblical evidence,[59] and, if general cultural diffusion is not accepted as a sufficient explanation, this provided an obvious channel through which he might have become immediately acquainted with Babylonian modes of thought.[60]

So far as we can tell from Neo-Babylonian inscriptions, the ideas which Jeremiah would have met amongst Babylonian contemporaries would have had different emphases from those of the Assyrians who came into cultural contact with Judah over a century earlier.[61] Judging by Nebuchadrezzar's own inscriptions, Jeremiah would have found little indication of the theology of holy war which had been so marked both in Israel and in Assyria. The idea is very little represented in Nebuchadrezzar's inscriptions, for example, that wars waged by Nebuchadrezzar were really Marduk's wars, being conducted by Nebuchadrezzar simply as the god's agent.[62] It might be argued that the reason for absence of indication of such an attitude was the absence in Babylonia of accounts of campaigns of the Assyrian type. But this argument can be reversed. Assyrian and Babylonian royal inscriptions both developed from the same basis, that is, from Sumerian dedication inscriptions, but only the Assyrians evolved from this the type of inscription which made what was effectively, and in some instances formally,[63] a report to the god about the king's military campaigns. That the Neo-Babylonian kings did not develop this element, nor borrow it from their Assyrian predecessors (although in some instances they borrowed quite extensive phrases for other sections of their inscriptions) is a strong indication that their deities were not interested in the details of their military campaigns. Certainly we sometimes find, in the prayer at the end of a Neo-Babylonian building inscription, not only mention of the desire for long life and continuation of the dynasty, but also a request for the presence of the god with the king and his army, and the overthrowing of enemies.[64] However, there are two points to notice about this: firstly, such clauses are quite general, having no reference to any particular military action or to any particular enemy; and secondly, they correspond to clauses which already existed in a corresponding position in some Assyrian royal inscriptions,[65] so that they cannot be taken as a vestigial summary of details given in *extenso* in the narrative portion of Assyrian inscriptions.

Significant in the inscriptions of Nebuchadrezzar are certain phrases which claim explicitly that Marduk had from the beginning granted the king supremacy over all mankind. A typical example, which (with minor variants) occurs frequently, is: 'O Marduk, Lord, Wise One, Great God, Splendid One, you created me, you entrusted to me the kingship over the totality of people.'[66] Elsewhere Nebuchadrezzar states: 'The widespread people, with whom Marduk the Lord filled my hand, I made subject to

Babylon.'[67] In the last passage quoted, we see a specific distinction between Marduk's granting control of the people to Nebuchadrezzar, which was the god's plan and must come to pass, and the implementation of the plan by warfare, which was Nebuchadrezzar's doing. Nebuchadrezzar's conquests were indeed part of Marduk's plan, but Nebuchadrezzar was not waging war on behalf of Marduk as the Assyrian kings had done on behalf of Ashur and the Israelite kings on behalf of Yahweh.

The basic attitude was no longer that (as predominantly in Assyria) the national god controlled the lands because he was mighty in war, but rather that because the god had decided a plan, this would be fulfilled. This was one co-ordinate of the Babylonian view of the supreme god, as likely to have been encountered by Jeremiah. Another was the belief that Marduk was creator of heaven and earth. In parallel with these views, Jeremiah now claimed that it was Yahweh who had created the earth and that he could give it to whom he saw fit. It was something new and positive that Jeremiah was asserting, and in this sense von Rad's distinction between old beliefs about creation by Yahweh and new doctrines on the matter is justified.

Jeremiah's statement of the theological claim that Yahweh was cosmic creator presented him as Lord of all the kingdoms of the earth, with no peculiar concern for Israel. With this development there were now two views of God's action in history which, if not necessarily actively in conflict, were at least in tension. The tension was only resolved by Deutero-Isaiah's assertion that God's care for Israel, as represented in the doctrine of Salvation History, was a particular aspect of God's care for the world which stemmed from his activity as cosmic creator. With the two doctrines so connected, the election of Israel and the settlement in the promised land could be presented as an end towards which creation was directed. In the final development, von Rad is justified in saying: 'Presumptuous as it may sound, Creation is part of the aetiology of Israel!'[68] But that was in the picture presented when the Pentateuch was edited into its final form in the post-Exilic period: the context in which Jeremiah saw Yahweh as creator was

not the limited one mentioned by von Rad. For Jeremiah
certainly, and possibly even for Deutero-Isaiah, God's purpose in
creation went beyond concern for Israel.

Even if Jeremiah was in his time almost alone in facing the
implications of the problem 'Who is cosmic creator?', by the
period of Deutero-Isaiah the matter must have become a conscious
issue in the thought of the Jews in Babylonia. In their environment
they could hardly have failed to note the Babylonian belief that
Marduk was cosmic creator, and any Jew had either to deny and
counter this or to renounce Yahwism.[69] An actual denial of the
cosmic creative power of pagan gods is found in a late Aramaic
gloss in Jer. 10:11:

You shall say this to them: 'The gods who did not make heaven and
earth shall perish from the earth and from under these heavens.'

With the question 'Who is cosmic creator?' once explicitly raised,
the only possible answer for a Jew was 'Yahweh'. This was
associated with the absolute denial of the reality of other gods. But
to place these two claims together gave a further problem. The
cosmic creator, even though he might choose one nation as his
special people, could not reject the rest of his created world. How
then could Yahweh identify himself as the god who, though in a
particular relationship to Israel, was also creator of the gentiles?
The mechanism was ready at hand in the old hypostasis El. In
Israelite tradition Yahweh had anciently been known as El, and
the god El anciently bore, both in Israel and elsewhere, the title
'creator of heaven and earth'.[70] It is perhaps not an accident that
Deutero-Isaiah's identifications of Yahweh with El come predominantly in the context of a challenge to the nations.[71] A further
factor favourable to making explicit the equation of Yahweh with
El was that, to judge by the absence of literary evidence, the
cosmic creative activity of El does not appear to have been
expressed in Israel in mythological terms; the latter fact does not
conclusively prove that no mythological cosmogony associated
with El was known in Israel, but if one existed it must have
enjoyed only very limited currency, to have left no indisputable

traces in Israelite literature. This absence (or insignificance) of a mythology of cosmogony entailed the advantage that the identification of Yahweh with the god El, long known as cosmic creator, could be explicitly re-stated and stressed without introducing any offensive pagan mythological associations.[72]

But Deutero-Isaiah did not only stress the identification of Yahweh with El afresh. He went right back to re-emphasize certain aspects of the pre-Yahwistic concept of God. By this means he re-introduced in particular a universalism latent in patriarchal religion but largely lost in the mainstream of Mosaic Yahwism, despite occasional protests by earlier prophets. Deutero-Isaiah recognized the problem inherent in the old exclusiveness of the doctrine of the election of Israel. By all human standards, there was no evidence, in the present low state of Israel's fortunes, of the special divine care for her postulated in the old view of election. Deutero-Isaiah asked:

> Why do you complain, O Jacob,
> and you, O Israel, why do you say,
> 'My plight is hidden from Yahweh
> and my cause has passed out of God's notice'? (40:27.)

and showed in the preceding and following verses that it was the concept of Yahweh as cosmic creator that resolved the problem. Israel was indeed a chosen people and had a special place in Yahweh's purpose and would receive vindication from Yahweh against its enemies. But the special place of Israel in creation was not an end in itself, so that present adversity did not represent a denial or abrogation of divine election. The fate of Israel had to be seen in relation to creation as a whole. Yahweh had created and now guided the whole universe and all peoples, and the election of Israel was to be understood as Israel having been formed

> to be a light to all peoples,
> a beacon for the nations,
> to open eyes that are blind,
> to bring captives out of prison,
> out of the dungeons where they lie in darkness. (42:6–7.)

Whilst God had a special care for Israel, his care was not for Israel alone. Israel was Yahweh's instrument to reveal himself to all men.

The foregoing argument has been directed to establishing that although the development of the theological doctrine of creation in Israel came to be linked with the old idea of the election of Israel, it is not explicable as a development or mere peripheral extension of ideas which one may loosely refer to as the doctrine of Salvation History. Rather it grew out of a recognition, in the light of cultural contacts with Babylonia, of the inadequacy of the old religious attitudes subsumed under that term. Inasmuch as this involved a conscious attempt by religious teachers to answer certain problems which arose as Judah's cultural horizons widened, this takes us out of the history of religion into theology. The theological answer to the problems so raised was eventually systematized in its fullest form in the cosmic creation story of Gen. 1:1–2:4a.

Whether or not this creation story is to be designated a myth depends upon one's understanding of the term 'myth', which is a subject of continuing discussion. What is beyond dispute, however, is that it is completely free of personal beings other than God. The view has often been taken, since Gunkel, that this is the result of demythologization of an earlier form in which *tehom* ('the deep'), and possibly other elements in the story, were personal beings. There is, however, little evidence to support such an hypothesis. It seems more probable that the details of the story, as well as the theological ideas it conveys, represent neither a development out of original Israelite concepts nor a direct adaptation of borrowed Mesopotamian concepts, but rather a reaction to Mesopotamian concepts. On this hypothesis, it has been argued that the arrangement of the sections dealing with the stages of creation is consciously intended to counter, or indeed to attack, ancient Near Eastern ideas.[73] In the Genesis creation story the function of the sun and moon seems to be minimized. This is reflected in the creation of light being separated from the creation of the heavenly bodies, but it is not limited to this distinction, which can be paralleled in Egypt; it goes beyond that distinction to represent the creation of light as actually occurring before that of the heavenly bodies. This is an anomaly with no relevant parallel in the ancient Near East.[74] Pettazoni attempted to relate the belief that light was created before the sun to the fact that at dawn the light appears before the sun, and at dusk persists after the sun has disappeared.[75] However, this is demonstrably inadequate. Mesopotamia is in the same latitude as Palestine and so enjoys identical phenomena at dawn and dusk, but yet no corresponding cosmogonic ideas are attested on the relationship between light and the sun. Pettazoni's explanation thus disregards part of the data and must be rejected. It seems more reasonable to accept that in the Genesis creation story the deliberate separation of light from the sun and moon, with priority denied to the two latter, had a theological purpose. This purpose was to combat the idea that the heavenly bodies were divine beings, or symbols of divine beings, with an independent part to play in control of the cosmos.

It is not only the existence of light before the heavenly bodies that requires explanation. It is also to be noticed that one of the functions actually bestowed upon the heavenly bodies in Gen. 1:18—to separate light and darkness—had already been effected by God in Gen. 1:4. This further emphasizes the subordinate status of the heavenly bodies. This is an additional indication that the whole form of the Genesis story of cosmic creation was directed against ideas associated with Mesopotamian mythology, so that what the Babylonians thought of as astral deities, or the symbols of astral deities, might be seen as mere physical instruments working the purpose of the one God.

The second Genesis creation story, in 2:4b–22, is in no way concerned with cosmic creation, and will be considered later in connection with the nature of man. However, there remains for consideration another group of Old Testament myth fragments, commonly taken as reflecting residual traces of Israelite mythological concepts of cosmic creation.

It is well known that the Babylonian creation myth, *Enūma Eliš*, has the cosmos created as a sequel to a combat of the god Marduk with the primordial she-monster Tiamat. Hermann Gunkel, in his classic work *Schöpfung und Chaos in Urzeit und Endzeit*, published in 1895, has a section of 86 pages on 'Allusions to the myth of Marduk's fight against Tiamat in the Old Testament, apart from Gen. 1'. This is sub-divided into 62 pages on the Dragon tradition, 21 on the tradition of the Primordial Sea, and three pages on comparison of the Old Testament Dragon and Primordial Sea traditions with the Babylonian Tiamat tradition.[76] At the end of the final pages of detailed comparison Gunkel claims: 'This then is our result: the Babylonian Tiamat-Marduk myth has been taken over by Israel and has here become a Yahweh myth.'

An interesting feature of this summary, supposedly relating to creation myths, is that the word 'Schöpfung' ('creation') occurs in it only twice. The first occurrence is in the introductory sentence: 'We have found in Israel a great and rich history of the world-creation-chaos myth',[77] which is of course simply an assertion of the point to be proved. The other mention of creation is in the passage reading:

The Babylonian myth records that Tiamat was divided into two pieces, the waters above and below. A Hebrew recension that explicitly expressed the latter is not available; none the less Ps. 74:13 speaks of the 'splitting' of the sea and also Job 26:13 knows the 'bolt of heaven'. At all events, in the Hebrew as in the Babylonian the creation of the world follows on the overcoming of the monster.[78]

The final sentence states as a conclusion what is in fact the main point at issue, but it is difficult to accept that Gunkel has proved this conclusion. What Gunkel proved was that there were on the one hand many fragmentary references to Yahweh overcoming a monster or the primordial sea, and on the other references to Yahweh operative in creation. The evidence Gunkel actually adduced for an essential connection between the two series of mythological concepts is very slight; it consists of no more than two passages from Psalms in which God's ownership and control of the world is mentioned alongside his victory over Leviathan or Rahab.[79] These two themes are not necessarily causally connected, and the two series of myths could have existed side by side unrelated.

Despite these considerations, many Old Testament scholars follow Gunkel in extending the term 'creation myth' to include any story about the struggle of a god to establish a settled order which culminates in his sovereignty and in fertility upon earth.[80] Ringgren, an advocate of this view, puts it in the following way:

Several Old Testament passages contain clear allusions to mythological ideas that are connected with creation, ideas that stand much closer to the Babylonian account. In them we hear of a terrible battle fought by Yahweh against a dragon, which is called Rahab or Leviathan or else simply 'the dragon' (*tannín*).[81]

Ringgren then adduces Ps. 74:13f. and Job 26:12–13, and adds: 'The context shows that in each case the battle with the dragon goes together with the creation of the world.' *Pace* Ringgren, it is by no means certain that in Ps. 74:13–14 the destruction of *tannín* (NEB 'the sea-serpent', RSV 'the dragons') and Leviathan was thought of as a prelude to creation: indeed, there are strong indications that it was not. Part of the world's fauna (NEB 'sharks', RSV 'the creatures of the wilderness') already existed, to whom Yahweh gave Leviathan as food; whilst, moreover, such natural features as perennial rivers were already in being, and were dried up by Yahweh. It is true that it could be argued that the perennial rivers dried up by God were themselves primordially existent waters overcome by Yahweh. But were this so, it would have to be recognized that they are here fully demythologized and so from quite a different stratum of belief from *tannín* and Leviathan. This would equally be against the conclusion that the passage Ps. 74:12–17 is the relic of a single consecutive myth, rather than a miscellany of allusions to mighty deeds of Yahweh in mythic time. In Job 26, if the verses preceding the mention of the defeat of the sea-monster (or monsters) do refer to cosmic creation (and they could equally refer to God currently and constantly maintaining the universe), they do not make cosmic creation the culmination

of a *Chaoskampf* (as Gunkel's argument requires), but either antecedent or parallel to it. The hypothesis deriving from Gunkel has
been summarized usefully by D. J. McCarthy, who is sceptical of
its validity and asks whether in fact 'the *Chaoskampf* with all its
attendant themes is really a story of creation in any meaningful
sense'.[82]

The biblical passages called in evidence by Gunkel have been
re-examined in this connection many times, and will not be considered *in extenso* here.[83] What seems clear from an analysis of
these passages is that where there is certain mention of God's
victory, or assertion of control, over some monster (usually
associated with the sea), there is no proved reference to cosmic
creation as a sequel. On the other hand, in those passages where
there is explicit mention of cosmic creation, there is no antecedent
Leviathan, no dragon, no serpent, no Rahab. To create a marriage
between the two series of mythic themes is to join together what
Israelite thought kept asunder.

None the less, it continues to be claimed that these two themes,
the divine combat with a monster and cosmic creation, do
essentially belong together, and it is instructive to examine the
type of argument used to support the claim. An explicit argument
on this point is given by M. K. Wakeman. She points to what she
regards as the 'conspicuous parallel' between Job 40:29a (41:5a in
RSV and NEB) and Ps. 104:26. The former reads (in RSV) 'Will
you play with him [i.e. Leviathan] as with a bird?', and the latter
'Leviathan which thou didst form to sport in it [the sea]'. Dr.
Wakeman comments:

What is interesting here is that the warring Leviathan is found in Job
where there is no reference to the time of creation, whereas in the
context of this creation hymn [Ps. 104], . . . Leviathan is just another
creature, God's plaything. One suspects a conscious attempt to refute
the implication of the myth that not all the world has always been
subject to God's will.[84]

What Dr. Wakeman is pointing out is that in neither passage is a
battle between God and Leviathan linked with creation. This is

true beyond question. What can be objected to is Dr. Wakeman's explanation of this fact. The existence of something called 'the myth'—a single all-embracing myth—is postulated, and the assumption is also made that we know substantially all the details of this hypothetical myth. The absence of particular details of the hypothetical myth where they might be expected is then taken not as a ground for querying the hypothetical reconstruction but, on the contrary, as proof of the accuracy of the reconstruction. Formally analysed, the argument appears to run thus:

X is absent.

If present, X would have been objectionable.

Therefore X must have been deleted because of its objectionable nature.

Therefore X must originally have been present.

The basic assumption of Gunkel and his many followers, that there was one myth which included both divine combat with a primordial monster and cosmic creation causally related to the god's victory, requires to be re-examined. Here it is useful to go back to Gunkel's starting point, *Enūma Eliš*, commonly known as the Babylonian Creation Myth.

It is now clear, as Gunkel was not in a position to know, that *Enūma Eliš* is neither a paradigm for ancient Near Eastern creation myths, nor indeed early. W. G. Lambert well describes it as 'a sectarian and aberrant combination of mythological threads'.[85] It contains a number of themes which elsewhere occur separately, and the chronological point of origin of *Enūma Eliš* relative to other myths does not give *Enūma Eliš* priority. The situation is not that *Enūma Eliš* is one great original unitary myth which has later disintegrated to re-appear in fragmentary form in other sources, but rather that it is a conflation of a number of myths originally separate and distinct. Separate myths, other than that of Marduk's actual combat with Tiamat, which can be identified within the final form of *Enūma Eliš*, include the following:

(1) a myth of the origin of the gods and all things, from the mingling of the waters of Tiamat and Apsu, thought of not as principles of evil but beneficent,[86] Tiamat having the title 'Mother

Hubur, who fashions all things' (II 19). We have a probable allusion to this mythic theme elsewhere, where Tiamat is called 'the wet nurse of Enlil'.[87]

(2) a myth of the vanquishing of the cosmic waters Apsu, and usurpation of his powers, by Ea, employing not personal combat but magic (I 60–76).[88]

(3) a myth of a rebellion of the gods against Anshar, head of the pantheon (II 14–15).

(4) a myth of the creation of sky, constellations, moon and sun (V 1–44).

(5) a myth of the creation of man, of which the planning was attributed to Marduk but the execution to Ea (VI 34–8).

(6) a myth of the building by the gods of Babylon with its temple and ziggurat (VI 57–72).

The amount of space given in *Enūma Eliš* to the various themes is interesting. Out of the seven tablets, there is less than one tablet dealing with Marduk's actual combat and less than half a tablet concerned with cosmic creation. But every tablet contains material glorifying and exalting Marduk, and except for a brief section on the creation of man, the whole of the last two and a half tablets are directly concerned either with the building of Babylon or with the glorifying of Marduk. Other themes, not originally connected with Marduk, are introduced in such a way that they serve to glorify Marduk. Thus, the theme of Ea vanquishing Apsu and then making his abode within Apsu seems to have the purpose of allowing Marduk, who has secondarily been identified with Asalluhi to make him Ea's son, to be born within Apsu, the primordial sweet waters; by this means he achieves a link with the primordial forces. The old myth of the creation of man is given a setting which enables Marduk to receive credit for it, even though the actual operation of the creation of man could not credibly be transferred to Marduk. To read the total work without pre-conceptions surely leaves the impression that the central theme was not creation (either cosmic or human) but assertion and justification of the supremacy of Marduk and of his city Babylon. Brandon has in fact spoken of a 'propaganda factor' in *Enūma*

Eliš,[89] and the term is well merited. *Enūma Eliš* was a conscious creation for a particular religio-political end. For Marduk of Babylon to be supreme, the claim had to be justified for him that he was cosmic creator. But he was a junior god, and it would have received no credence to claim this directly. The end could only be achieved by the theological adaptation—indeed, manipulation —of existing myths. There was an old myth according to which life began by the movement of the primeval waters. It was impossible, with the existing characteristics of Marduk, to bring him directly into relation with this, by transmogrifying him immediately, on the mythic plane, into the primeval beings. There was, however, another theme available by which he might be enabled to acquire their powers and functions—the old theme of divine combat. This had long been known in several myths. Thus, in the myth *Ninurta and Asag*, the god Ninurta fought a monster Asag, whose function was to hold back the primeval waters.[90] But this particular divine combat was not part of a creation myth, since agriculture already existed.[91] Another old myth of divine combat was the myth of Anzu, in which a divine bird-monster Anzu stole the tablet of destinies and was challenged by successive gods until one finally overcame him.[92] This again was not a creation myth, since the whole pantheon and light already existed.[93] In one extant passage Lugalbanda is given the epithet 'the mountain that trampled on the sea',[94] reflecting another myth of primeval combat, but the passage offers no hint that this was in the context of cosmic creation. The theme of divine combat therefore had no essential connection with creation. Its introduction into *Enūma Eliš* was part of the theological means by which Marduk was enabled to usurp the totality of creative powers originally associated with the primordial beings.

That in Mesopotamian thought cosmic creation did not of necessity involve a divine combat is quite clear from a number of early instances of myth fragments in which creation occurred without combat. An example has already been noted within *Enūma Eliš*, in the creation of the beginning of the pantheon simply from the mingling of the waters. There are further traces in

Sumerian myths of the idea of the origin of things in the separation of earth and heaven,[95] without any indication of a combat. Also, an Akkadian myth contains the line 'When Anu had created the heavens',[96] again with no suggestion of a primeval struggle.

In view of these facts, it appears difficult to maintain the view taken by Gunkel, and most recently stated explicitly by M. K. Wakeman, that there was one all-embracing myth in which cosmic creation was necessarily linked with a divine combat, and on the basis of this hypothesis to create a synthesis in which Old Testament allusions to God's control of a monster and Old Testament references to cosmic creation fall together as examples of the postulated myth occurring in the Israelite tradition.

The status of the monsters controlled by Yahweh in the Old Testament is not so well assured on the basis of the Mesopotamian evidence as it has often been assumed to be. The usual assumption is that the monsters were originally primordial, pre-existent, and opposed to Yahweh. But such properties may not properly be assumed on the basis of supposed Mesopotamian parallels, since we find there monsters which are not primordial, not pre-existent, and not necessarily opposed to the gods. In *Enūma Eliš* itself there are monsters which are neither primordial nor pre-existent; such are those created by Tiamat *ad hoc* for the coming fight with Marduk.[97] There are mythical monsters of the deep mentioned as though still existing in historical times, fully analogous with the Leviathan whom Yahweh created to sport in the sea: 'Shamash, your rays reach down to the abyss, so that the Lahmu of the ocean behold your light.'[98] Elsewhere '50 monsters of the sea' are said to praise Ea, suggesting that they are Ea's creatures and not his adversaries.[99] Therefore there is no reason, on the basis of Mesopotamian evidence, to seek to resist the clear indication of several biblical passages (Isa. 27:1; Job 3:8; Ps. 104:26, 148:7 [RSV]; Amos 9:3) that the sea monsters referred to in connection with Yahweh's power were monsters regarded as existing in historical, and not merely mythic, time, and that, far from being pre-existent rivals of Yahweh, according to some passages the

monsters had been created by Yahweh, and were his agents.
There is no reason independent of supposed parallels to look for a
pre-existent being behind the plain references in Job 26:12–13 to
Rahab and the crooked serpent, or to see Leviathan as originally
other than a monster placed in the waters by Yahweh, and
subject to him.

If we insist upon seeing, in the background of Israelite thought,
a primordial monster whom Yahweh has to overcome in order to
effect creation, this clearly supposes a dualism.[100] But once it is
recognized that there is no compelling evidence for such an
interpretation of the myth fragments, this problem disappears and
the Israelite view becomes uncompromisingly monist.

There is one obvious difference between the status of the creator
god in Israelite religion and in *Enūma Eliš*, in that in the latter the
cosmic creator was himself created. Fohrer has argued that because
Yahweh was an eternal god, the idea of a theogony for him was
inconceivable: 'the world had a beginning, but not Yahweh (Ps.
90:2)'.[101] However, in view of the demonstration by Eissfeldt of
the possibility of a concept that Yahweh was at one stage the most
powerful divine being in a pantheon headed by El, this statement
might be better put in a slightly modified form, without destroy-
ing Fohrer's point. The Israelite god Yahweh, in the fully developed form in which he subsumed the old High God El, existed
from eternity, and therefore a theogony did not develop.

It has been suggested that there is an important difference
between Israelite and Mesopotamian ideas of cosmic creation in
that God existed before the universe, whereas the Mesopotamian
gods were themselves born and lived within the physical universe.[102] But the antithesis in this bold form can be challenged.
On the Israelite side, it is by no means certain that God was pre-
existent relative to all aspects of the universe. The syntax of Gen.
1:1–2 can be taken in either of two ways, one way leaving the
question open whether or not the primeval waters pre-existed
alongside God, and the other making it clear that they did. On the
Mesopotamian side, in *Enūma Eliš* it is true that the deities of the
pantheon are presented as born, but this needs qualification.

Firstly, though the gods of the historical pantheon were not pre-existent, the primeval beings Tiamat and Apsu were, and it was from these that the gods derived and had their being. Secondly, though indeed the gods of the historical pantheon were born, they were not born within the physical universe: they were born 'when the heavens had not been named, when dry land had not been called by name'.[103] Thirdly, the mythological statement of the birth of the gods in syzygies needs to be seen within the context of the purpose of *Enūma Eliš*, which was to exalt Marduk. Marduk, earlier a minor god, had to be placed in an appropriate mytho-logical framework which would enable him to take over the functions of the great gods. The syzygies contributed to this: it is explicitly said that Anshar and Kishar, the second generation from the primeval beings, surpassed their parents, and also that Ea, Marduk's father, was greater than his own grandfather Anshar.[104] Marduk in turn was said to be greater than all the gods that preceded him.[105] When he was born, he sucked the breasts of goddesses, thus imbibing their qualities.[106] Thus it seems that the purpose of the syzygies, as well as of the claim that the young god was suckled by goddesses, was the theological one of piling up the qualities of the older deities within the person of the heir of the ages, Marduk. He was even brought into relationship with Tiamat through one of the fifty names accorded to him at the end of *Enūma Eliš*—'Mummu, creator of heaven and earth', Mummu being an epithet of Tiamat.[107] The whole emphasis in the the-ogony is upon the means by which Marduk acquired the qualities of all the great gods: he was born within the Apsu, which was primeval and pre-existent, and there is nowhere any suggestion that he was born within time and inside the existing physical universe, which, indeed, he himself subsequently created.

In addition to the foregoing considerations, it must be noted that *Enūma Eliš* is not necessarily to be taken as incorporating an account of a standard Mesopotamian view of cosmic creation. There is no other detailed account of the creation of the heavens and earth extant in the cuneiform sources, but there are allusions to this matter. In these there is no hint of a primeval struggle; in one such allusion it is the gods in assembly who had effected the work of creation, and in another it is Anu.[108] In both these cases the gods clearly existed before the universe took its final form, just as God did in Gen. 1:1. Whilst individual gods might be created or born within the universe, the great gods generically existed before and outside the universe. Demons, speaking of their creation by Anu, said 'heaven and earth [or the underworld] were created with us',[109] clearly implying the existence of Anu before the universe. It is therefore not legitimate to accept that there is a basic difference between the Israelite and Mesopotamian views of the divine powers in that the Israelites saw the divine as standing outside the physical universe, whilst to the Mesopotamians the divine was itself part of it.

The Divine in History

There have been repeated attempts to identify the difference between Israelite religion and the religions of other parts of the ancient Near East in terms of a different way of looking at history. The basic premiss is that the Israelites saw their God as active within history in an immediate and direct manner not found in the thought of other ancient Near Eastern peoples.

This view has been developed in several different directions. In one direction it has had considerable influence in the modern presentation of Old Testament theology. In many works on Old Testament theology, or on Old Testament history or religion written from a theological approach, there is repeated mention of 'salvation history' or 'saving acts' or 'saving institutions' in relation to ancient Israel. These saving acts or institutions are supposed to be related to divine interventions in Israelite history. Such concepts are treated as central to the Old Testament, sometimes to the obscuration of other aspects of the religion of Israel. Thus von Rad writes:

It has been shown that practically the entire literature of the Old Testament is attached, in the form of larger or smaller accumulations of tradition, to a few saving institutions ordained by God; and this means that Israel was incessantly at work upon making her God's saving acts and institutions actual.[1]

In the following pages some criticisms are made not only of the concepts but also of the terminology associated with the 'salvation history' interpretation of Israelite religion. In the case of criticisms of the terminology, the arguments are (unless otherwise stated) in relation to the English terms translating von Rad's German. It should not be overlooked that the English terms have in most cases a different semantic spread, different overtones, and a different religious cultural context from the German, so that some criticisms valid for the English terminology used by British followers of the traditio-historical school may not be equally applicable to the German terminology originally employed by von Rad.

What one fails to find in works in English referring to 'salvation history' or 'saving acts' or 'saving institutions' is a satisfactory explanation of what is meant by 'salvation' or 'saving' in such contexts.[2] These heavily loaded emotive, and sometimes ambiguous, terms seem to be left undefined to allow them the better to serve as a lubrication by which to slide imperceptibly from concepts of the Old Testament to concepts of Christian theology. 'Salvation' in English usage does not connote a static situation but rather something dynamic—the saving of some individual or group either from something or for something or both. In Christian theology the sense of 'salvation' is clear enough: it is the saving of the individual soul from destruction or damnation by sin, for eternal life. But clearly, when Old Testament theologians of von Rad's school speak of 'salvation history' or 'saving acts', they are not using the terms in that sense; they apply them not to individuals but to some entity referred to as 'Israel', without any overt definition of the sense being attached to that term. There are various senses in which the term 'Israel' may be used. There was an historical religio-ethnic entity bearing that name. It consisted of a group of men, women and children who had, or at least claimed, common ancestry, and who practised a common pattern of social and religious behaviour. Like their neighbours, they passed their time in such activities as ploughing, gathering the olive harvest, cooking, weaving, making love with their own or other people's spouses, stealing, participating in festivals, complaining about taxation, recounting old myths and folk-tales, and keeping the children in order. But there is no indication that it is this flesh-and-blood Israel of which the Salvation History theologians are thinking. Von Rad's Israel seems to be a purely theological abstraction that does such things as being 'incessantly at work upon making her God's saving acts and institutions actual',[3] learning 'to look at herself from outside',[4] having 'the assurance of being able at all times to reach [Yahweh's] heart',[5] working 'for a long time on the Decalogue before it became . . . capable of standing for an adequate outline of the whole will of Yahweh',[6] recognizing 'the Decalogue [not] as an absolute moral law prescribing ethic [but] . . . as a revelation vouchsafed to her at a particular moment in her history, through which she was offered the saving gift of life'.[7] Looking at that final phrase, one may fairly ask: who received this so-called 'saving gift of life', and what was it? Above all, what was Israel (whether the abstraction or the historical entity) being saved from, or saved for? An explicit answer, other than in terms of Christian theology, does not appear to be offered by the Salvation History school; but it would seem that the fate from which Israel secured escape by means of the so-called 'salvation' was, when one blows off the froth of theological sophistry, simply its extinction as a religio-ethnic entity. That is, God repeatedly intervened in history to preserve a particular ethnic stock. This is certainly the implication of von Rad's taking Deut. 26: 5–9 as the central Credo of Israelite religion.[8] This passage summarizes Jacob's descent into Egypt, the rapid increase of his descendants, the Egyptian bondage, the Exodus and the Settlement; and on it von Rad comments:

these words are . . . out and out a confession of faith. They recapitulate the main events in the saving history from the time of the patriarchs . . . down to the Conquest, and they do this with close concentration on the objective historical facts. . . there is no reference at all to promulgated revelations, promises, or teaching. . .[9]

If this represents what is understood by 'saving history', then 'saving history' basically means no more than that God maintained a particular religio-ethnic group in existence, when the operation of normal political and social factors might have been expected to result in its extinction.[10] That is, whilst Israel was historically only one of a number of ethnic groups, amongst them Egyptians, Greeks and Persians, which continued to exist as recognizable social entities throughout the first millennium B.C., despite numerous political and social pressures, the survival of Israel is taken as a special case involving 'salvation', the unique factor being a special divine intervention in history. It is not always made clear, in writings on 'salvation history', whether the special divine intervention is accepted as an objective reality, or whether it is only thought of as a subjective element in the Israelite interpretation of its own history.[11] What is certainly postulated on the 'salvation history' approach to the Old Testament material, is that whether or not actual divine interventions occurred in Israelite history, the Israelites not only believed there were such interventions, but also held that belief in such a form and with such emphasis, and drew such theological conclusions from it, that this belief was not just an aspect of, but was the very heart of, the assumed distinction between Israelite religion and all others.

Von Rad's approach is open to another criticism in his use of the concept 'faith' in relation to Israelite religion. He thinks of Israelite religion in terms of acceptance or rejection of 'the message' of 'the living word of Yahweh coming on and on to Israel for ever',[12] that is, in terms of (a word specifically used in the English translation of his writings) a 'faith'. In this approach von Rad is making the fundamental methodological error of imposing upon ancient religion the approach and attitudes of modern German Protestantism. Faith implies a system of belief voluntarily adopted from more than one possibility (including non-belief as a possibility). But this is a modern concept, not an ancient one. An ancient religion was not a faith in that sense but a way of regarding and reacting to the cosmos which was an inescapable part of the society as a whole. There was no question of the devotee deciding that he would believe one complex of propositions after consideration of various alternatives: the religious ideas of the ancient Israelite or Mesopotamian involved not things that he believed (in the sense of accepting by conscious decision) but things that he thought he knew. Thus Job says 'I know [not 'I believe'] that my vindicator lives' (19:25), the point about the distinction between supposed knowledge and belief being independent of the exact sense of the verse. The Israelite was born into a culture in which a certain view of the world was held. Because it was not a completely closed culture, there were certain tensions, with the opportunity of inclining to one or other alternative explanations of phenomena and answers to related theological problems—such as the problem of who gave fertility, or who was creator—but the opportunity for alternative views was restricted within quite close limits.

In the religions of the modern world, a person identifies himself with a particular religion by subscribing to a certain Credo, and can dissociate himself by refusing to subscribe. But to think of something definitive called 'Israel's faith', to which (by implication) an individual Israelite, or Israelites collectively, might subscribe by confessing a Credo, or from which an Israelite might withdraw by refusing to utter a Credo, is imposing upon the Old Testament evidence categories which do not derive from the Old Testament. There exist specific statements of the manner in which a non-Israelite might become a member of the Israelite community, and also of the manner in which an Israelite might be cut off from the community, and in neither case is a Credo involved.[13] By imposing the concepts of 'faith' and 'Credo' upon the Old Testament data, von Rad is attempting to force the evidence into a Christian straitjacket.[14]

A theologian is entitled to use his own categories for analysing and synthesizing the evidence from the religion he is studying, and in the course of this may legitimately utilize categories which do not derive from his sources. What is not legitimate is to read back into the sources categories which come not from the sources themselves but from the theologian's methodology, and then to base arguments upon the falsely postulated presence of those categories within the source material. 'Israel's faith', in the sense in which that term is used by von Rad, is a concept deriving from his own abstraction from the sources rather than from the actualities of Israelite religion. To base arguments, as von Rad does, upon the existence in Israel of something called 'Israel's faith', taking this to mean not the sum of religious beliefs but a conscious decision upon and definition of beliefs in the modern Protestant manner, is methodologically invalid.

Whether or not divine intervention occurred at particular

points in history is a matter of modern faith and not a problem susceptible to investigation. It is, however, possible to discuss whether or not Israel was distinguished from other religio-ethnic groups of the ancient Near East by the view that God constantly intervened in history on her behalf, to preserve the nation's existence, or, to use the more impressive-sounding terminology of von Rad, to give it 'the saving gift of life'.

A number of other scholars, who would not subscribe to the Salvation History interpretation of Israelite religion in the form presented by the school of von Rad, none the less argue for a distinctive Israelite way of looking at history. This view is stated in its baldest form by Mowinckel: 'While the other peoples experienced the deity in the eternal cyclic process of nature, the Israelites experienced God in History.'[15] Fohrer, although he does not accept the view in question, gives a useful representation of it in the following terms:

That Yahwism is definable as a theology of history, that all the basic confessional statements of the O[ld] T[estament] refer to history as the locus of Yahweh's actions, and that his revelation or activity takes place in or through history seems to be the characteristic principle for the so-called historical books of the O[ld] T[estament] and for prophecy. In this linkage with history we seem to see the true difference between Yahwism and other religions, with their timeless or non-historical basis, and thus the revelatory nature of Yahwism.[16]

This interpretation of the difference between Israelite and other ancient Near Eastern religions has been challenged by B. Albrektson in his monograph *History and the Gods*.[17] Albrektson, whilst modestly calling himself no more than 'an amateur in Assyriology',[18] has made a valuable comparative study of a number of Sumerian and Akkadian texts which specifically speak of actual or potential interventions of gods in human affairs, not in mythic time but in historical time. His general conclusion may be summed up in what he concludes from one particular text; that is, that the Mesopotamian texts bear

testimony to the belief that historical events are in one way or another

caused by supernatural agents, that the gods create history. The idea
that their main sphere of activity is nature does not even begin to
emerge: here they are all concerned with what happens in the relations
of states and men.[19]

Examining the Old Testament data, Albrektson claims to show
that it

does not speak so much of a divine 'plan' in a proper sense as is commonly assumed, and that the ideas of the deity's purposeful control of
history and of the belief in the course of events as a realization of divine
intentions are common to the ancient Near East.[20]

By this approach, Albrektson challenged some of the most
cherished ideas of the theological establishment, and the reviews
reflect the considerable interest aroused.[21] In some reviews, there
was a tendency to overlook that Albrektson was neither attempting to deny the uniqueness commonly claimed for Israelite
religion nor purporting to give a definitive statement of the relationship between Israelite religion and the religions of neigh-
bouring peoples, but merely clearing away 'too facile definitions
of [the] distinctiveness'[22] of Israelite religion as a preliminary to a
more correct description. It is thus hardly a relevant criticism of
Albrektson's work that he 'had merely selected similar aspects as
between the Hebrews and other nations, and not investigated the
differences';[23] he selected similar aspects because the predominant
view of Israelite religion assumed the absence of such similarities.

W. G. Lambert has, in response to Albrektson's monograph,
offered an interesting restatement of the basic differences between
the Israelite and the ancient Mesopotamian attitudes to the activity
of God in history.[24] This important, even though brief, study of
one aspect of the subject merits some attention.

Professor Lambert begins from the premiss that 'Israel was
distinctive in her ancient Near Eastern context',[25] and then proceeds to examine, as one aspect of this claimed distinctiveness, the
differences between 'the Hebrew and the ancient Mesopotamian
ideas of destiny and divine intervention in human affairs'.[26] It is
clear from the context that when Professor Lambert speaks of the

distinctiveness of Israel, he is not thinking merely of ways in which Israelite thought differed from that of ancient Mesopotamia: he is thinking of ways in which Israelite thought was distinguished from that of all other ancient Near Eastern cultures. It is therefore proper to point out that differences which one may succeed in establishing between Israel and ancient Mesopotamia do not necessarily establish the distinctiveness of Israel in the absolute sense: there is the possibility that the mode of thought in ancient Mesopotamia might have stood on one side, over against a mode of thought on the other which not only belonged to Israel but also was shared by some of her neighbours, so that it could have been the mode of thought of ancient Mesopotamia, not of Israel, which was distinctive in the sense of being unique—if, indeed, there did exist a conceptual chasm between the two sides.

Professor Lambert offers a summary of the characteristics of ancient Mesopotamian modes of thought. According to him, the Sumerians, Babylonians and Assyrians saw a world subject to various disasters, such as plague and flood, which were, however, never total. What held the forces of disaster in check was something called n a m . t a r in Sumerian and *šimtu* in Akkadian; these terms are conventionally translated 'destiny' in English.[27] Another term, m e in Sumerian and *parṣu* in Akkadian, often rendered 'decree', falls in the same semantic area.[28] Lists of the things denoted by the latter term occur in some texts;[29] they include such functions or concepts as godship, the throne of kingship, shepherdship (as a royal function), the royal insignia, various priestly offices, truth, sexual intercourse, prostitution, music, falsehood, various crafts, various kinds of religious awe or dread,[30] judgement and decision.[31] Professor Lambert, following Landsberger,[32] shows that these terms refer to the essential function in society or nature which an object, class of persons or institution was primevally invested with by the gods; the existence of such permanent functions was a basic concept in Mesopotamian civilization. He summarizes his conclusions by saying that

in the ancient Mesopotamian view every aspect of human society was decreed by the gods. Nothing was left to be chosen by the human race as suitable and convenient for it at a particular stage of development and in a particular geographical location.[33]

It may be useful to add two qualifications to this statement. Firstly, gods were not restricted to primeval time for decreeing fates. Thus, in a poem on the Sumerian city Kesh, it is repeatedly stated that the god An decreed its fate (apparently favourable for the future) after its destruction,[34] that is, in historical time. Secondly, divine decrees were not unalterable. Thus, it is stated in connection with the death of the Sumerian king Ur-Nammu:

> An altered his holy word . . .;
> Enlil . . . changed his decree of fate.[35]

Though Professor Lambert's statement of the situation in Mesopotamian thought is substantially acceptable, it is possible to question the correlated suggestion that the Mesopotamian view on the divine decreeing of the framework of human life and society was conceptually wholly distinct from the situation in Israelite thought. Professor Lambert says: 'The Hebrews lacked of course any idea of a series of impersonal regulations governing the whole universe. Yahweh laid down rules and could change them.'[36] The validity of this statement, as the basis of a distinction between the Israelite and Mesopotamian situation, may be questioned. It is difficult to understand why in the Mesopotamian context the destinies or decrees governing the universe are regarded as necessarily impersonal. In a number of cases—for example, in the myth *Enki and the World Order*—it is specifically stated that a named god bestowed the particular qualities, or 'destiny', upon the thing, place, group, or institution. Thus the decreeing of the destiny of the city of Ur is stated in the following terms:

He went to the shrine of Ur,
Enki, the lord of the *apsu*, decreed (its) destiny:
'City, possessing all that is appropriate, cleansed by water, firm-standing ox,
Dais of abundance that extends over the highland, green like a mountain,
Hashur-forest with wide-spreading shade, self-confident,
May your perfected decrees operate aright.

The great mountain, Enlil, has pronounced your great name in heaven
    and earth;
City, whose destiny Enki has decreed,
Shrine Ur, may you raise your neck to heaven.[37]

A destiny decreed by a named god in a polytheism is no more
impersonal than, say, such a decree as that of the sequence night
and day in the setting of Israelite monotheism.

A further point must be made on the comparison of Mesopotamian and Israelite data in relation to divine decrees. In this
comparison, it is necessary to distinguish between the existence of
concepts and the existence of categorization of concepts. It would
have been possible for the idea to be held that there had existed
from primeval times something called kingship, and something
called marriage and something called music, and so on, without
the superimposed concept that there was a general category to
which each and all of these concepts belonged. There is evidence
suggesting that though Israelites did not achieve the categorization
of the concepts regarded as divine decrees, the concepts themselves
existed.

Thus, although it is certainly true that there are no terms in
Hebrew serving as near equivalents of the Sumerian n a m . t a r
and m e , it is possible to challenge the assertion of Professor
Lambert that in Israel 'there is no . . . divine will manifested in the
precise forms of human social life and the arts of civilization'.[38]
One might argue that human marriage is a very clear example of
something decreed by God as a permanent institution in Israel no
less than in Mesopotamia. However, Professor Lambert attempts
to forestall this argument by suggesting that a crucial difference
existed between the Israelite and the Mesopotamian situations. He
says:

Marriage . . . was to the Hebrews a divinely appointed institution, but
there is no evidence that the precise details of the marriage rites were
held to have been laid down once for all by God, and were as such
immutable. No doubt traditional forms of the wedding ceremony were
clung to tenaciously amongst the Hebrews as elsewhere, but this was
not an article of faith. In contrast the Babylonians of one period were

enjoined to observe a celebration of nine days' duration because the mother goddess had so decreed at the creation of man.[39]

What is proved by the data adduced is that in Israel marriage as a social institution had been laid down by God in primeval times, and in Mesopotamia the details of weddings had been laid down by a deity in primeval times. It is difficult to follow the argument that, because there was in Israel no fixed length for a wedding, or if there was a fixed length we do not know it, the concept behind the divine appointment of the institution of marriage in Israel was totally different from that in Mesopotamia.

There are other instances which can be adduced of God in Israel having determined destinies in primeval times, in the sense (already accepted as found in Mesopotamia) of decreeing particular aspects of nature or of human society.

One clear example is represented by the words of God in Gen. 3:19: 'to dust you shall return'. In our terms this merely aetiologically explains an observed phenomenon, but then so does the determining of destinies for the various aspects of nature or society in Mesopotamia. Clearly, from the Israelite point of view, the disintegration of a dead body is represented as a divine decision in primeval times, and God could equally well have determined that the dead body should remain without corruption or should turn to ashes or be exposed to wild beasts and vultures, or it might have been decreed that men should—as Tertullian alleged was the case with the people of Pontus—'carve up their fathers' corpses along with mutton, to gulp down at banquets'.[40]

A second example of God in Israel decreeing a destiny in the sense established for Mesopotamia is found in Gen. 8:22:

> While the earth lasts
> seedtime and harvest, cold and heat,
> summer and winter, day and night,
> shall never cease.

This is a divine decree relating both to nature and to human society, inasmuch as the mention of seedtime and harvest is meaningless without reference to human agricultural activities.

Similarly, the preceding example, of the return of the body to dust —rather than being cremated, mummified, eaten cannibalistically or exposed to creatures of the wild—unquestionably presupposes the human institution of burial.

A clear example of a primeval divine decree fixing the framework of human life occurs in Gen. 6:3, recording God's decision that man 'shall live for a hundred and twenty years'. God did, indeed, later change his mind and reduce the period to seventy years, but this is no different in principle from the gods' treatment of some of their decrees in Mesopotamia. Kingship, for example, though a m e or 'decree', could be withdrawn from earth and taken back to heaven, as it was at the time of the Flood.[41]

Another passage, Gen. 9:6, without question makes God decree the institution of the blood feud:

> He that sheds the blood of a man,
> for that man his blood shall be shed.

The seventh-day Sabbath, as an aspect of human society decreed by God in primeval times, comes into the same category, at least in the late Priestly source (Gen. 2:3), though here there is the possibility that the concept of fixing the exact details of an institution in primeval times might have been directly influenced by Mesopotamian thought. Such influence is hardly possible, however, in the J story of God decreeing labour pains in primeval times as a permanent aspect of human life (Gen. 3:16).

Another instance, showing a clear parallel between Mesopotamian and Israelite modes of thought about the permanent nature of certain aspects of society, is seen in two references to the campaign season. Sargon II of Assyria refers to a certain month as being one which the Lord of Wisdom, Ninshiku, had prescribed in an ancient tablet for mustering the army.[42] One may set this alongside the statement in 2 Sam. 11:1 that King David started a campaign 'at the turn of the year, when kings take the field'. Granted, the biblical passage does not say that it was Yahweh who had decided that kings should follow this practice; but it was clearly thought of as a part of the scheme of society, fixed—

whether personally by Yahweh or by some impersonal power—in ancient times. Both in Assyria and in Israel the campaign season was a fixed institution, anciently pre-ordained as a facet of human society, not a matter upon which particular kings might decide for themselves.

In the light of such data, it seems difficult to accept that there was absent from Israelite religion the concept of divinely ordained and permanent regulations, decreed in primeval times, governing both the universe and human institutions. It is therefore not valid to find an antithesis between Mesopotamian and Israelite thought which might be summed up by saying (as Professor Lambert asserts) that in Mesopotamia 'the contrast was not, as among the Hebrews, between morally right and wrong, but between order and disorder'.[43] In all the Israelite examples given above, the fulfilment of the divine plan is a question of order or disorder, not of morally right or wrong. There was, for example, surely nothing morally wrong in a woman in childbirth in Israel not suffering labour pains; the fact was simply that this was part of human life as God had decreed it. This idea is, indeed, so strongly emphasized in the Genesis story, that the passage concerned could still be adduced in the nineteenth century A.D. for the argument that it would be impious, and a frustration of the divine intention, to employ anaesthetic methods in childbirth.

Thus it is as difficult to concur with the view that there was a total absence from Israelite thought of the concept of 'destiny' (in the sense earlier defined) as to accept the earlier suggestion that the gods were not, in Mesopotamian thought, believed to intervene directly in history. Both ideas are present in both cultures, and the supposed absence of one idea from one side or the other cannot be used to explain the distinctiveness of one side or the other. One may certainly feel that there is a greater emphasis upon direct intervention in history in Israel and upon destiny in Mesopotamia, but this impression can hardly be quantified, and even if it is factually based, represents differences of degree, not of principle.

Some scholars have gone beyond Albrektson's demonstration that in Mesopotamia as in Israel the gods were accepted as intervening in history, to see parallels not only in principle but also in detail. Thus, a number of writers have used terminology suggesting the presence in Mesopotamia of that particular view of divine intervention in history known by Old Testament scholars as the Deuteronomic theory of history, which predominates in the Bible in the books from Deuteronomy to Kings. This Deuteronomic view of history has two elements: it sees history as cyclic, and it sees the fortunes of a nation or a dynasty as directly linked to observance or disregard of the will of Yahweh. In the Bible both elements together are seen most clearly demonstrated in the Book of Judges, where this particular interpretation of history is set out in paradigm form. Thus, we find the following typical example:

The Israelites did what was wrong in the eyes of Yahweh; they forgot Yahweh their God and worshipped the Baalim and the Asheroth. Yahweh was angry with Israel and he sold them to Cushan-rishathaim ..., who kept them in subjection for eight years. Then the Israelites cried to Yahweh for help and he raised up a man to deliver them, Othniel ..., and he set them free. The spirit of Yahweh came upon him and he became judge over Israel. He took the field, and Yahweh delivered Cushan-rishathaim ... into his hands... Thus the land was at peace for forty years until Othniel ... died. Once again the Israelites did what was wrong in the eyes of Yahweh. (Jud. 3:7–12.)

The view of the cyclic nature of historical events is very clearly seen. Adversity led people to call to Yahweh, Yahweh raised up a deliverer, the deliverer gave security, security led to religious laxity, religious laxity brought down adversity upon the people. In the Books of Kings the retributive element remains very clearly seen, but the cyclic element is much less marked, although still present, being shown for example in weal under Hezekiah following his penitence (2 Kgs. 20:6), succeeded by disaster consequent upon the evil-doing in the time of Manasseh (2 Kgs. 21:9–12).

Some scholars have applied the terminology of the Deuteronomic theory of history to what is called the Tummal inscription, a Sumerian composition from the beginning of the second millennium. Tummal was a district in the city Nippur containing a shrine of the goddess Ninlil, spouse of the national god Enlil, and the inscription gives a schematic history of the fortunes of this shrine from its foundation to the time of the text's composition. It takes the following pattern:

For the second [third, fourth, etc.] time, the Tummal fell into ruins.
X built a building in the complex of Enlil's temple.
Y, son of X,
brought Ninlil to the Tummal.
For the third [fourth, fifth, etc.] time, the Tummal fell into ruins.[44]

This certainly expresses a cyclic view of history, but whether it is proper to regard it as presenting a Deuteronomic view seems less assured. It is certainly the case that, except at the end of the text, the falling into ruins of the Tummal is mentioned immediately before a ruler of a new dynasty exercising the kingship in Sumer. There is, however, no positive indication that the change in dynasty was thought of as a consequence of the Tummal's falling into ruins, and the absence of a specific statement that the Tummal fell into ruins immediately before the rise of the final dynast mentioned is against this view. The purpose of the text could equally well have been to promote the interests of the Tummal shrine, by demonstrating that all the greatest rulers made a point of restoring it. Oppenheim might be right by intuition in saying that the Tummal inscription serves 'to illustrate [the] belief that pious rulers received divine favors and those who did not respect the temple fell by divine interference',[45] but evidence to prove such an interpretation does not appear to be at present available.

Another Mesopotamian text for which an attempt has been made to establish the presence of a Deuteronomic view of history is the Weidner Chronicle.[46] This badly damaged text comprises a summary narrative of rulers of third-millennium dynasties. The piety of some, and the impiety of others, is mentioned, and related to the favour or disfavour of the gods towards the particular ruler. But whilst the retributive element is plain, it is difficult to see here a cyclic element, in the sense in which that is demonstrable in the biblical Deuteronomic history or in the Tummal inscription. The picture is not, as in Israel, of the fortunes of the state rising and falling in consequence of the piety or impiety of the ruler or of the people, but of the shifting of the power centre in accordance with the actions of particular rulers or dynasties, without any mention of the fortunes of the state itself. Certainly this shows, if further proof were needed, that the divine powers were thought in Mesopotamia to intervene in history to reward pious and to punish impious rulers, just as in Israel, but the case does not appear to have been made out for this intervention to have constituted a regular cyclic pattern of disobedience, disaster, repentance, divine support.[47]

This raises the wider point of whether, under a common acceptance in Israel and Mesopotamia of the possibility of divine intervention in history, there may have been quite different theological assumptions. Professor W. G. Lambert takes the view that there was such a difference. His argument is that in Israel the understanding of the events related to Abraham and his descendants implied 'a concept of history as including the working out of a plan',[48] and that this notion of a dynamic divine plan in the working out of history was not found in the Mesopotamian cultural area.

This is a very significant point, which deserves examination. In comparing the two civilizations in relation to this matter, it is particularly important to ensure that we are comparing like with like. Ideally, what we need to be able to compare is the concept of history held by contemporaries of similar social groups in the two cultural areas, for example, the kings Sargon II and Sennacherib in Assyria and Hezekiah in Judah. A difficulty is that although we have documents bearing on the matter from both sides, not only is there no reason to suppose that the two groups of documents were drawn up for the same purpose, but also the Old Testament documents, unlike the Assyrian documents in the main, are not in the raw state; they have been edited through many stages, and by the time of the final recension there had been abundant opportunities for introducing reflections upon Israelite history from a much later period, and with these reflections, concepts which were not those of the Israelite contemporaries of Sargon and Sennacherib. Source criticism reduces this difficulty, but does not eliminate it entirely; to appreciate the possible non-conclusiveness of source criticism, one has only to think of the areas of doubt still remaining about what may be accepted as originating from the eponyms themselves in the books of the three major prophets.

We may first examine the concept of the working out of a divine plan as attested in Israel in the pre-exilic period. In view of the fact that Yahwism was the religion associated with two distinct political entities, it might be productive to examine the concept comparatively between the two kingdoms of Israel and Judah. Since part of the divine plan as understood in Judah was specifically related to the Davidic monarchy, and as there was no comparable permanent dynasty in the political kingdom Israel, there must certainly have been some differences of concept in this area, though not necessarily major ones.[49] However, this itself would require a substantial monograph for adequate treatment, and for the present purpose discussion will be limited to the overall picture presented by the Old Testament, based mainly on evidence relating to Judah.

Eliminating any demonstrably post-exilic developments, and disregarding the superstructure built on the evidence by some modern theologians, we may recognize in the Old Testament, during the Monarchy period, two lines of thought about a divine plan in history. One saw a covenant of Yahweh with Abraham and his descendants, the other a covenant with David and his dynastic descendants. In terms of belief in a divine plan in history, the meaning of the so-called 'covenants' (or, better, 'treaties', to use a term without tendentious theological overtones) was that God had promised continued existence to the Israelite ethnic group, and to the line of David. Although it is true that some prophets actually questioned the popular understanding of the divine promises in such categorical terms,[50] this serves only to confirm that the predominant pre-exilic concept of a divine plan was centred on nothing other than the absolute belief in God's intention to preserve both the ethnic group and the dynasty. It is

not denied that exilic and post-exilic reflection upon the cata-
strophic end of the Judaean kingdom produced developments and
modifications of these beliefs, but these are not relevant to the
point at issue, which concerns the general pre-exilic Israelite view
of history, not theological extrapolations from it engendered by a
particular trauma.

In Mesopotamia, as in the Israelite cultural area, there is the
possibility, and indeed the strong likelihood, that different views of
history were held in the two kingdoms. This is indicated by the
fact that royal inscriptions of the Annals type, characteristic of
later Assyria, never developed in Babylonia. It is in later Assyria
that belief in a divine plan in history is most clearly discernible. To
establish an Assyrian belief in a divine plan in history, it is not
necessary to prove in the Assyrian sources indications of a view
precisely analogous with that in Israel, containing the concept of a
covenant between God and man—though one scholar has indeed
gone so far as to use 'covenant' terminology of one aspect of
Assyrian religion.[51] What is needed to prove the presence of the
concept of plan is to establish that the activities of the gods were
thought of as directed to some more remote objective than the
achievement of the immediate event, and that they were thought
of as operating a continuing intervention in history to that end.

Now it is precisely the claim of some of the Assyrian kings that
their elevation to the kingship is directed towards fulfilment of a
divine plan. Thus Sargon II ascribes his succession to the favour of
Ashur, and says of him that

(in order) to renew the cultus of the temple, to make the ritual perfect,
to make the cult-centre splendid, he steadfastly gazed on me amongst all
the black-headed (people) and promoted me. He fully made over the
land of Assyria into my hands for administration and direction; he made
my weapons bitter over the four (world) regions.[52]

Here it is indisputable that Sargon II claimed that Ashur was using
him as the instrument by which to prosecute a plan, with both
cultic and political implications. This is comparable with the
claims made for Yahweh's use of Judaean rulers. The same

Assyrian text gives further indications of a divine plan, not in the sense of something established by divine decree in primeval times and unchangeable, but of something which the god had decided should be effected within history. The text speaks of the city Ashur as 'the exalted cult-centre which (the god) Ashur its lord had chosen for the (world) region (as) the central base of kingship',[53] and then states that Sargon's predecessor had 'brought his hand to that city for evil'.[54] In consequence 'the Enlil of the gods in the anger of his heart overthrew his reign',[55] and, as Sargon put it, 'me, Sargon, the legitimate king, he promoted; he made me grasp sceptre, throne (and) crown'.[56] It is difficult to see how the overthrow of an Assyrian king by the god Ashur because of offences against his cult-city can be regarded as differing in principle from, for example, the overthrow by Jehu, at Yahweh's direction, of the dynasty of Ahab for cultic offences, or indeed, from the threat of death (subsequently modified) made against Hezekiah in 2 Kgs. 20:1-19. In all cases—Israelite and Assyrian—the change or threatened change is related to the prosecution of a supposed divine plan.

That it was the intention of the gods that the ruling Assyrian dynasty should endure, just as it was assumed to be part of Yahweh's plan that the Davidic dynasty should endure, is shown in numerous passages. Thus Tiglath-Pileser I, a century before King David, already claimed that the gods had given his dynasty a promise of eternal rule. Addressing the gods, and speaking of himself in the third person, he says:

You have given to him his lordly destiny for power, and said that his high-priestly seed should stand for ever in the temple Ehursagkurkurra [the temple of the national god Ashur].[57]

This is no less definite, as marking a divine plan, than the covenant of Yahweh with the house of David. One sees the same belief, in the concern of the Assyrian gods for the dynasty, some four centuries later under Esarhaddon. Esarhaddon's father and predecessor Sennacherib had been murdered, and there was rivalry over the succession. Esarhaddon records:

In the matter of exercising the kingship of my father's house I clapped
my hands. To Ashur, Sin, Shamash, Bel, Nabu and Nergal, Ishtar of
Nineveh and Ishtar of Arbela, I raised my hands (in prayer) and they
responded favourably to my utterance.[58]

Here it is unquestioningly assumed that it was the plan of the gods
that the kingship should remain with the particular dynasty. The
only question was which of the sons should succeed, and this
problem was not different at all from that which arose at the death
of David in Israel. There the eternal kingship was already assured
by the divine will to David's house, but there was room for dispute
as to which of David's sons was the destined heir. To settle this
dispute in his own favour, the steps which Solomon took, which
involved obtaining formal divine approval for his own claim and
besmirching and then murdering possible rivals, were similar to
those Esarhaddon took later.

There are other passages in Esarhaddon's inscriptions which
reinforce the view that the gods of Assyria had a plan in history,
effected through the continuance of one particular dynasty.
Esarhaddon makes the specific claim of a continuing dynasty of
Assyrian kings caring for the temple of Ashur, from Ushpia, the
original builder, through named rulers of the second millennium,
down to himself.[59] His own restoration of the temple was more
than a matter of ensuring the proper continuance of the cult: he
specifically stated that for the purpose of rebuilding he employed
captives from other lands, so that other peoples might observe the
might of the god Ashur, to which end he ensured that they saw
him himself (Esarhaddon) carrying the building-hod on his head.[60]
He specifically claimed '[the gods] commissioned me myself
against (any) land that sinned against Ashur', and added 'Ashur,
father of the gods, filled my hand (with power) to disrupt and to
settle, to make broad the boundary of the land of Assyria.'[61]
Clearly, to preserve the royal dynasty, to lead the Assyrian armies
victoriously into foreign lands, to punish rebellion against Ashur,
to extend the Assyrian boundaries, and to show the might of
Ashur to all mankind, both by the god's conquests and by his
splendour in the Assyrian capital, were all aspects of the divine

plan, in the view of Esarhaddon. The divine plan for the continuation of the dynasty, for the purpose of exalting the might of Ashur, is frequently alluded to elsewhere in Esarhaddon's inscriptions. Thus he refers to himself, with his genealogy given through his immediate predecessors, as of 'the eternal seed of kingship of Bel-bani son of Adasi, founder of the kingship of the land Assyria',[62] and this is in the context both of restoration of temples and of the gods bringing all lands into submission under his feet. Sennacherib equally thought in terms of the gods willing the continuation of the dynasty for ever, subject to due piety to the gods. He set up a stele which should say to Ashur: 'May his sons and grandsons abide . . . for ever',[63] with the exhortation to dynastic successors to restore the temple if it fell into ruins and to anoint the stele; the inscription contained further the threat that any successor who failed in this duty would be met with the divine curse and the overthrow of his kingship.[64]

The very epithets applied to Ashur as national god of the military state of Assyria reflect his divine plan, which was to ensure the dominion of Assyria and to quell those who sought to disturb the *pax Assyriaca*. He is the one 'who overthrows all the disobedient', 'who scatters the wicked', 'who acts against him who does not fear his word';[65] the one 'from whose net the evil-doer cannot flee';[66] the one who 'as to him who does not fear his word, who trusts in his own strength and, forgetting the might of his divinity, speaks arrogance, rushes against him furiously in the clash of battle and shatters his weapons'.[67] The various instances of evil mentioned in these phrases refer to particular offences against the god Ashur in the form of opposition to the military might of Assyria, which clearly supports the view that Ashur had a plan in history for Assyrian imperialism, and that any opposition to Assyria was an impiety against him. W. von Soden speaks in connection with Assyrian imperial expansion of 'a kind of theology of holy war',[68] in which the dominant theme was that the god Ashur had made the claim to rule over all men. The idea that Assyrian military activity was in prosecution of a plan of the god can be exemplified again and again. Thus we find Sargon II using phrases such as 'At the command of Ashur I defeated them', 'I mustered the mighty hosts of Ashur', 'I raised my hand to Ashur that the Mannaean land might be avenged'.[69] Evidence of this kind, which could be much multiplied, shows that the gods, in particular Ashur, were promoting Assyrian imperialism, not in terms of a destiny decreed in primeval times, but as an activity within history relating to extending the might of the nation Assyria and perpetuating the dynasty. Whilst it is true that we do not find covenant terminology used for these concepts, it is difficult to see how the situation differs in principle from that relating to the divine plan for the continuance of the nation deriving from Abraham and the line founded by David in Israel. Such differences as there are between Israel and Assyria in this respect must be looked for in terms of relative emphasis, not of basic principle.

There is one piece of evidence, not relating specifically to the Assyrians, that could be adduced as an explicit, and possibly native, statement of a wholly static view of society in Mesopotamia, contradicting the idea of a continuing dynamic plan. This comes in a fragment attributed to the third-century B.C. Babylonian priest Berossos, as quoted by Alexander Polyhistor. The passage in question refers to the appearance of the divine being Oannes to the people of Mesopotamia in primeval times, and reads:

(Oannes) [the god of Wisdom] gave men acquaintance with letters and skills and crafts of every kind. (He taught them) to build cities, to found temples, and to frame laws... He showed them seeds and how to harvest the fruits; all in all, he bestowed on men everything tending to make life comfortable. From that time, nothing further has been discovered.[70]

This might appear to be conclusive as a representation of Mesopotamian attitudes, since the earlier part of the quotation is a substantially accurate reflection of traditions and attitudes found in original cuneiform sources. Yet one may fairly ask whether the conclusion to the section—'From that time, nothing further has been discovered'—really does represent an encapsulation of a traditional Babylonian view, or whether it might not be a later deduction from the earlier traditions under the influence of Hellenistic thought. It should be remembered that a Jewish contemporary of Berossos expressed very much the same view as that just quoted:

> What has been is what will be,
> and what has been done is what will be done;
> and there is nothing new under the sun.
> Is there a thing of which it is said,
> 'See, this is new'?
> It has been already,
> in the ages before us. (Eccles. 1:9–10 [RSV].)

It would be grossly misleading to take this as representing the characteristic Israelite view during the monarchy, and we must therefore be chary of accepting the view ascribed, at the end of the previous quotation, to Berossos, as typical of earlier Babylonians and Assyrians.

It is, in fact, easy to demonstrate that the Assyrians of the first millennium did not think in terms of details of life primevally fixed, to which nothing new could be added or in which nothing could be altered. We know of many instances in Assyria in which humans recognized that they had made new technological advances. In some cases they piously said that the gods had revealed the new discovery to them, but even so that revelation, and the new process or material or architectural form, came in their own lifetime, not in primeval mythic time. Sennacherib, for example, recorded a number of changes from what had been done in older times. He re-designed Nineveh, and although he did indeed refer to its plan as having been 'designed from of old', he then went on to say that the site of the palace there had become too small, and that no previous ruler had thought 'to lay out the streets of the city, to widen the squares, to dig a canal, to plant trees'.[71] Despite the theoretical primeval plan, Sennacherib held that it was according to the will of the gods that he should make considerable alterations quite out of keeping with the earlier scheme of things. This included altering the channel of one of the tributaries of the Tigris.[72] The gods also showed him various sources of minerals which had not been discovered before.[73] As a result of the clever understanding which the god Ninshiku had given him, Sennacherib pondered over the problem of casting large objects in bronze and worked out a technique which no one had ever used before.[74] There was nothing about this piece of technology having always existed hidden in the womb of time; Sennacherib was quite specific about having thought it out for himself. He claimed:

Through the clever understanding which the noble Ninshiku had given me, in my own wisdom I pondered deeply the matter of carrying out that task. Following the guidance of my head and the prompting of my heart, I fashioned a work of bronze and skilfully achieved it.

Other kings introduced architectural innovations;[75] it is true that these were borrowed from Syria rather than invented from scratch, but even allowing that the Mesopotamian gods had 'decreed the destiny' of particular types of building in Syria (and this is nowhere claimed or even hinted at), it has to be accepted that those gods had left it to human initiative to discover the appropriateness of such buildings for Mesopotamia.

The foregoing evidence has been adduced against the suggestion that the people of ancient Mesopotamia saw their gods as having decreed everything in primeval times, with no place left for divine intervention and the development of a divine plan within history. The other side of the claim that Israelite religious thought was distinctive in that it alone saw God as acting in history is that the people of ancient Mesopotamia saw the divine in the cyclic process of nature and that in this they differed significantly from the Israelites. Yet there are very clear indications that in some quarters and periods in Israel Yahweh was also recognized as operating in and through nature. It is, indeed, not always possible to make a sharp distinction between intervention in history and operation in the realm of nature, as one may be an aspect of, or the mechanism of, the other; obvious cases are famine, flood, or the giving or withholding of rain and fertility.

It must be conceded, however, that the activity of Yahweh in and through nature was sometimes questioned. Yet it is significant that this questioning came not primarily from Yahwists concerned to preserve the distinction between Yahweh and gods representing aspects of nature; on the contrary, it originally came from polytheistic quarters, in which it was claimed that some other deity, and not Yahweh, controlled particular aspects of nature. The latter situation was clearly operative when Hosea found it necessary to insist that it was Yahweh, not Baal, who granted fertility. He represented Yahweh as saying: '[Israel] does not know that it is I who gave her corn, new wine, and oil' (2:8). Furthermore, the question of the control over nature appears to have been one aspect of the contest between Elijah and the prophets of Baal at Carmel; this is certainly suggested by the coming of rain, to break the long drought, which immediately followed upon the vindication of Yahweh in the contest (1 Kgs. 18:41).[76]

Such evidence, which has been amply discussed in the standard works on Israelite religion,[77] makes it clear that, whatever the precise form of the link between Yahweh and nature, Yahweh was certainly thought to act in nature, not only in the primeval creation but also within history. J. L. Crenshaw, one of the scholars to touch upon this problem most recently, is certainly justified in concluding that both Yahweh and the Mesopotamian gods were regarded as controlling both history and nature.[78]

Yet even though the operation of both Yahweh and the Mesopotamian gods could be recognized in the cyclic process of nature, there remains the possibility of a significant difference in the mechanism. One possibility which requires examination is the suggestion that, albeit he controlled nature equally with the Mesopotamian gods, Yahweh stood outside nature in a way the Mesopotamian gods did not.

Th. Jacobsen (not, it may be noted, writing in the context of a direct comparison between Israel and Mesopotamia) states the Sumerian situation for the relationship of the gods to natural phenomena in these terms:

Utu is the numinous power that comes into being as the sun, the sun-god, and the visible form which that power takes is the flaming sun disk; the language allows no distinction between the two.[79]

It is, however, doubtful if the claimed lack of possibility of differentiation can be maintained in the rigid terms in which Jacobsen states it. One does in fact find passages where a distinction is made between the Sun-god and the physical sun. Thus, in the myth *Enki and the World Order* we read:

The valiant Utu [the Sun-god], the firm-standing bull . . .,
The father of the great city, the place where rises the sun, the great herald of holy Anu.[80]

Here undoubtedly the god and the physical sun are distinguished, the latter not being marked with the god determinative. Yet it has to be added that two lines later the distinction becomes blurred, for the text continues:

The judge, . . .
The one wearing a beard of lapis lazuli, who rises from the horizon to the pure heaven.[81]

Here the epithets clearly refer to the Sun-god, not merely to the sun, and it is the Sun-god himself who moves across the sky. The situation as to the phenomenon and the numen might therefore be re-stated in the following terms. The Mesopotamian was consciously aware that the phenomenon was not the actual divine being. Yet he felt so vividly the numinous power behind the visible object that the latter immediately made real for him the presence of the god himself. That is, there was a very strong sense of the immanence of the divine in the natural world, although this stopped short of pantheism.

Jacobsen elsewhere adduces a text which offers a striking example to substantiate both this sense of the immanence of the divine in nature, and at the same time the clear recognition of the distinction between the divine being and nature. The text, commenting on the death of the god Dumuzi, reads (in Jacobsen's translation):

You who are not the cream were poured out with the cream,
You who are not the milk were drunk with the milk.[82]

Unmistakably, this text on the one hand makes a positive distinction between the god and the milk, and on the other sees the numinous power of the god as present in the milk.

Other examples of the immediate relationship between the numinous power and the divine being may be adduced. Thus, just as it is possible to say that Utu represented both the Sun-god and the sun-disk, so Ishkur represented both the Sumerian Weather-god and the south wind. But this statement again requires some refinement. We have a hymn which contains the following lines:

When Father Ishkur goes out of his house, he is a roaring stormwind,
When he goes out of his house, out of his city, he is a young wild ox;
When he roars from the storm to heaven, he is a booming stormwind.[83]

This might appear to be conclusive for the identification 'Ishkur equals stormwind'. But it was not quite so simple. That this straightforward identification did not fully cover the concept is clear from what is said elsewhere in the hymn. In one group of lines the god is praised as 'Father Ishkur, who rides on a stormwind', and in another place in the same composition he is told by Enlil:

My son, I have given you the stormwinds, I have harnessed the stormwinds for you, . . .
I have harnessed the seven winds for you like a team, I have harnessed the stormwinds for you.[84]

Here the stormwinds are something distinct from and controlled by Ishkur. The Sumerian was conscious that the stormwinds were not Ishkur. None the less, they had a numinous quality which for the Sumerian meant that Ishkur was indeed immanent in the stormwinds.

When we turn to the Old Testament we find that some of the things quoted as said about Utu the Sun-god or Ishkur the Weather-god could in Israel be said about Yahweh. Thus he might ride on the clouds or the wings of the wind.[85] But, contrary to the situation in Mesopotamian religion, he could never be directly equated with the physical sun or with the wind.

That last categorical statement requires to be justified, in the face of evidence which some would say exists for sun-worship in Israel.[86] There is a passage in Job which bears directly on this:

If I ever looked on the sun in splendour
or the moon moving in her glory,
and was led astray in my secret heart
and raised my hand in homage;
this would have been an offence before the law,
for I should have been unfaithful to God [El] on high. (31:26-8.)

Also, astral worship is specifically forbidden in Deut. 4:19 and 17:3, implying knowledge of it in Israel. Some have also taken Ps. 19 to contain lines borrowed from a hymn to the sun, but even if one accepts this improbable suggestion, it is irrelevant to the discussion of Israelite religion, since, as Ringgren points out, this Psalm 'never equates Yahweh with the sun; instead, Yahweh (or El) is the creator of the sun'.[87]

The passages from Job and Deuteronomy, on the other hand, certainly envisage the possibility of sun-worship in Israel. However, they clearly regard such a thing as apostasy from Yahweh. This, therefore, reinforces the idea that the sun could not be thought of as simply an aspect of Yahweh; if one worshipped the sun one was not worshipping Yahweh in another manifestation, one was worshipping something other than Yahweh. The sun is merely a part of Yahweh's creation, and wholly distinct from him. Yahweh is never regarded as being immanent in the sun.

A corresponding situation applied for the stormwind. Indeed, to emphasize this, we have the story of the theophany to Elijah at Horeb. Yahweh was passing by, and there was first a hurricane, then an earthquake, and then fire. Yahweh was present in none of these, but in what came finally—not 'a still small voice' as conventionally rendered, but rather 'a numinous silence'.[88] Yahweh controlled all the forces of nature, but was immanent in none of them.

This suggests a new direction in which to look in seeking a principle to which to attach the differences ascertainable between Israelite and Mesopotamian religion. The usual procedure has been to look for something positive in Israelite religion which is not found elsewhere, such as a particular view of history or a particular view of the nature of man. Here, however, in the Israelite view of God in history and nature, we find close parallels between the Israelite and Mesopotamian concepts right up to the final question of the being of God himself. At this point comes a marked divergence; the sense of Israelite religious thought is given by a negative—not by what God is but by what he is not. He is not immanent in the heavenly bodies or the wind, and—by another negative in another context—God is not representable in human form or animal form, and—by yet another negative—the divine has not a multiplicity of forms. Furthermore, as we shall see later, he is not approachable by certain techniques. It might well be productive to re-examine the whole of Israelite religious thought not in terms of positives but in terms of negatives, to identify not new concepts added by Israel but common ancient Near Eastern concepts rejected. If indeed Israelite religion was unique, it is possible that the essence of that uniqueness lay in the recognition of what God was not.

The Divine in Relation to Good and Evil

In ancient Israelite society a man received a measure of protection from human enemies by group-solidarity of the clan and the institution of blood-vengeance, and knew that any evil done by himself against another man would be liable to corresponding sanctions. In Mesopotamia, where the tribal system had been largely superseded by the city-state organization as early as the third millennium, it was the state that protected a man from his enemies and the state to which he was answerable for his own misdeeds. Thus, despite the considerable differences between the structures of the two societies, in both of them a man was able to recognize a direct relationship between human evil-doing and human retribution.

It was, however, common experience that evil could befall a man which had no apparent human activation. Obvious examples are natural disasters such as flooding, drought or earthquake, and personal misfortunes such as painful illness and untimely death. Man was therefore faced with the problem of explaining the origin of such evils, not merely as a theological problem, but also with the hope, in understanding their origin, of finding means to circumvent them.

One primitive view of the nature of evil and evil-doing, still evidenced in both the Mesopotamian texts and the Bible, was that it was an invisible physical substance or contagion. A probable instance of this comes in the scapegoat ritual in Lev. 16:20-2 (though this is speaking specifically of human sins):

When Aaron has finished making expiation . . ., he shall bring forward the live goat. He shall lay both his hands on its head and confess over it all the iniquities of the Israelites and all their acts of rebellion, that is all their sins; he shall lay them on the head of the goat and send it away into the wilderness in charge of a man who is waiting ready. The goat shall carry all their iniquities upon itself into some barren waste and the man shall let it go, there in the wilderness.[1]

In Mesopotamia, magical rituals in which people or buildings were wiped with various objects to absorb evil are relics of a similar view of the physical nature of evil.[2] The same idea is reflected in texts which mention the removing, driving away, or wiping out of such things as sins or curses, or which speak of their disposal by their going up to heaven like smoke, being carried to the bottom of a river, or being consumed like a flame.[3]

Yet despite these residual traces of the idea of evil as a physical substance acting in a non-deistic setting, the predominant concept was that evil was a circumstance brought upon a man by some will; the two ideas could of course be linked, and sometimes were, by evil being thought of as a noxious substance directed by a will.

Evils which befell a man could be secretly activated by human wills of malevolent witches,[4] but this falls outside the scope of our theme. Except for evils so explained, man had to see them either as the random result of blind chance, or as originating in the sphere of the divine. But neither in Mesopotamia, where the gods had decreed the form of society, nor in Israel, where God ruled over all, was the concept of blind chance acceptable; wherefore evils with no manifest human activation had to be explained as having their origin in the supernatural sphere. There were two main possibilities: such evils could arrive because the gods had willed them, or they could owe their existence to the fact that alongside the gods there existed malevolent powers which the gods had not held in check.

Beings in the numinous world were by no means limited to those which might be called gods. Even in Israelite religion, for example, there were, alongside Yahweh himself, such supernatural beings as cherubim, seraphim, and the Destroyer (or Angel of Death, a being distinct from Yahweh, though acting for him, in the tenth plague of Egypt). In the religion of Mesopotamia, the official pantheon, considerable as it was, was far from comprising all numinous beings, for apart from the gods, demons

—good, neutral or bad, but especially bad—roamed the earth and might make themselves felt in almost any aspect of life. In view of the evil with which demons were often associated, an examination of them in the two cultures may shed some light on the attitude of the two peoples to the divine in relation to good and evil.

G. Van der Leeuw, looking at demons from the point of view of the phenomenology of religion generally, though with glances at the Mesopotamian data, reached the conclusion that 'no essential difference can be admitted between demon and god'.[5] He qualified this by adding that 'everywhere demons are older than gods', and that a demon 'may become a god—if he does not become a devil'. E. Ebeling, speaking from his unrivalled knowledge of Mesopotamian religious texts, similarly expressed the view that 'there is no intrinsic difference between [demons] and the great gods, only a matter of degree'.[6]

Although Van der Leeuw was unable to accept demons as being different in essence from gods, he did pinpoint one significant difference in behaviour, that is, the basic irrationality and arbitrariness of demons. As he put it, 'the demons' behaviour is arbitrary, purposeless, even clumsy and ridiculous, but despite this it is no less terrifying'.[7] This purposelessness of the behaviour of demons is clearly seen in Mesopotamia.[8] Not only might they kill a man in the open country, motivelessly, without reference to his relationship with the gods nor in retribution for anything he might have done or left undone; but they might even pointlessly interfere with the animal world, disturbing pigeons and other birds in their nests or hidey-holes, or lashing cattle and sheep to make them run and scatter.[9] They were also responsible for such inexplicable behaviour as a bride or bridegroom running away from their own wedding.[10] Whatever the situation when humans suffered, there was clearly nothing essentially evil about pigeon-poking; it was merely pointless mischief. It was not evil itself which marked the activities of demons, nor was the distinction between good and evil behaviour a means of differentiating between gods and demons. Such a god as Enlil could act immorally or amorally or unwisely, but he did not act motivelessly.

In general, less attention has been paid to demons in the study of Mesopotamian religion than their existential importance would warrant. The main factor underlying this situation is that to the elitist social stratum through whose eyes we mainly view Mesopotamian religion—that is, the professional scribes—the demons were not quite respectable; though clearly of considerable significance to the ordinary man, they were in the official theology regarded as subordinate to the gods of the pantheon, despite traces in myth fragments of this not always having been so. Inasmuch as scholars dealing with Mesopotamian religion have (not unreasonably) usually approached it via the evidence from within the cultus, there has been a tendency to treat beliefs related to demons as less significant—or at least less worthy of serious research—than the official theology incorporated in such categories of texts as hymns, prayers, myths and theogonies. This attitude has been reinforced by a tendency amongst Assyriologists to make a Frazerian division between magic and religion, and to treat demons, insofar as they have been regarded as worthy of consideration at all, as an aspect of magic rather than of religion. Thus in Edouard Dhorme's *Les religions de Babylonie et d'Assyrie* (Paris, 1949), an important book of over 300 pages, demons receive a mere three pages, and that in the middle of the chapter 'Magie, divination, astrologie'. In Bruno Meissner's *Babylonien und Assyrien*, II (Heidelberg, 1925), the allocation of space to demons is rather more generous, though there also the main discussion of them comes in the chapter on Magic.

There is substantial evidence that belief in demons was of at least as much practical significance in the everyday life of the ordinary man in Mesopotamia as was belief in the gods. Not only do apotropaic incantations against demons form the central subject-matter of one major and several associated minor text series,[11] but in addition there are innumerable references and allusions to the activities of demons scattered throughout the whole of Sumerian and Akkadian literature, and not a few representations of them in the form of amulets.[12] The sheer quantity and diversity of the data makes it very difficult to formulate any irrefutable generalizations about the nature of Mesopotamian demons, or to isolate in what respects, if any, they differed from gods. There are, however, a few points of difference between gods and demons which may tentatively be identified, in addition to the arbitrariness of demons noted by Van der Leeuw. Demons, unlike gods, are never complete personalities; they seldom have individual names (the few apparent exceptions, such as Lamashtu and Pazuzu, spill over into being generic names), they are never creators, and they have no function in the world-order. On the positive side, a demon possesses one property which does not appear to be attributed to any god, namely, the ability to enter into (or attach itself to) a man's body:[13] good as well as evil demons could do this.[14]

These points will be returned to later. Meanwhile, we may note one significant difference between Ebeling and Van der Leeuw in their view of the relationship between gods and demons. Ebeling, though not questioning the identity of essence between gods and demons, is prepared to admit a difference of degree between beings of the two categories, but Van der Leeuw does not accept this. Speaking of the situation in relation to Greek religion, Van der Leeuw expressly states the view that the *daimon* does not 'by any means imply an inferior being' relative to a *theos*.[15] Against Ebeling, what Van der Leeuw urges for the Greek situation can be shown to be true for at least one group of Mesopotamian demons; such demons were not necessarily inferior in degree to the great gods, and could even be designated by the same term *ilu*. There are several instances in which the powers of a particular group of demons were matched with, and even temporarily proved superior to, those of particular great gods. The best known instance is that of demons attacking the Moon-god at the time of the eclipse:

In the broad heavens, the dwelling of Anu, the king,
They take their stand for evil, there is none to oppose.
. . .
When the seven of them, the evil *ilū*, forced their way into the vault of
  the heavens,

They clustered angrily round Nanna, the Moon-god;

. . .

So he was dark by night and day, he did not sit in his lordly dwelling place.[16]

The Moon-god had to be rescued by other gods. Elsewhere we have mention of the demons overcoming the god Nergal, Lord of the Underworld,[17] and in another passage they appear to challenge the gods in heaven.[18]

It will be noticed that in the passage just quoted the evil numinous beings, generally referred to as 'the Seven', are called 'evil *ilū* [gods]'. As elsewhere 'the Seven' are designated by terms specifically applied to demons,[19] this supports the view that there was no intrinsic difference between gods and at least these particular demons. It may also be noted that even a great god could be spoken of as becoming a demon in respect to a particular person,[20] but this was (when an evil demon was meant) probably a secondary metaphorical usage, simply implying that the god would act in the same maliciously hostile manner as eventually came to be thought of as characteristic for a demon.

Demons are most clearly catalogued and categorized in the text series *Utukkū Lemnūtu*, 'Evil demons', although there are also lists of types of demons in other series and in individual texts. Leaving aside 'the Seven' at present, we find that the main lists of demons are divisible into three main groups.

First comes a group of six types of demon, all of them regularly qualified in these lists by the epithet *lemnu* 'evil'.[21] The use of the epithet indicates that demons in these categories were not evil in essence; had they been so, the adjective would have been tautologous. That they were not essentially evil is confirmed by the fact that one does sometimes find, in other texts, beings of several of these categories qualified as 'good'.[22]

Alongside the six demons just mentioned are two other groups of three each, which are never (in the catalogues of demons in *Utukkū Lemnūtu*) specified as 'evil';[23] in their case, as it is quite clear that they are always thought of as acting evilly, the evil must be inherent in their nature. This difference in essential nature suggests that these six represent a different stratum of religious concept and that they originated at a later stage than the former six. One of these two groups centred on a female demon (or class of demon) called Lamashtu, who attacked babies and women after childbirth, and the other comprised Lilitu (the prototype of biblical Lilith) and two related beings.[24] Occasionally further demons, such as Death, Evil Fate, Fever, intrude into the standard lists just mentioned.[25]

This brief analysis has disregarded the group known as 'the Seven', whom we have already met. Some scholars have attempted to identify them as comprising seven specific categories from amongst those named in the principal lists,[26] but this is demonstrably artificial, since the grouping into six, three and three is consistent and many times repeated, whilst groups which include seven named types of demon are rare and inconsistent. When 'the Seven' are described, they are seen to have certain characteristics—mainly negative—setting them apart from other demons. They are sexless,[27] nameless,[28] and formless—indeed, their formlessness is such that they 'are not even recognizable by the wise gods'.[29] J. Lewy has argued that this group is identical with some divine beings known as 'the seven sons of Enmesharra',[30] although it must be added that whilst 'the Seven' are of frequent mention in *Utukkū Lemnūtu*, the name of Enmesharra occurs there only as that of one of the gods by whom demons are exorcized.[31]

According to a well known text of the late Assyrian period, Enmesharra was a god who voluntarily abdicated power to the subsequent heads of the pantheon, An and Enlil.[32] In an alternative form of the myth, Enmesharra did not abdicate voluntarily but was forcibly ejected from his position of supremacy;[33] it was in the light of this form of the myth that Enmesharra and his sons came to have applied to them the description 'the bound gods'.[34] Various conclusions could be drawn from this ambivalent view of Enmesharra and his sons. The two different attitudes could be correlated with a good and a bad side of 'the Seven', since 'the seven sons of Enmesharra' sometimes appear to have a benevolent nature.[35] On the other hand, some scholars take the view that there were distinct groups of seven good beings and seven evil beings within this area, only one group being identifiable with the sons of Enmesharra.[36]

The references in myth fragments to Enmesharra are usually taken as evidence that he was a primeval god who had once been supreme, and with this view the meaning of the name—'Lord of the numinous power of everything'[37]—would appear to accord. Also in agreement with this hypothesis is the fact that in the theogonies Enmesharra constituted the generation antecedent to Enlil, or even a god outside the Enlil theogony.[38]

Accordingly, some scholars have thought of the sons of Enmesharra as gods of an older pantheon, or of an older stage of the existing pantheon, who had been superseded and reduced to demons.[39] There are, however, indications that the development was rather more complex.

If in fact Enmesharra had been a relic of an old sub-stratum pantheon, older than the pantheon of the historical period headed by An, Enlil and Enki, one would expect the name Enmesharra to show some indication of sub-stratum origin. But neither in language nor in concept does it manifest any sub-stratum features. It is of the same type as the names Enlil and Enki, the initial syllable e n marking the bearer of the name as the lord of some aspect of existence; and it is indubitably Sumerian. As to the concept it expresses—'Lord of the numinous power of everything'—, this seems to be more, not less, sophisticated than the concepts underlying either the name Enlil ('Lord Wind') or Enki ('Lord Earth'). The name appears to represent an abstraction, comprehending the totality of the supernatural powers experienced by the early Sumerians.[40]

Beyond points already noticed, there is relatively little data about Enmesharra, except to indicate that he possessed certain chthonic features.[41] Other than his putative former headship of the pantheon, he appears to have no function and no properties.

The most conspicuous fact about Enmesharra was his seven sons. Now these seven sons, if it is correct to identify them with 'the Seven', originally lacked names, forms, and anthropomorphic features:[42] they were simply invisible formless numinous forces. It is therefore suggested that Enmesharra originated simply as an abstraction to comprehend the totality of the concept included in the formless nameless numina known as 'the Seven'.[43]

According to the specific statement of the ancient texts, 'the Seven' were winds.[44] This being so, it might appear odd that Enmesharra, if indeed father of 'the Seven', shows no connection with winds either in his name or in his characteristics. This apparent anomaly would, however, be readily explicable if Enmesharra was not, in the religio-historical sense, the point of origin of 'the Seven', but merely the abstract summation of their numinous properties. Now alongside the fact that Enmesharra, nominally the earlier head of the pantheon, had no overt connection with winds, we have to place the fact that the god Enlil, effectively current head of the pantheon, was, by the very meaning of his name, 'Lord Wind'. In the theogonies, as we have already noted, Enlil derived immediately (though not ultimately) from Enmesharra.[45] Logically, of course, Enmesharra's seven sons also derived immediately from him. Enlil was thus theologically a substitute form or equivalent of, the seven sons of Enmesharra in name, function, and theogony. Enlil differed from 'the Seven', which represented wind numina but were nameless and formless, in that he as 'Lord Wind' was in anthropomorphic form.

It is therefore suggested that the suppression of the seven sons of Enmesharra represented the stage at which the anthropomorphic form of Enlil arose, so that the older non-anthropomorphic representations of the same forces, as formless winds, became suppressed. A corresponding development has been shown by Jacobsen for Abzu, the primordial waters, defeated and superseded by the god Enki, and for Imdugud, the numen of the stormclouds, similarly replaced by the god Ninurta.[46] In each case the old numen lived on, retaining a pre-anthropomorphic form, alongside the anthropomorphic god who had in some respects replaced it. The very primitive numina replaced by Enlil retained not only non-anthropomorphic but even animistic forms.[47]

The view that Enmesharra had his origin in theological speculation rather than that he was an otiose deity of popular religion receives added support from the fact that later theogonies introduced a number of further generations back beyond Enmesharra. The list is variable and the deities concerned have already been recognized as originating in scribal speculative theology, as a means of increasing the separation between Enlil and his ultimate source Earth.[48]

This interpretation of the relationship between the wind numina, Enmesharra and Enlil accords with the general view expressed by Van der Leeuw that demons were older than gods. On the other hand, his statement that 'demons might become gods' could well be modified; it might be better to say rather (at least in relation to Mesopotamian religion) that demons might represent an earlier form of those numinous forces which at another level of religion actually became gods. This situation provides material for comparison with the data from ancient Israel, where some scholars have suggested that certain narratives about Yahweh demonstrate the incorporation into him of earlier demons.

The foregoing argument is limited to one particular group of Mesopotamian demons, 'the Seven'. Other groups can be shown to have had quite a different origin and background, and some of them were certainly not reduced gods, nor even ancient numina.

One of the best known, and most feared, of demons was a female demon (or class of demon) bearing the name Lamashtu.[49] Our knowledge of this demon goes back to the beginning of the second millennium, when we meet her in both Old Assyrian and Old Babylonian incantations, though in the former not by name but by her description (common later), 'daughter of Anu'.[50]

In the Old Assyrian text mentioned, there is reference to a myth according to which the Sky-god Anu cast his daughter out from heaven to earth, because of bad counsel and rebellious advice.[51] The text goes on to describe the daughter of Anu: her hair hangs free and her loincloth is stripped off. Clearly this being is fully

anthropomorphic, and cannot *prima facie* be brought into connection with any old pre-anthropomorphic numen. The description of her is significant: she is a woman naked and completely
helpless. It is therefore interesting to see what she developed into.
She became above all the demon who attacked women in childbirth and babies, and there is already allusion to her effect upon
babies in the Old Assyrian text.[52] It is easy enough to suggest
glibly that Lamashtu was a personification of the dangers that
faced a woman and her child at and after childbirth, but there is no
immediate clue as to why such a figure should be identified with
the daughter of the supreme god, nor why that divine figure
should have been cast out of heaven.

In the *Atrahasis* myth, a demon was specifically created after the
Flood as one of the mechanisms by which the number of the
human race might be kept within reasonable bounds. This demon
was designated by a term, *pāšittu*, which was also applied to the
daughter of Anu.[53] Whilst this does not conclusively prove a
connection between the destructive demon in the *Atrahasis* myth
and Lamashtu, it is significant that *Atrahasis* was specifically linked
with a ritual of childbirth,[54] that is, with the very *rite de passage* in
which Lamashtu was particularly active.

It is thus possible to see in the background of the mythology of
the daughter of Anu, alias *pāšittu*, alias Lamashtu, two distinct
views on a theological problem. The problem was: why is there a
demon who attacks nursing mothers and babies? Two conflicting
answers were available. One was that the attacking being, although
divine and powerful and indeed daughter of the supreme god, was
a rebel divinity, and had already suffered punishment from the
supreme god for rebellion against the divine will: this bore the
implication that Lamashtu's malevolence against a particularly
helpless segment of humanity was not in accordance with the will
of the great gods. On this view, Lamashtu represented an evil
principle in opposition to the divine. The alternative and sharply
conflicting answer was that the activities of this demon were
actually part of the divine plan, intended to control the numbers
of the human race.

Some other demons were manifestly personifications of particular symptoms, attitudes or mental states, such as 'Headache-disease', Fate, Temper (*niziqtum*). That they were personifications is clear from the fact that in the texts the terms oscillate between denoting the symptom (or attitude or mental state) and denoting a being whose appearance could be described. Thus *di'u* ('Headache-disease') could be the disease itself,[55] but it could also actually be a demon, in which form it was described as having the appearance of a Lamashtu (with the epithet *pāšittu*), with the head of an Alû-demon and the body of an Abubu-monster.[56]

We have noted the view that there is no distinction of essence between gods and demons. This is true of the primordial demons such as 'the Seven', but there were demons of later secondary origin to which this would not apply. An evil Alû-demon could, for example, be of purely human origin, the product of a man's nocturnal emission.[57] It could be trapped in an inverted basin, which was unthinkable of any god.[58] No cult was directed to demons, in the form of hymns and prayers, and indeed it is specifically said that they had no understanding of prayers.[59] Offerings of food and drink were sometimes made to them, but these were not offerings comparable to those made to the great gods, but rather were in the nature of grave offerings to bribe the demons to return to the underworld.[60]

It has been said above that demons seldom had individual names. This statement requires qualification, since there are instances in which individuals from particular groups of demons were equated with named gods. An example is provided by the Asakku demons, who both possessed shrines[61] and were equated with such deities as Latarak, Lugal-edinna, and Muhra[62]—all chthonic, and the two last known as forms of Nergal.[63] It might be argued that this proves that the demons in question (and perhaps other classes) were reduced chthonic gods, the equations mentioned being relics of their former divine status. Against this is a chronological fact: the equation of these demons with gods only occurs at a relatively late period. At earlier periods they are mentioned simply as demons, their only direct connection with gods being that, according to a fragment of a myth, they were conquered by Ninurta.[64] Such a development can be explained without the assumption that these particular demons were reduced gods. With the development of social institutions and technology came an increasing sense of the gods' control of the universe, alongside which the place of demons as independent beings acting arbitrarily became increasingly anomalous. There was therefore a movement towards bringing the activities of the demons under the control of the great gods. This happened by stages. The demons, originally independent of the gods and sometimes hostile to them, first had their independence of action circumscribed, and came to be thought of as acting as agents of the gods, subject to their control.[65] They were at this stage given such descriptions as 'messengers of Enlil'[66] or 'throne-bearers of Ereshkigal'[67] (goddess of the Underworld), or were said to 'march before Nergal'.[68] From this it was but a step to the demons being seen not as independent beings at all but as aspects or hypostases of the great gods.

We thus see three stages in the development of Mesopotamian demons. Those which arose from ancient numina, in the beginning acting wholly independently of the gods, might move to become agents of the gods, and finally begin to become hypostases of the gods. This represents a theological process in which there was a progressive denial of the place of the irrational in life. With the reduction of demons to agents, and even in some cases aspects, of the great gods, all that happened now lay within the will of the great gods.

We turn now to consider demons in Israelite religion. In this connection we must first turn our attention to a topic which has given rise to a considerable literature, namely, what is commonly called 'the demonic in Yahweh'. The wide currency of this phrase is traceable back to Paul Volz's monograph *Das Dämonische in Jahwe*, published in 1924.[69] Volz himself defined his use of the word 'demonic' as 'in the more limited sense of the sinister, dreadful, pernicious, cruel, hostile and almost satanic',[70] with particular application to instances of divine hostility which cannot convincingly be attributed to divine anger brought about by sin against the holiness of God. Volz illustrated his use of the term by reference to such incidents as Yahweh's surprise attack upon Moses on his way to Egypt (Exod. 4:24); the death of Uzzah for touching the Ark, even though merely to steady it when it toppled (2 Sam. 6:6–7); and the divine wrath at David's census (2 Sam. 24:1).[71] Later in his monograph Volz gave many further examples of how he applied the term: for him, instances of 'the demonic in Yahweh' included such matters as the bronze serpent Nehushtan destroyed by Hezekiah (2 Kgs. 18:4); the covenant-making rite involving the dismemberment of animals in Gen. 15:10, 17; and Yahweh's command for fire sacrifice of human firstborn, referred to in Ezek. 20:26.[72] He emphasized the view that 'the demonic in Yahweh' was not a mere accidental survival of primitive traits: 'the demonic Yahweh is not something belonging to the pre-Mosaic period as a "primitive fiend", that, having survived the work of Moses, finds expression here and there in isolated instances and finally vanishes. Rather it belongs to the essential stock of the Old Testament belief in God generally.'[73]

One of the biblical examples adduced by Volz may be used to illustrate more precisely how he applied the term 'the demonic in Yahweh'. In Exod. 4:24, when Moses was on his way to Egypt at Yahweh's instructions, Yahweh met him at a night stop and attempted to kill him because he was uncircumcised. There is no indication anywhere in the story, as it at present exists, of the intervention of any being which might be described as a demon, whether independent or an agent of Yahweh: it is Yahweh himself, and he alone, who acts. This does not, of course, preclude the possibility that the story is based on a piece of folklore in which it was a demon who attempted to kill Moses, but there is no trace whatever of this in the existing form of the story, and it was not this possibility that led Volz to apply the incident as an example of 'the demonic in Yahweh'. If ever there was a form of this story in which an independent demon acted against Moses, this has been totally eliminated; what remains conveys an implicit denial that there were any demons existing who could act independently of Yahweh, and an insistence that whatever was done, good or ill, just or unjust, was done by Yahweh himself and no other.

Volz explained the origin of the situation as he understood it in this way. He accepted the Decalogue as Mosaic, and took the starting point of Moses' teaching as monotheism—not incipient monotheism but full explicit monotheism. The first commandment was in Volz's view

a prohibition directed less against the revering of the gods of other peoples—the Egyptians and Babylonians, etc.—than against the revering of all other El-beings—tribal numina, ghosts, demons, and especially any kind of cult of ancestors and the dead. For every event in nature, history, and the lives of men, Yahweh must be the sole originator... What in other religions was divided up amongst different gods . . . for the pious of Israel had to be united in the one God. . . With Yahweh as the sole causality, Moses cut off all belief in demons, and all activities that were generally ascribed to demons. Thus all service that would have been rendered to demons . . . was here comprehended in the one Yahweh.[74]

In a subsequent stage of biblical editing, according to Volz, the Yahwist, fully accepting the monotheistic teaching of Moses, 'transferred the old demonic sagas, that he would not or could not dispense with, in bold faith to Yahweh. Thus the demon became Yahweh and Yahweh became a demon.'[75] He gave as an example of the postulated development 'the Fear of Isaac' of Gen. 31:42, 53, which, though finally a title of Yahweh, was (he suggests) originally perhaps a local demon.[76]

Volz argued that this kind of development occurred not only with the narratives but also with the rites of ancient Israel. There, old usages and ideas of animistic origin were taken over into the cult of the monotheistic Yahweh—'the bells, through which demons were scared off; the magic through which hostile night-demons were exorcized; the blood that was poured into the earth to the chthonic deity.'[77] These are (for Volz) examples of things originally demonic that were adopted into the worship of

Yahweh, as a consequence of the teaching that in Israel only Yahweh should be revered.

By this means, according to Volz, 'Yahweh became demonic, and ... because Yahweh absorbed everything demonic and was himself the most powerful demon, there was no further need in Israel for demons.'[78] Furthermore, before Yahweh, who now united all power both divine and demonic, magic likewise dwindled away, since in face of such a Being, who was not merely demon but also God, magic was of no avail.

In consequence of this, Volz argued, there arose the fact that whilst everywhere else in the world gods and demons stood side by side in belief and cult, in Israel the one Yahweh encompassed all; whereas everywhere else Dualism was the basic view of things, the Israelite view was bound up with monotheism.

Volz made a distinction which it is important to bear in mind in considering his interpretation of Israelite religion. He emphasized that whilst Yahweh absorbed the idea of the demonic, it would be a mistake to think of him as absorbing actual demons.[79] In the final resort the demonic was not something taken into the being of Yahweh but something which was part of his essential nature, given the monotheistic premiss of Mosaic religion.[80] Later there were attempts to detach and remove this demonic element from Yahweh, which are seen in the existence of such concepts as the angel (mal'akh) of Yahweh, the spirit (ruaḥ) of Yahweh, the Lying Spirit sent by Yahweh in 1 Kgs. 22:22, and Satan himself.

It becomes clear that throughout his monograph Volz was operating with his own definition of 'demonic', based on the use of the term in German literature, and that in using the term 'demonic in Yahweh' he was making certain implicit assumptions as to essential differences between the divine nature and the demonic nature, the principal difference being that for him the divine nature was essentially good and the demonic nature essentially bad. The phrase 'the demonic in Yahweh' is used to refer to aspects of Yahweh's behaviour which show him as responsible for actions that, on human understanding, are arbitrary, contrary to justice, unexplainedly malevolent, or simply

amoral or immoral. The term did not for Volz indicate a view
that the god Yahweh subsumed the characteristics of beings earlier
known as demons; rather, it referred specifically to aspects of the
nature of Yahweh himself which conflicted with the nature
postulated for him in the doctrine of ethical monotheism. This is
emphasized by a revealing comparison Volz made between
Israelite and Babylonian religion. 'In Bel of the Babylonians', he
said, 'the demonic nature does not surprise us; but that the
glorious, pure, spiritual, universal God of Moses and his successors
should make himself known in such a way . . . is a riddle'.[81] This
shows a misleading usage, if not an actual misunderstanding, of
the concept 'demonic' in relation to ancient religion; in Babylonian religion there were specific supernatural beings called
demons, not equated with Bel, and this makes it difficult to see in
what sense we may properly speak of 'the demonic nature' of Bel.

The term 'the demonic in Yahweh' is probably too well
established for it to be quickly abandoned now, but it is regrettable
that it has gained such wide currency, since it implies a particular
direction in which to seek for the solution of the problem it posits.
Such a use of the term 'demonic' can only lead at the best to
obscuration (as a smoke-screen behind which to hide the theological dilemma) and at the worst to confusion. 'Demonic', if it
means anything, describes either action of a demon, or action
which is like that of a demon. Used in the latter sense of action by
Yahweh himself, within the sphere which has been called 'the dark
side'[82] of Yahweh's nature, the usage has implicit within it the
premiss that the proper sphere of action of a god is the good,
whilst anything which is not good falls within the sphere of action
of a demon.[83] Indeed, the phrase 'the demonic in Yahweh' is
sometimes explicitly used as the antithesis of 'the goodness of
God'.[84] Even if such terminology stops short of predicating
dualism, it is certainly open to two objections. Firstly, it involves
a logical contradiction: one is describing the action of a god by a
term which by definition denotes the manner in which a god does
not act. Secondly, the terminology also involves an illegitimate
methodology in Comparative Religion, in that it is founded upon

an arbitrary assumption about a matter basic to the investigation—
the area and mode of action of a deity. To characterize the anti-
goodness of God as 'the demonic' immediately muddies comparison with Mesopotamian religion. In Mesopotamia, whilst
demons might be the source of anti-goodness either as the instruments of a god or independently of a god or even contrary to the
will of a god, it was also possible for a god himself by his own
nature to bring about anti-good, without the agency of a demon.
For these reasons it is desirable to avoid the term 'the demonic'
except with reference to supernatural beings distinguishable from
gods. For what Volz made it fashionable to call 'the demonic in
Yahweh', it is better to use either the term 'the sinister side of
Yahweh',[85] or 'Yahweh's amorality'.

This insistence upon a distinction of terminology between the
situation in which amoral or immoral or arbitrary action is
attributed to an aspect of the supernatural other than the divine,
and that in which it is attributed directly to the divine, in no way
denies that historically one may come to be replaced by the other,
or even that there may be some biblical passages in which a flux
between the two concepts is clearly visible.

A possible instance of such a flux is the story of Jacob's wrestling
at Jabbok (Gen. 32:24–30), which one scholar has recently spoken
of as a 'demonic attack upon the fleeing Jacob'.[86] The danger of
such phraseology is that it suggests that there was an attack by
Yahweh himself acting in the form of a demon. This would be
misleading. It is quite probable that the story contains a demonic
element, but, as von Rad clearly brings out,[87] the story as we have
it retains traces of a more ancient as well as of a more recent form;
the demonic element belongs to one form of the story, and the
great god Yahweh to the other, which has sought to suppress the
demonic. It is not accurate to think of this as an instance of an old
demon assimilated by Yahweh; it was rather a demon suppressed
by Yahweh. If von Rad's analysis is correct, the original form of
the story contained the classic elements of the demonic as described
by Van der Leeuw—'behaviour which is arbitrary, purposeless,
even clumsy and ridiculous'. But in the final form of the story the

arbitrariness of the incident gives way to purpose: the purpose is to give Jacob a theophany and a blessing and (through the omen of his new name) a promise.

In the more ancient form of the story, as analysed by von Rad, Jacob's antagonist was a numen in human form, who might legitimately be called a demon, a kind of troll who wantonly attacked the last person remaining from a party crossing a ford. The powers of this demon were limited, since not only did its effective activity cease with the coming of dawn, but also Jacob almost succeeded in defeating his supernatural adversary. Subsequently, the import of the story changed. The antagonist became understood as Yahweh himself, and (as von Rad shows) certain intrusive insertions were made into the original story to accommodate this conception.

It needs to be emphasized that this story is not an instance of Yahweh beginning as a demon and ending as a god. What we find here is not religious evolution but deliberate adaptation of a story on theological grounds. Theologically it was not tolerable to suppose that there could exist demons acting outside the providence of Yahweh. The demon was not absorbed by Yahweh; he was suppressed and replaced by Yahweh, and the details of the story had to be altered to fit the new situation. The story does not show that Yahweh was at some stage an overgrown demon, but on the contrary that the theological understanding of the activity of Yahweh was such that at no time would it fit within the framework of demonic activity.

Apart from the traces in the Jabbok story, instances of action by demons are rare in the Old Testament, and instances of action of demons other than in implementation of Yahweh's will are almost non-existent. Some of the possible instances are doubtful. In Jud. 9:23 Yahweh is said to have sent an evil spirit between Abimelech and the men of Shechem, but there is no certainty that this refers to an actual demonic being, and those scholars may be correct who take it as merely meaning something like 'anger'.[88] But even if 'evil spirit' is to be taken here as a personal being, it was quite clearly a being wholly under the control of Yahweh and acting as his instrument. The will operating is specifically the will of Yahweh, and not of some independent being. The same is true of the evil spirit which tormented King Saul: the spirit is said to be 'from Yahweh'.[89] Even if these instances involve demons, they are not instances of independent action: they represent divine action in which a wholly subordinate demon is used as the instrument.

A certain instance of a spirit acting for evil is found in 1 Kgs. 22:19–22. Here Yahweh, sitting upon his heavenly throne surrounded by the host of heaven, invited a volunteer to entice King Ahab to his destruction. There followed a discussion in which 'one said this and another said that' until finally one being volunteered to be a lying spirit. Although the members of Yahweh's heavenly court are sometimes called *'elohim* 'gods', this term is not used in this instance and the spirit (*ruaḥ*) might well be regarded as a demon. But even so, and even though he was able to exercise freewill to the extent of deciding whether or not to volunteer, he remained strictly an instrument of Yahweh's will. The suggestion has been made (very tentatively) that behind this account there may lie 'the conception of an evil spirit or demon'—presumably assumed to have been originally independent—'which here appears subordinate to Yahweh in the interests of monism'.[90] This suggestion has no validity in the immediate context of the story: the purpose of the story was specifically to give the explanation of the action Yahweh had (according to the prophet Micaiah ben Imlah) taken to bring about the destruction of King Ahab, so that if at any staęg in the tradition the lying message given by the spirit had derived from any other will than the will of Yahweh, the whole point of the story would have been lost. What one may perhaps accept from the suggestion referred to is that there may have been an ancient popular belief in demons who could give lying messages about the future, and that Micaiah ben Imlah utilized this within a Yahwistic setting. But it is clear that both by Micaiah and by his opponents monism was unquestioningly accepted. Therefore, when Micaiah devised a fable on the basis of an old belief in demons, he never doubted that a demon could in the last resort only operate as an instrument of Yahweh's will: the subordination of the demon to Yahweh was a basic premiss of the story from its origin.

The sinister side of Yahweh is again seen in the background to the census instituted by King David. Here, in 2 Sam. 24:1, 'the anger of Yahweh was kindled against Israel, and he incited David against them, saying, "Go, number Israel and Judah" ' (RSV). The parallel passage in 1 Chron. 21:1 has a significant alteration: there it is stated that 'Satan stood up against Israel, and incited David to number Israel' (RSV). A clear distinction is discernible between 'Satan' in the latter passage, where the word has become a proper name, and the same word with the definite article in Hebrew ('the Satan') in the prologue to the Book of Job and in Zech. 3:1–2, where it is a title denoting a member of the heavenly court, not essentially evil, who is in God's service as a kind of prosecuting counsel.

Problems arising from the two accounts of David's census have been frequently discussed.[91] It is significant that the mention of Satan, as a pseudo-independent demon, occurs in what is manifestly the later form of the story. This makes it difficult to argue that the concept of Satan here goes back to an older concept of an independent demon, which has been subordinated to Yahweh in the interests of monism. Clearly, the introduction of Satan in the Chronicles passage is a relatively late development 'to account for evil and misfortune'.[92] Kluger expresses this rather well in saying that 'the detachment . . . of the dark side of God [has] now reached a state of complete separation. It appears now as . . . a separate personality.'[93]

Thus in Israelite religion there can be seen three strata of demons.[94] There are traces of an original concept of independent demons, though with no indication that these were ever accepted alongside Yahweh. There was a well-established belief in the possibility of demons who might act evilly at Yahweh's decree. Finally, at a late date, new independent demons arose from hypostatization of the sinister side of Yahweh. The two former stages are very marked in Mesopotamia, much more so than in Israel;

but though there is plenty of evidence for hypostatization of certain divine qualities in Mesopotamia—such as, for example, ᵃkittu and ᵃmišaru (god Justice and god Righteousness)—there is little evidence of the late development of new demons from the hypostatization of the sinister side of the gods.

The difference in development in this last respect between the two cultural areas might suggest that the problem of divine responsibility for evil presented a graver problem in Israel than in Mesopotamia. But it is certain that, though there may have been a difference of emphasis, the problem of the sinister side of deity was not restricted to Israel; it was also evident in Mesopotamia. It was recognized in Mesopotamia that the gods could act deceitfully towards mankind by altering their own decrees. Thus, in connection with the death of the Sumerian king Ur-Nammu, there occurs the passage, already quoted:

> An altered his holy word . . .
> Enlil . . . changed his decree of fate.[95]

But gods, unlike demons, were expected to act rationally and in accordance with human concepts of justice, and their failure to do so could lead to complaint. Thus Ur-Nammu complained:

This is how I have been treated;
Although I had done the gods service, . . .
Had brought about great prosperity for the Anunnaki,
. . .
No god stood by me. . .
What has been accepted of my efforts, as one who has served the
  gods? . . .[96]

There also exists a Sumerian composition of the early second millennium which deals specifically with this problem.[97] S. N. Kramer, who has edited the work, speaks of it as 'dealing with suffering and submission, a theme made famous . . . by the Biblical Book of Job',[98] though it is questionable whether it can properly be thought of as embodying the Job motif; as W. von Soden has pointed out, the latter requires not only a complaint over unmerited suffering but also a questioning of divine justice,[99] and the second element is no more than adumbrated in the Sumerian composition under discussion. The work is in the form of an address to his personal god by a man who complains:

> My righteous word has been turned into a lie,
> ...
> You have doled out to me suffering ever anew.
> ...
> My companion says not a true word to me,
> My friend gives the lie to my righteous word,
> The man of deceit has conspired against me,
> And you, my god, do not thwart him.[100]

The sufferer's troubles are then enumerated. There then follow some very significant lines, translated by Professor Kramer as follows:

> They say—valiant sages—a word righteous and straightforward:
> 'Never has a sinless child been born to its mother,
> ... a sinless youth has not existed from of old.'[101]

Knowledge of Sumerian is still such that even the most competent Sumerologists would not claim to catch nuances. None the less, it would appear beyond question that in the context this passage is offering an explanation of suffering, and that that explanation is based on a belief in original sin. It will be seen subsequently that this idea is attested from a later period. Such a solution provides an explanation of suffering without the need to postulate the activity of hostile independent demons or to challenge the justice of the gods, that is, to bring in what we have called 'the sinister side of deity'. In this Sumerian composition the idea of the essential justice of the gods is reinforced by a happy ending to the sufferer's trouble, with the moral—specifically stated at the beginning of the work—that the god will see his worshipper righted if only he applies to him earnestly and constantly.

W. von Soden has offered a valuable comparative treatment of the problem that arises within the religions of Israel and Mesopotamia when apparently undeserved suffering is seen, not as deriving from pure chance or from some demonic power independent of or opposed to God or the gods, but as due to deity itself.[102] For brevity he calls this 'the Job motif'. He argues that four conditions are necessary before the problem is likely to become a significant issue in any culture, and holds that in both the cultures in question these conditions were eventually achieved. The conditions he proposes are these.[103] Firstly, the element of taboo within the religion must be sufficiently circumscribed that misfortunes cannot be automatically attributed to the consequence of an unwitting breach of taboo. (However, whilst theoretically this seems valid, it must be said that it is difficult either to establish that the taboo element in the religion of either Israel or Mesopotamia progressively decreased with time or, if it did, to decide at what point this condition was fulfilled.) Secondly, the form of society must have evolved to such a stage that the individual enjoys some significance other than as part of a larger social unit. Thirdly, if the religion is not monotheistic, tensions within the pantheon must have been resolved to the point where there is no longer a multiplicity of conflicting divine wills; so long as the divine wills are thought of (as in some pantheons) as in mutual strife, the misfortunes of a good man can simply be attributed to his having offended one deity in seeking to please another. This condition was manifestly satisfied in Israel before the middle of the first millennium; von Soden argues that it also came to be satisfied in Mesopotamia, where religion developed, by the identification of deities or by the recognition of some deities as hypostases of others, in the direction of a kind of monotheism, or what, following Landsberger, he prefers to call monotheotetism.[104] The fourth condition proposed is that there must be no idea that the final requital of good and evil conduct takes place in the afterworld.

Professor von Soden goes on to argue that in the late second millennium in Mesopotamia—or, more specifically, in Babylonia—there arose a marked consciousness of sin, linked to developments in certain texts. There was an old idea that when a man suffered, it was because of attack by some evil influence, demonic or magical, to which some offence against the gods had exposed him. Magical rituals and incantations existed to remove such influences; but for them to be effective, it was first necessary to identify either the evil influence or its cause. In the case of demons, the demon (or class of demon) itself had to be identified. In the case of evil brought upon a man as the consequence of a particular offence against the gods, it was the offence that had to be named. On this basis there grew up the Incantation Series known as *Šurpu*,[105] which contains long lists of possible offences, some ritual (such as eating tabooed food), some ethical (such as lying or cheating), and others social (such as causing estrangement within a family group). On the literary level these exhaustive collections of possible sins were simply an aspect of the Mesopotamian scribal passion for listing and classifying everything, from names of gods to terms relating to doors.[106] Professor von Soden suggests that these lists of sins had the theological consequence of making Babylonians feel, with this plethora of possible sins made explicit, that no one could claim to be free from sin.[107] In this connection he adduces a text in which a worshipper, addressing Marduk, says:

> Who has not sinned, who has not committed offence?
> Who can discern the way of the gods?[108]

It is questionable, however, whether *Šurpu* contributed to the concept of the sinfulness of man, or whether it merely reflected it. We have seen that the idea of man's basic sinfulness was already stated in a Sumerian composition of the beginning of the second millennium. Moreover, to ask 'Who can discern the way of the gods?' surely implies not merely that no man can be free of the consciousness of sin but also that he may be guilty of unwitting offence against the gods. In view of the latter, the catalogues of possible sins in *Šurpu* would have had little theological (as distinct from therapeutic) relevance, since even if a man kept within the guide-lines provided by *Šurpu*, he could still have no assurance of avoiding sin. The consequence of such views was clearly that everyone merited punishment. Therefore divine punishment of an apparently good man did not call in question the justice of the gods.

This topic is dealt with at length in a Babylonian poem, probably of the twelfth century,[109] often called 'The Righteous Sufferer', or in Akkadian (from its initial line) *Ludlul bēl nēmeqi*.[110] This presents the speaker, a high official, as deserted by the gods, expelled from office and estates, slandered, encompassed by hostility, smitten by diseases, paralysed, in pain. In view of the customary English title, it is important to notice what claims are, or are not, made for the righteousness of the sufferer. He complains that he is being treated like a person who has not made appropriate food and drink offerings to the gods, and who has not engaged in the proper cultic rites. Yet, so he insists, he has conscientiously done all that was proper in the matter of prayer, sacrifice and cultus generally.[111] It is specially to be noticed that the sufferer claims only to have been guiltless in relation to the area of worship and cult. There is no claim that he was sinless in the absolute sense, and, indeed, at the end of the third tablet there is a passage, broken but retaining enough text to be intelligible, which refers to the sufferer's guilt, punishment, offence, and sins of negligence being carried off after Marduk had shown him mercy.[112]

The sufferer's conclusion about the source of his troubles, after recording the evidence of his cultic piety, was that the god's view of these things might not be the human view:

> What is proper to oneself is an offence to one's god,
> What in one's own heart seems despicable is proper to one's god.
> Who knows the will of the gods in heaven?
> . . .
> Where have mortals learnt the way of a god?[113]

This answer to the problem of unmerited suffering avoids imputing injustice to the gods by denying that man can know the hidden will of the divine powers. In the context this was a startling conclusion. The sufferer was not speaking of good and evil conduct in general life. He had specifically defined these in relation to strict observance of the cult. Now the standard view would have been that whatever the situation as to other spheres of activity, in which a man might have to decide for himself what was right, at least in the matter of the cult there could be no doubt at all as to what was the will of the gods: the plans of the temples, the rituals, and the very wording of the incantations used, were all believed to have been prescribed by the gods themselves in primeval times. In doubting man's ability to know the will of the gods in this context, the writer was implying scepticism about the value of the cultus as a means by which man could implement the will of the gods. Although this implicit scepticism about the cultus is not further developed, this latent denial of the value of the cult in fulfilling the will of the gods should be a warning against too readily rejecting the surface sense of Israelite prophetic utterances which appear to convey denigration of the cult, such as 'loyalty is my desire, not sacrifice' (Hos. 6:6), taken by some modern commentators to mean nothing more revolutionary than 'I desire kindness greater than that expressed in sacrifice'.[114]

Another Babylonian composition, perhaps of about 1000 B.C.,[115] displays a more radical scepticism. This work, known as 'the Babylonian Theodicy', takes the form of a dialogue between a sufferer and a friend, the sufferer making his complaint against the injustice of things, the friend giving the conventional unsatisfying answers of Babylonian piety.[116] The sufferer begins by mentioning the details of his own plight—he had been an orphan from infancy and had bad health and insufficient food and drink. With conventional piety his friend assures him that reverence to the gods will finally be rewarded with prosperity. The sufferer denies the postulated connection between well-doing and divine reward by pointing to examples of those who prosper without giving any heed to the gods—the wild ass that helps itself to the growing corn, the ravaging lion that attacks the herds, and the human profiteer. Back comes the friend with the answer that all these will surely pay the penalty for their misdeeds in due time. The sufferer disputes this on the ground of common experience: whilst he himself has always shown piety, rogues have got ahead of him.

Clearly, it was the prosperity of the wicked man, more than the suffering of the apparently good man, that made the problem acute. Whilst one could never be sure that even an apparently good

man had not secretly or unwittingly offended the gods, one could
hardly doubt that a blatantly bad man was constantly doing so and
certainly deserved condign punishment. The sufferer in the poem
directly questions the justice of the gods on this ground:

Those who neglect the god go the way of prosperity,
While those who pray to the goddess are impoverished and dispossessed.
In my youth I sought the will of my god
. . .
But . . . my god decreed destitution instead of wealth.
. . .
The rogue has got on, but I have been brought low.[117]

Later, the sufferer points to the arbitrary injustice of society as a
whole:

People extol the word of a strong man who is trained in murder,
But bring down the powerless who has done no wrong.
. . .
They fill the oppressor's hoard with gold,
But empty the beggar's store of its morsel of food.[118]

With this final proposition the friend agrees, and thereupon offers
an answer to the problem. This answer seems to go right back to
the idea in the Sumerian text adduced earlier:[119] When the gods
created men, so the friend says, 'With lies, and not truth, they
endowed them for ever'.[120] That is, the evil that men experience is
attributable not directly to injustice of the gods, but to the original
sin of man himself, as he was created by the gods. The final
conclusion therefore is that there can be no such thing as suffering
of the good, since all men without exception are evil.[121] The
sufferer, accepting this, concludes that his only recourse is to
throw himself upon the divine mercy.[122]

When we turn back to Israel, we find that the problem of the
arbitrary nature of apparent divine favour had been recognized
long before Job. This is clearly seen in the story of Cain and Abel:

The day came when Cain brought some of the produce of the soil as a
gift to Yahweh; and Abel brought some of the first-born of his flock,

the fat portions of them. Yahweh received Abel and his gift with favour; but Cain and his gift he did not receive. Cain was very angry and his face fell. (Gen. 4:3-5.)

There follows a very difficult and obscure passage in which Yahweh gives an explanation of sorts; this may (or may not) mean that doing right is an end in itself, irrespective of any consequent rewards. What is, however, clear, is that it was accepted that there could be an element in Yahweh's activities which, whether or not it might properly be called arbitrary, at least would be un-intelligible to humans. This corresponded to the solution found at some stages in Mesopotamian thought, represented in the view that man cannot know the way of the gods.

The same principle recurs in another J story, the call of Abram in Gen. 11:28-30 and 12:1-3. We are given no statement as to why Yahweh chose Abram rather than Nahor; it is simply accepted that Yahweh has the right to choose one man and dis-regard or even reject another. This stands out very clearly when one compares it with the story of Abraham's arguing with Yahweh over the destruction of the cities of the plain in Gen. 18:22b-33, a section which Eissfeldt regards as secondary.[123] In this latter narrative Abraham specifically challenges Yahweh on indiscrimi-nate punishment:

Far be it from thee to do this—to kill good and bad together; for then the good would suffer with the bad. . . Shall not the judge of all the earth do what is just?

Between the two former Genesis passages adduced and the last, there has been a change in Israelite religious thought. It is no longer accepted that Yahweh has the right to act arbitrarily. As judge, he is bound by considerations of justice. Moreover, the justice in question is regarded as something absolute and know-able. The old idea that the ways of God may be unknown is in this respect rejected: the principles he has revealed and laid down for man's behaviour represent part of his own nature, to which he necessarily conforms.[124]

The idea, which developed after the period in the early first millennium represented by the compilation of the J source, that it was an essential part of the nature of Yahweh that he acted justly, had a corollary. If a man met with misfortune, this showed that he was an evil-doer, even though the fact might not be evident to his fellow-men; in Browning's pithy phrase, 'He must be wicked to deserve such pain'.[125] This view held the field in Israelite, and later Jewish, thought, not only until the appearance of the Book of Job, but in some quarters long after that time. We find it still reflected in the New Testament, when Jesus' disciples, commenting on a blind man, asked: 'Who sinned, this man or his parents? Why was he born blind? Is it not that this man or his parents sinned?' (Joh. 9:1–2). In the Old Testament, the general belief in reward for good and punishment for evil is explicitly stated as a supposed matter of common knowledge:

I have been young, and now am old; yet I have not seen the righteous forsaken or his children begging bread. (Ps. 37:25 RSV; NEB emends.)

This is from a Wisdom psalm in acrostic form; the whole tenor of it suggests that the problem of the flourishing of those who are manifestly wicked is beginning to assert itself, but the psalm insists on the doctrine of retribution, and claims that the prosperity of the wicked is only temporary and that sooner or later they will receive their deserts. Though it is difficult to give a date to it with any assurance, this psalm is certainly not early.[126] Thus, despite the early recognition of the apparently arbitrary nature of divine acceptance or rejection, the general view of undeserved suffering in Israel remained one that denied the problem: God was just and would—sooner or later—reward the good and punish the bad. This represents in principle the same view as the conventional piety of Mesopotamia, reflected in the earlier parts of the friend's arguments in the Babylonian Theodicy; the wicked suffer and the good prosper. But there is a difference of detail which was ultimately to have considerable significance. In Mesopotamia, the usual view was that evil befell a man because he had offended the god, so that the god deserted him or ignored him, leaving him unprotected against hostile demonic or magical powers. Typically the ordinary man of Mesopotamia was not of sufficient significance to the great gods that they, directly and in person, would strike him with disaster. Thus it was not the great gods who took away a man's child to punish him; it was the demoness Lamashtu who snatched the child from the man, able to do so because the gods had ceased to protect him.[127] But in Israel, Yahweh himself was so intimately concerned with each individual that it was he himself who was acting when disaster struck. Thus, the death of Bath-sheba's child was not at the hand of a demon because Yahweh had withdrawn his protection; it was at the hand of Yahweh himself.[128] The personal divine intervention in the affairs of the individual was a measure of the divine concern for the individual; this is well expressed in the words: 'As a man disciplines his son, Yahweh your God disciplines you' (Deut. 8:5 RSV). Thus the idea developed that divine sending of what appeared to be evil was not necessarily a mere automatic punishment for sin, but could be a mark of God's concern for the individual.

This specifically Israelite development out of the old general ancient Near Eastern doctrine of divine retribution gave a new dimension to the problem. Suffering could be not only punishment, but also a mark of God's moulding and testing the individual and bringing the sufferer to him. When the question was re-opened in the Book of Job, and the old glib answers rejected, this development was to the fore.

Professor von Soden points out that in terms of chronology and literary genre, the author of the Book of Job might have been acquainted with, and even have borrowed from, the correspond-ing Babylonian poems.[129] Job may indeed owe something to cross-cultural fertilization, but it must be said that the author, utilizing the Babylonian dialogue form, and taking the latent Israelite idea of suffering as a testing, develops the treatment of the problem beyond anything adumbrated in either culture. The author of Job neither denies the fact of unmerited suffering with the generality of earlier Israelites, nor solves the problem with the Babylonians by a theory of original sin or of the unknowability of the ways of God. He does not indeed solve the problem at all, but on the theological level he transcends it. He accepts that the purpose of suffering is ultimately unknowable, and that the ways of God are past understanding. But God himself is knowable, and Job enters at the last into personal communion with God. And in that personal communion with the divine, suffering dissolves into nothingness. But this development falls in the realm of theology and mysticism, and is outside the scope of Comparative Religion.

Communication with the Divine

Man's quest for assurance of the future in an uncertain world leads him along many strange paths, amongst them, in modern times, political utopias and technological science-fiction. In the ancient Near East the typical means by which man sought his assurance for the future was through the cluster of techniques which we subsume under the general term 'divination'. Unless otherwise indicated, the latter term will be used here in its widest permissible sense, to include prophecy.

Belief in the validity of divination rested upon certain views of the nature of the future, the basic one being that the future was not blindly random but was related to existing circumstances.[1] There was, however, no single embracing hypothesis of the nature of the relationship between present and future circumstances; rather, two distinct and conflicting views can be recognized as underlying the divinatory techniques attested.

One view, which is not infrequently explicitly stated, operated on the assumption that divine beings controlled the shape of future events by their decisions, and that they might reveal to man their intentions or wishes for the future.[2] The future, though shaped by divine intention, was not mechanistically determined. This is made clear in several ways. Firstly, the divine intention was not necessarily self-fulfilling; man could to some extent hinder the fruition of the divine intention by failing to conform to it, though this was at his peril. Thus we find a wife writing to her husband reporting on omens she had had taken on his behalf. Speaking of her husband in the third person, she adds: 'May my lord act in accordance with the true sign from the mouth of the god.'[3] This indicates that the will of the gods as discovered by omens was not a mere neutral matter which it was useful to know, but a directed intention to which the devotee would be well advised to conform (though he need not).

A second aspect of the view that the future was not mechanistically determined but rather directed by the will of the god, was that a man could approach a god not only to ask him to reveal the future, to which man would then for his own well-being conform, but also to seek the god's promise that the future would be in accordance with the wishes of the suppliant.

But, conflicting with the foregoing in principle, was another view of the nature of the relationship between present and future; and this view was essentially non-deistic. As far as I am aware, the theoretical basis of this view is never explicitly stated in the ancient texts. This may well have been because its origin went back into prehistoric times, whereas the deistic view was a rationalization of divination which developed after the rise of anthropomorphic deities.

On this second principle, a consequential relationship was postulated between a present incident X and a future incident Y. Thus, if a snake fell from a roof near a man, this would indicate some future incident or situation for the man. But the future incident or situation was unrelated to any personal activity, either of the man or of a god. It was not a circumstance that a god had willed for a particular man at a particular time, nor was it related by way of reward or punishment to anything the man had done. If incident X happened to anyone at any time, incident Y would follow, unless (assuming incident Y to be unpleasant) steps were taken to deflect it. One way of deflecting a presaged evil, if the potentially affected person was a king, was for another person to take over his role temporarily.[4] In the case of other people, magical means of prophylaxis, or the intervention of a god, might be sought. The logical contradiction inherent in the idea of taking steps to frustrate destiny does not appear to have been faced in the ancient Near East.[5]

Traces of ideas related to non-deistic divination are probably to be recognized in the Old Testament. The same underlying principle of a magical (not causal) relationship between two incidents may be seen in the idea that the deliberate performance of certain actions would magically (not causally) be followed by

certain situations.[6] An example of this occurs in connection with
Elisha in 2 Kgs. 13:14–19. The dying prophet was visited by King
Joash of Israel, who lamented the forthcoming loss of the prophet,
as the power behind Israel in its wars with Syria. Elisha thereupon
told the king to take a bow and arrows and to shoot out of the
window 'Yahweh's arrow of victory, the arrow of victory over
Syria' (RSV). The king was then instructed to strike the ground
with the arrows, which he did to the extent of three times. At this
Elisha became angry, saying that if the king had struck the ground
five or six times he would have finished off Syria completely, but
now would only defeat it three times. It is quite clear here that the
action performed by the king was not understood as simply giving
a clue to the future which a man knowing the key could understand, but was thought of as actively affecting the future, independently of any divine will.[7]

The importance attached to divination in ancient Mesopotamia
is reflected both in the extensive literary remains relating to that
activity, and in the reputation left behind in the Hellenistic world,
where the term 'Chaldaean', properly relating to the last native
Babylonian dynasty, became a synonym for soothsayer or astro-
loger.[8] There were in Mesopotamia many different methods and
techniques of divination. For example, the message given could
either arrive spontaneously or come by means of some mechanism
which needed to be activated; and its form could be either binary
—that is, the response 'yes' or 'no' in relation to a particular
problem—or specific. If specific, it could either be immediately
intelligible to a layman or could require interpretation by a
qualified expert. But such differences of detail are of concern for
the present purpose only insofar as they admit of the possibility of
different underlying views of the supernatural world.

What strikes one forcibly about Mesopotamian divination is
that the questions put to the supernatural powers where a mechanism has to be activated, and the presages given by spontaneous
omens, predominantly offer no indication of interest in the future
other than as it directly concerned the person to whom the omen
applied, whether private citizen or king. The typical prognosis of

Mesopotamian omens in the case of a private person relates to his own or his family's health, prosperity and long life, or the opposite; and in the case of the king to success or otherwise in military undertakings, or to the well-being of the kingdom, or to the appropriateness of a proposed administrative appointment. One text summarizes matters for which extispicy was appropriate as follows:

for the well-being of the king, for weapons, for a military expedition, for the capture of a city, for the well-being of a sick man, for rain from the sky, for performance of desire.[9]

These are all anthropocentric, not theocentric. This makes it difficult to accept that there was basically any yearning to enter more fully into knowledge of the divine plan; there is no indication that the enquirer sought knowledge of the divine will other than in relation to his immediate temporal advantage, so that, forewarned, he might be enabled the better to grasp incipient good fortune or to take steps to escape potential bad fortune.

The predominating forms of divination in ancient Mesopotamia differed with period, place, and social stratum. Amongst the principal techniques were divination by inspection of the liver or other internal organs of a sacrificed animal, by observation of the patterns of oil on water, by astronomical and meteorological phenomena, by the movement of birds, by events in everyday life such as the behaviour of animals or insects or the pattern made by spilt water, by portents in monstrous births or abortions, by dreams, by the configuration of incense smoke.

These can be divided into two main divisions: those, such as liver divination, in which an officiant activated a process; and those, such as the observation of astronomical phenomena, where the initiative had to come from the supernatural powers.

As the best known type of technique requiring human activation, we may consider extispicy, subsuming under that term both liver-divination (hepatoscopy) and divination by examination of the entrails more generally (haruspicy). Oppenheim has indeed argued that hepatoscopy and haruspicy represent respectively an older and a later level of development,[10] and he is probably correct;[11] but as there is no indication that a basically different view of the supernatural underlay the two sub-divisions, this point is irrelevant for the present purpose. Extispicy is widely attested in Mesopotamia from the beginning of the second millennium to the late first millennium, and the technique was disseminated (not necessarily unchanged) beyond Mesopotamia, as far afield as Etruria.[12] It was certainly known in Palestine, since clay models of livers, marked as keys for hepatoscopy, have been found in second millennium Hazor,[13] and Ezekiel referred to the technique, though specifically as used by the king of Babylon.[14]

There are collections of liver omens extant from the Old Babylonian period onwards, and these indicate that at some periods or by some techniques omens were treated as binary, giving an indication either 'yes (favourable)' or 'no (unfavourable)', whilst in other periods or circumstances omens could convey specific messages. As a random example to show the typical form of the latter in liver omens, the following will serve: 'If its "finger" [part of the liver] encloses the tip of the gall bladder, a fire will trap the man in his house.'[15]

The aetiology of omens seems to have been understood in different ways at different cultural levels. At the most sophisticated level the theory was that the god or gods of omens deliberately gave a message by certain signs to which experts possessed the key. This was explicit in some late documents relating to extispicy,[16] employed to obtain answers to problems about certain state matters placed before the god. However, as Oppenheim has observed, the invocation of the god or gods in such texts 'represents but a superficial "mythologization"' of an earlier 'a-deistic attitude' 'centered on an unindividualized divine power which is concerned about man but cannot be approached by him in prayers or cultic acts'.[17]

Details of the extispicy procedure varies with period and place, but in the procedure on which we are best informed there were three elements. The query was set before the god. The god was asked to write his answer on the internal organs of a sacrificial animal. The animal was slaughtered and the organs were examined for positive or negative indications. Two groups of texts, one late Assyrian and one Babylonian, enable us to see at least an outline of this procedure. There were minor differences between the two groups, and the following summary refers to one of the later Assyrian examples.[18]

The query was put to the Sun-god; typically this began with a request for a positive answer, followed by a statement of the period under investigation, and then the actual question. Thus:

O Shamash, great lord, on the matter about which I ask you, answer me a firm assent.
From this day, the third of this month, Ayyar [approximately May], until the eleventh of the month Ab [approximately August] of this year.
For these hundred days and hundred nights, the period stipulated for this extispicy, . . .
Will either . . . the troops of the Cimmerians, or the troops of the Medes, or the troops of the Mannaeans, or any enemy whatever,
Strive and plot (against me)?[19]

Details of possible ways in which potential enemies might take such hostile action—whether by conspiracy or various military, economic or other means—were then specified more closely.

Some clauses followed in which the Sun-god was asked to disregard certain circumstances which might affect the answer, after which the question was repeated. A brief prayer was addressed to the Sun-god asking him to give favourable omens and a firm 'yes'.[20] A sheep was then sacrificed and eviscerated, and the entrails were examined by the officiant, who noted the various ominous features. These were checked against the canonical collection of exta omens, and the protases of the appropriate omens recorded. Since the specific prognostications of the omens were not given,[21] one must conclude that the answer was arrived at on the basis of taking each prediction as either positive or negative, and finding whether the majority was favourable or unfavourable. Three things in particular emerge here. Firstly, the enquirer was not concerned about the divine will in any but the most practical and immediate sense. The Assyrian king might well have echoed the hymn

> I do not ask to see
> The distant scene; one step enough for me.

What interested him was not the more remote divine plan but the severely practical and immediate issue of what was in store for the current campaign season of the next hundred days. Secondly, the enquiry was not a neutral seeking of knowledge of the god's will, but a quest for assurance of the god's approval of a course of action decided upon by humans. The Assyrian king knew what he wanted and asked the Lord of Omens to bend indications of the future to the king's desires; there was no resigned 'Thy will be done'. Cases are known in which, when the god failed to give approval to the proposed course of action, the king flouted the intention of the god.[22] It is true that the cases attested are mainly those quoted as dreadful warnings of the consequences of such impious conduct, but such warnings doubtless emanated from those professionally interested to maintain the prestige of extispicy, and the fact that such instances did occur makes it clear that kings were not always disposed to pander to the stubborn will of unco-operative gods.

A further point noticeable in the extispicy procedure is that although a specific god Shamash (in other texts conjoined with Adad) is invoked, the invocation is a markedly bald one. By contrast with the long series of epithets found in many other genres of texts, one finds here only the title 'great lord'. The structure of the text is almost independent of the phrase 'Shamash, great lord', which could be deleted from the three or four points at which it typically occurs with minimal disturbance. This suggests the possibility that the mention of the god of omens was no more than a pious modification to a formula which was in origin non-deistic.

The non-deistic origin of at least some forms of divination is suggested by another consideration. The great antiquity of divination in some of its forms was recognized, as is shown by the fact that, for example, the origin of hepatoscopy (and also lecanomancy) was attributed to Enmeduranki, a king of Sippar from before the Flood.[23] But one of the gods with whom hepatoscopy came to be particularly linked was Adad; and Adad did not, so far as we know, enter the Mesopotamian pantheon until well after the cultural period with which the Flood tradition must be associated. That is to say, tradition took the origin of hepatoscopy back to long before the arrival of Adad in Mesopotamia, so that the connection of the two must be secondary.[24]

That the omens were basically non-deistic is further a conclusion from the fact that it is usual for a particular circumstance always to presage the same particular area of ill or good fortune. The omen thus represented not a god's decision upon a situation but rather a recognized correlation between past and future phenomena. The gods came into the matter only as the divine beings able to intervene to cut the web.

The non-deistic basis of divination can be seen clearly behind certain dream omens.[25] The data on dreams in ancient Mesopotamia fall into two main divisions. On the one hand we have a few accounts of actual dreams in a personal historical context, conveying a message from a deity. Oppenheim regards these as basically theophanies in the form of dreams.[26] On the other hand— and much more numerous—we have collections of possible incidents in dreams, with ominous significance, arranged in Dream Books, together with conjurations and rituals for eliminating the evil of any dream of bad portent.[27]

There are significant differences in the two categories of dream data. Firstly, whilst the accounts of actual dreams of a named person may be highly specific, the dream incidents of the Dream Books are predominantly very general and relate to a standard limited area: favourable dreams prognosticate wealth and prosperity, long life, honour, good luck or good news, association with a protective spirit, peace of mind, or the birth of sons; and unfavourable dreams the opposite—poverty or hunger, disease, a short life, death of the dreamer or one of his family, possession by an evil spirit, sorrow or a troubled mind, no sons, attack by an enemy, robbery, imprisonment, or dishonour.[28]

The second apparent characteristic of the dream incidents of the Dream Books is their general non-deistic attitude. Whilst deities are indeed spasmodically mentioned, sometimes in the protasis of the omen and sometimes in the apodosis, this is in such a way that there is no implication that the dream is sent by the god referred to. Thus we find the dream omen:

If (in a dream a man) does the work of a sailor,
    the god Enlil has a claim against him for a neglected vow.[29]

However, this in no way implied a warning sent by Enlil. This is clear from the fact that the omen occurs as one of a group which includes the following:

If (in a dream a man) does the work of a seal-cutter,
his son will die.
If he does the work of a fuller,
for a poor man (it means) his misfortunes will leave him.
If he does the work of a carpenter, . . .
decrease is in store for him.[30]

Clearly, Enlil had no more bearing on the aetiology of the dream than had the sailor, seal-cutter, fuller or carpenter.

Mention is, however, found of a god of dreams, in the Dream Rituals and elsewhere.[31] But this does not necessarily conflict with indications that the type of dream omen found in the Dream Books was originally and basically non-deistic. The Dream-god had no clearly definable characteristics—it was even unclear whether this being was a god or a goddess[32]—and he (or she) appears to have had no function beyond incorporating in personified form old non-deistic ideas about the aetiology of dreams. Oppenheim expresses a similar view thus: 'The existence of a "god of Dreams" . . . can only be understood in light of . . . the demonic nature of certain dream-experiences. The Dream-god exists only with respect to this specific aspect.'[33]

There are conflicting indications as to the aetiology and essential nature of a dream. In some instances the dream seems to have been thought of as a physical entity serving as the vehicle of a good or evil influence which clung to the dreamer. Even though a man had forgotten his dream and could not recall so much about it as whether it was good or bad, he might still be concerned about it;[34] this suggests that the dream was thought of as a real entity, independent of the dreamer's memory of it, and that the dream somehow became attached to the dreamer. This interpretation is reflected in the practice, if the import of a dream was evil, of the dreamer seeking to remove the evil by various physical means, such as by washing it off from his body with water or by absorbing the evil by rubbing himself all over with a lump of clay.[35]

But there were other concepts of the aetiology and nature of a dream. Thus, there was the belief that the dreamer could change a dream of bad portent into a good one. This might be effected by the non-deistic technique of a magical ritual and spell, or by the overtly deistic means of prayer to the Sun-god, or by the two techniques jointly.[36] This would imply that the evil of the dream was not after all an actual substance which clung to the man and had to be physically removed, but rather an unfavourable situation foreshadowed for the man, which could be cancelled, thwarted, or reversed by suitable counter-magic or by the favourable intervention of a deity.

Yet a third view of dreams, implied by some of the rituals, was that dreams were an aspect of demonic activity, and that the evil they might bring upon a man could be frustrated by outwitting the demon. This seems to be the implication of a ritual by which the dreamer, whilst repeating a magical formula three times, touched his foot on the ground on the side of the bed on which he had been sleeping—presumably as a decoy for the lurking demon—and then sprang out of bed on the other side.[37]

One element of common ground between all these different concepts of the aetiology of dreams is the absence of any marked indication of the involvement of a personal divine power seeking to give the dreamer either advice, warning or foreknowledge of events in general.

A significant second common element is that whatever the

aetiology attributed to the non-message dream, it was held that any evil foretold by it could be prevented.[38] That is, the dream omen (and the same is true of omens obtained by other techniques) was not related to ineluctable fate. There is a clash here with the idea, so abundantly evidenced elsewhere in Mesopotamian religion, of fate decreed by the gods. This contradiction hints again at the non-deistic basis of Mesopotamian divination. A prayer to a god is, indeed, sometimes incorporated in the ritual tablets used to remove the consequences of a dream, and it might be argued that this is contrary to the suggestion that much of the background of divination was non-deistic. But in such prayers the god is invoked as a divine power who can counter the evil influence: he is not the source of the evil influence.

A corresponding lack of indication of deistic background is shown throughout the great series of random omens known by an Akkadian title translatable as 'If a town is set on a hill'.[39] A few examples may be quoted to illustrate the type of omen material this vast series contains:

If water is poured out at the door of a man's house, and it looks like a snake, he will experience evil.

If a *birṣu* [a certain light phenomenon, possibly a shimmering reflection] is seen in a man's house, (this foretells) scattering of the man's household.

If a wild bull is seen in front of the (city) gate, the enemy will invest the city.[40]

Another section comprises a string of omens of the form 'if a sow kindles', and goes through the possible number of the litter from three to seven and possible colour combinations, with the usual kinds of presages of the type 'the man's house will be scattered', or 'man and wife will separate'.[41] Throughout all this vast series there is nothing to indicate that behind the omen given there was a personal deity offering communication to man. In some instances rituals are provided for averting the ill of the omen, and in these too the basic attitude is non-deistic. For example, in the averting ritual (n a m . b ú r . b i) dealing with the possible evils foreboded by light phenomena, magical operations involving certain plants and kinds of wood had to be performed at dawn, but there is no mention of a god at all.[42]

Similar indications of non-deistic background are given by physiognomic omens; for example:

If a man is covered with warts, he will have food to eat (even) in a famine.[43]

This manifestly does not represent a decision made by a god for a particular man in particular circumstances, but a recognition of the supposed relationship between phenomena. Whenever one circumstance occurred, the other would follow, without any divine will intervening *ad hoc*.

One might suppose that the deistic element would be more marked in astrological omens, inasmuch as the heavenly bodies were the visible manifestations, or at least the symbols, of certain gods. Sometimes the expected connection is found, as in references to astrological omens which occur in inscriptions of Esarhaddon,[44] but this may be a pious secondary development. Usually, in astrological omens outside royal inscriptions, the heavenly bodies are not overtly treated as manifestations of the divine. Thus, the moon is characteristically treated merely as a celestial phenomenon, the behaviour of which is on the same prognostic level as, for example, the shape taken by spilt water; there is no indication of the thought that a god is, if not actually visible in the form of the celestial body, at least active behind it and manipulating its appearance to give a direct message. A few specimens of astrological omens may be quoted in substantiation of this view. Thus we read:

When Mars again returns from the head of Leo and touches Cancer and Gemini, this is its interpretation: 'End of the reign of the king of Amurru'.[45]

Another report states:

When Jupiter stands behind the moon, this is its interpretation: 'There will be hostilities in the country'.[46]

It is considerations such as these which lead to the conclusion that the attitude behind the great mass of Mesopotamian omen material was basically non-deistic. This is not to deny that divination was taken under the umbrella of deistic religion at a fairly early date, certainly not later than the Old Babylonian period, though probably not earlier than that either. This may explain the conflicting indications of divinatory techniques having on the one hand been revealed before the Flood and yet on the other leaving but very little trace in texts earlier than the Old Babylonian period. Divination originated in, and in some areas remained fundamentally based upon, a non-deistic Weltanschauung.

This is an appropriate point at which to consider a bold, though very tentative, suggestion made by the French scholar Jean Nougayrol about the whole background of divination. Nougayrol has posed the significant question of the religious function of divination. He asserts that in the modern world, and probably in the Roman Empire, widespread belief in divination may be seen as filling a void left by the decline of deep religious faith; but he points out that we have no reason to assume a similar basis for the extensive occurrence of divination in ancient Mesopotamia. He therefore asks if it is possible that, in the absence of any concept of salvation in ancient Mesopotamia, divination might have been a means by which man might gain a more intimate contact with another world and a sense of participation in the divine order; were this so, divination might then be seen not as a secondary element but as the very heart of Babylonian religion.[47]

It appears to be a premiss of Nougayrol's tentative argument that outside ancient Mesopotamia the popularity of divinatory practices is correlated with decline in religious belief. This does not appear to be well founded. In regard to the evidence from the Roman Empire, the view of a Church Historian may be noted that 'contrary to what has often been maintained, one can say that interest in religion . . . was more real and more widespread in the third and fourth centuries than at any other period of ancient history'.[48] As to acceptance of divination being characteristic of the modern period of decline of religious belief, it seems probable that divination was, despite the official condemnation of the Church, as rife in mediaeval Christian Europe as today.[49] Thus it is clear that divination can flourish equally in periods in which deistic religion is widely accepted and in times of religious decline. This conforms with the view that Mesopotamian divination and its later counterparts are basically non-deistic, and that, as activities unrelated to and independent of deistic religion, they can on the one hand exist alongside the latter, and on the other can continue to thrive when religious faith withers. This latter is particularly facilitated by the fact that, unlike either cultic or personal religion, divination makes no demands—devotional, doctrinal, social or ethical—upon the practitioner.

The conclusion arrived at above, of the predominantly non-deistic basis of Mesopotamian divination, does not imply the view that there were no instances in Mesopotamia in which a personal divine being communicated his intentions, or his will, to humans. Personal communications from deities relating to future events are well attested, even though very much outweighed numerically by omen literature of the type already referred to. They fall into two main groups. The first comprises dreams in which a deity appears to a dreamer with a particular message, typically of advice, encouragement and promise of success in some enterprise under consideration: examples are known from the third millennium to the sixth century B.C.[50] This type of divine communication includes a case in which the god Ashur of Assyria appeared in a dream to a foreign king, Gyges of Lydia, urging him to become a vassal of Assyria, which would enable him to overcome his enemies;[51] this shows a belief in communications from Assyrian gods not bounded by narrow nationalism. In another case a whole army allegedly relied upon a dream from the goddess Ishtar promising them a safe crossing of a river in flood. The goddess told the army: 'I shall go in front of Ashurbanipal, the king whom I myself have created', and then, as the text says: 'The army relied upon this dream and safely crossed the river.'[52] This kind of report shows a spirit quite other than that of the dream omens. Here we have a personal deity who displays concern for the Assyrians, or at least for their king, and the troops react with personal trust in this expression of concern. Without question there is seen here direct communication of a deity with men.

The second type of direct communication from a deity comprises oracles. These are of particular interest from the point of view of Comparative Religion, in that there is a group of documents of this category, from first millennium Assyria, which seems at first sight closely comparable with the type of prophetic utterance known from the Old Testament. The oracles in question are attributed to named individuals in the reign of Esarhaddon, in the seventh century; in most cases (but not all) the individuals through whom the oracles came were women.[53] The texts tell nothing of the circumstances in which the messages were given, but make it clear that the persons named were thought to be vehicles for divine communications; what form the inspiration took is unknown. A typical oracle reads:

You shall not fear, O Esarhaddon. It is I, Bel, who speaks with you. I watch over your innermost heart, like your mother who gave you being. Sixty great gods have taken their stand with me to guard you. The god Sin is at your right hand, Shamash at your left. Sixty great gods stand round you, girt with the hurricane.[54] Rely not on mankind; cast your eyes on me, look on me. I am Ishtar of Arbela. Ashur has granted you well-being. When you were little I carried you.[55] Do not fear; revere me. Where is that enemy who has overwhelmed you?[56] It is I who am heedful. The latter things shall be like the former things. I am Nabu, Lord of the Stylus; revere me.[57]

It will be noticed that three different deities, Bel, Ishtar of Arbela, and Nabu, are represented as speaking. It is not clear whether the implication is that three distinct gods gave messages in the same oracle, or whether three oracles have been conflated in the one report, or whether the text implies that Bel, Ishtar and Nabu were all aspects of the one deity. What is, however, clear is that deities were thought to have a personal concern for a human being, albeit a king, and to be willing to send a message of assurance—and indeed love—to him, not in the vague terms of omen texts but in plain language.

In this particular text, the technical term for the woman through whom the oracle came is not given. But terms for such inspired persons are known, and in some instances the literal meanings of such terms may give a hint as to the original function of the person they describe. The word used in Assyria was *ragintu*,[58] meaning literally 'one who calls out'. We have letters in which the words of such people were reported to the king. In one such, a *ragintu* is quoted as saying—evidently in the name of a god, although a god is not mentioned in the extant part of the report—: 'I shall conquer the enemies of my king in the midst; I shall not give the throne except for the king my lord'.[59]

In the case quoted, the *ragintu* was certainly a cultic functionary, since she is referred to as bringing the king's garment, and this was used in the cult. In another instance the *ragintu* of a specified town is mentioned as though she was easily identifiable under that title, indicating that she had permanent cultic status.[60] But in other cases oracles were reported to the king from places otherwise unknown,[61] which suggests that they were minor places of negligible political or cultic importance. In such a setting the human vehicle of the oracle can hardly have been a regular cultic functionary, and is likely to have been a private person who had fallen into an ecstatic state and thereby been recognized as the channel for a message from a god.

The most specific Mesopotamian evidence for the giving of oracles through inspired persons comes from documents from Mari on the middle Euphrates, dating from the early second millennium. Between twenty and thirty letters from this source are now known referring to messages from deities.[62] Some of these relate only to dreams, and so would fall into the dream-theophany category discussed by Oppenheim; and others give no indication of the mechanism concerned. But in twelve of the letters there are references to messages given through a *muḫḫum* or *āpilum* or the female counterpart. By etymology *muḫḫum* should mean 'frenzied person'—an appropriate term for an ecstatic —whilst *āpilum* denotes 'one who gives an answer'. Several of the letters mention that a male or female *muḫḫum* or *āpilum* rose and

gave an oracle or that a person was in an ecstatic state (*immaḫû*);
and in five or six cases it was in a temple that this happened.[63]

Clearly, the giving of oracles through ecstatic persons was
known at Mari, and it was usually associated with cult functionaries. But the cultic connection was not invariable, for in one
instance the medium of the oracle was identified as the wife of
a freeman.[64] Had this lady enjoyed any personal cultic status,
she would surely have been identified in her own right, and not
simply by social class. This would therefore appear to be one
certain case of a divine message coming through a non-cultic
person in the ecstatic state. This would be a further indication that
direct communications from a deity could come to an individual
and not only through the cult.

A word may be said about the nature of the Mari oracles. There
is no indication that they were activated. Usually they were very
brief, and limited either to a message of encouragement to the king
or to instructions about religious rites. A typical passage reporting
such an oracle reads:

On the day I despatched this letter to my lord, a *muḫḫum* of the god
Dagan came and spoke an utterance to me thus: 'The god has sent me a
message: "Report to the king quickly. Let him present funerary
offerings for the ghost of Yahdun-Lim" .' That *muḫḫum* said this to me,
and I have duly reported to my lord. Let my lord do what seems good
to him.[65]

Such oracles were sometimes checked by omens from liver-
divination.[66] This is an indication that the latter was still considered the primary mechanism for ascertaining what we refer to
deistically as the divine will.

Clearly there is a case for examining the oracles from Mari and
Assyria in relationship to Old Testament prophecy.[67] However, it
must not be overlooked that methods recorded in the Old
Testament for discovering the divine will are not limited to
prophecy.[68] The best attested other technique is that of Urim and
Tummim.[69] At the beginning of the Monarchy this was accepted
as one of the three major and respectable methods of ascertaining

the divine will, since it is stated that when Saul inquired of Yahweh, 'Yahweh did not answer him, either by dreams, or by Urim, or by prophets' (1 Sam. 28:6 RSV). The system was binary,[70] the decision perhaps being given by which of the two objects called Urim and Tummim the priest drew from his pocket. Whilst it is clear that from the time of Saul onwards the use of Urim and Tummim was thought to give a decision from Yahweh, the possibility cannot be excluded that it was in origin a very ancient practice which did not necessarily postulate the existence of a personal divine will behind its operation: it need have been no more deistic in origin than tossing for heads or tails. An indication of the antiquity of the practice is given by the fact that the section of the 'Blessing of Moses' relating to Levi (Deut. 33:8) emphasizes Levi's operation of Urim and Tummim before referring to his priestly sacrificial function.

Dreams of the specific type (called by Oppenheim 'message dreams') were usually accepted in Israel as genuine channels for divine communications; this is exemplified in stories about dreams by Jacob, Joseph, Solomon and (from the very late period) characters in the Book of Daniel.[71] Yet by the end of the Monarchy period there were sceptics who regarded dream messages with suspicion. One such was Jeremiah. He refers to the prophets 'who speak lies in [Yahweh's] name and cry, "I have had a dream, a dream!" ' (23:25), and represents Yahweh as condemning prophets who do this. The succeeding command—'If a prophet has a dream, let him tell his dream; if he has my word, let him speak my word in truth' (23:28)—might appear to give some modified acceptance to the possibility that dreams could contain divine messages, but this has to be read in the light of the comment which follows it—' "What has chaff to do with grain?" says Yahweh.' Zechariah (10:2) took a similar view of the falseness of dreams as a means of learning Yahweh's will, putting this method on the same level as divination by *teraphim*, the portable household images well known from the story of Rachel's flight from her father Laban (Gen. 31:19–35). How *teraphim* were used for divination is unknown.

Several other methods of divining receive mention in the Old Testament. Thus, in the period of the Judges, the hero Gideon used a fleece for this purpose, taking God's decision upon a particular question as given by whether the fleece, when left out all night, absorbed moisture from the dew or remained dry (Jud. 6:36–40). There is also a casual mention of a silver cup being used by Joseph for the purpose of divination (Gen. 44:5), though no details are given of the technique concerned: in the context this was probably an Egyptian rather than an Israelite device, and the obvious guess (the evidence does not permit more) is that lecanomancy was involved.

There were other methods of divination used in Israel which were not merely suspect, like the use of dreams and *teraphim*, but which were—from the point of view of strict Yahwism—regarded as positively sinister and evil. Notable in this respect is the use of necromancy through mediums, which is referred to several times in terms of severe condemnation. Specific prohibitions of such practices are found in the laws,[72] and they are denounced in Isa. 8:19–20:

When they say to you, 'Consult the mediums and the wizards who chirp and mutter', should not a people consult their God? Should they consult the dead on behalf of the living? (RSV.)

The *New English Bible*, it should be said, offers a rendering of this passage which is significantly different at the crucial point. It reads:

But men will say to you,
'Seek guidance of ghosts and familiar spirits who squeak and gibber;
a nation may surely seek guidance of its gods,
of the dead on behalf of the living, for an oracle or a message?'

The crucial difference rests on the substitution of 'its gods' for 'their God' for Hebrew *'elohim* with pronominal suffix. The NEB rendering, though not wholly assured, could be justified in general, but if a translation on those lines is to be adopted, the term *'elohim* ought then to be rendered in this context not 'its gods' but 'its numina'. On the NEB interpretation of the passage, 'its *'elohim*' are clearly beings of the class to which ghosts and familiar spirits belong; and *'elohim*, when applied to ghosts, most assuredly did not mean 'gods' in the usual sense: the stock example of this is I Sam. 28:13, where the witch of Endor described the apparition of the dead Samuel as '*elohim*. However, despite the alternative ways of rendering the passage as a whole, it clearly establishes that Isaiah knew, and regarded as illicit, a method of divination involving necromancy.

In necromancy we have an area in which there is to be seen a marked contrast of attitude between official Yahwism and official Assyrian religion of the same period. For a few decades later than Isaiah's condemnation of necromancy—or, to use the euphemism employed for it in our own society, Spiritualism—we have evidence that the practice enjoyed respectability and favour in the heart of Assyrian society. A letter from the royal archives reads:

I shall show to the king my lord as follows:... They [presumably the necromancers] have said ... 'In connection with the office of Crown Prince, her ghost [that of the Crown Prince's dead mother] blesses him, since he has shown reverence to the ghost, and says "His line and seed shall rule over Assyria".'[73]

We turn finally to look at prophecy in Israel as a means of ascertaining the divine will. Here it is hardly necessary to point out that the volume of literature, primary and secondary, upon Israelite prophecy is so vast that consideration must be limited to a few points most directly relevant to the present comparison between Israelite and Mesopotamian religion.

Three points in particular may be noted. Firstly, the evidence for the giving of messages from a god directly through the utterance of an inspired person is much more abundant from ancient Israel than from ancient Mesopotamia. Secondly, Old Testament prophecy was not a single unitary phenomenon but comprised the receiving of divine communications both by a message which was a response to activation and one which came spontaneously. Thirdly, in Israel the prophetic function might be an individual and personal gift, and was not, as priesthood was, dependent upon ancestry and initiation. Some amplification may be offered of each of these points.

As to the quantitative aspect of the matter, it is indisputable that, even accepting for the immediate comparison that documents such as the Esarhaddon oracles and those Mari letters which record messages from the gods are all to be placed in the same category as Israelite prophetic literature, the latter far outweighs the Mesopotamian material. The disparity becomes still more marked when one takes into account the much larger population in Mesopotamia and the much longer period from which documentary evidence is available there.

The point that Old Testament prophecy was not a single unitary phenomenon is quite distinct from the much discussed problem of whether the Hebrew terms for 'seer' and 'prophet' originally denoted one, two or three types of functionary. The point being made is that alongside the form of prophecy in which the word of Yahweh came spontaneously to a prophet was another form, which needed to be activated: the person operating the latter was of the same class, and was sometimes the same person, as the man receiving the spontaneous message. We have clear examples of the activated type of prophecy being operated by a canonical prophet in events connected with King Hezekiah. Hezekiah, on receiving a letter from Assyrian emissaries, 'went up into the house of Yahweh, spread it out before Yahweh', and offered a prayer (2 Kgs. 19:14). This was the activation, and the response came in an utterance from Isaiah. Yet Isaiah certainly gave other divine messages to Hezekiah which arrived spontaneously and were not specifically activated: we see this in an incident when, as the prophet was leaving the palace after delivering a message, another message came to him and he had to return to modify what he had previously foretold (2 Kgs. 20:1–6). Thus, even if one is prepared to accept that Isaiah and other canonical prophets were cultic functionaries who gave oracles on demand in that capacity,[74] there is no difficulty in accepting that they might also on occasions have exercised the gift of prophecy outside the setting of a cultically controlled organization.

The evidence for the personal nature of the prophetic function is significant, in view of the emphasis which has sometimes been placed upon the cultic connections of the prophets. That a man might display prophetic phenomena spontaneously, without passing through selection, initiation and training, is clear from the case of Saul, who fell into prophetic ecstasy when he met a group of prophets,[75] and also from the odd incident of Num. 11:25-9, when during the time of Moses seventy elders were seized with the spirit of prophecy. This random nature of the prophetic function marks it off distinctly from such cultic functions as the office of liver-diviner in Mesopotamia or priest in Israel. In both the latter functions the initiate was theoretically the lineal descendant of an ancient worthy who had been invested with his professional prerogatives and knowledge by a deity; there is nothing corresponding with this for the prophet. Moreover, both the diviner in Mesopotamia and the priest in Israel[76] had to satisfy conditions not only of descent but also of freedom from physical deformity. Thus, the Mesopotamian diviner had to be 'offspring of Enmeduranki, king of Sippar, . . . begotten by a *nišakku*-priest of pure descent, . . . without blemish in body and limbs',[77] whilst in Israel not only were there divine sanctions against any person not descended from Aaron entering the priesthood (Num. 16:40), but even amongst those of suitable lineage any physical defect disqualified (Lev. 21:16-23). The absence of any comparable qualifications for exercising the function of prophecy is a strong indication that, even if there were prophets within the cult, prophecy as a function was never in Israel taken fully and formally under the organization and direction of the cultic system. Unlike the Israelite priest, whose office was—from early in the first millennium at least—subject to prescribed qualifications of ancestry and physique, the prophetic office depended only upon the personal consciousness, or claim, to be the vehicle of the word of Yahweh. This could take, as elsewhere noted, two distinct forms; the ability to receive the word of Yahweh through an activating process,[78] or a state in which the word of Yahweh came spontaneously, putting the prophet under an irresistible compulsion to utter it.[79]

It does not fall within the scope of the present work, in discussing

Old Testament prophecy, to attempt to evaluate the truth of the prophetic claim to be the vehicle for direct messages from God; this is a matter for theology and not for the comparative study of religions. It is, however, proper to consider whether or not there were any features of Old Testament prophecy which justify the claim that it was unique in the religio-historical context of the ancient Near East.

The mainstream of nineteenth-century biblical scholarship had a very clear view on this: canonical Old Testament prophecy was unique; the prophets were independent of cultic religion and often impatient of it, and were in direct and immediate communication with God. This postulated uniqueness is now, however, challenged by the evidence of apparently comparable prophetic activity elsewhere in the ancient Near East; whilst the independence of the prophets and their direct and immediate communication with God is called in question by the argument that the canonical prophets were in some (or even all) cases operating within the cult, or at the least were heavily conditioned by cultic concepts. Von Rad expresses the latter point of view dogmatically:

The prophets were never as original, or as individualistic, or in such direct communication with God and no one else, as they were [formerly] believed to be... Research has meanwhile clearly shown that the prophets were much more directly involved in concepts common to the ancient east, in cult and in myth, ... than ... was supposed. And this attachment to inherited traditions and ideas generally current at that time did not simply affect the circumference of their message: it went right to its heart. Consequently, the classical definition of the specific essence of prophecy, based as it then was, in particular, on the new ideas conceived by the prophets out of their own intimate communion with the deity, has been largely discredited. We have also abandoned the whole idea of a 'religion of the prophets' as a religion of the spirit diametrically opposed to the 'cultic religion of the priests'.[80]

The old interpretation of the data saw a deliberate turning away by the prophets from the old traditional forms of Yahwism associated with the cult. Whether there was, or was not, such a deliberate turning away is related to the interpretation of a number of disputed biblical passages which *prima facie* would appear to support the conclusion that some old forms and some old concepts were rejected by the prophets. Basically the main line of argument against accepting the obvious conclusion is that the prophets themselves did not reject the cultic framework as a whole. This is a point at which Mesopotamian data are relevant; such data show that it was quite possible to make a conscious rejection of old religious concepts associated with the cult and ancient myth, without breaking with the cult itself. Such a development in Mesopotamian religion has been investigated by W. von Soden. He has established that, in Mesopotamia at the period of the major canonical Old Testament prophets, there is demonstrable an attitude which he calls a 'secularizing tendency'.[81] This involved a questioning and conscious rejection of a number of the concepts long accepted in Mesopotamian religion. Yet there is no reason to think that those involved in this trend regarded themselves as breaking with the mainstream of Mesopotamian religion. If one transposes this to the Israelite situation, it admits the possibility that the prophets could equally have rejected some of the old concepts of Yahwism, without considering themselves as making a break with Israelite religion. That such a rejection certainly occurred in some Israelite circles is easily demonstrable. Thus we have the case of King Hezekiah, who destroyed the bronze serpent Nehushtan, a venerable old symbol of Yahwism closely associated in tradition with Moses himself.[82] In acting thus, he did not think of himself as breaking with older Yahwistic forms, although he was doing so; as he saw the situation, the element of the cultus he was throwing out was false. For another example of the rejection of older cultic aspects of Yahwism, one may point to Josiah's desecration of Bethel (2 Kgs. 23:15–16), a desecration provided with a theological apologia, but from the point of view of older Yahwism a desecration none the less, since Bethel had a venerable association with a Patriarch and had been the site of a major theophany.

The other point to be discussed arises from the occurrence in Mesopotamia of messages believed to come directly from the deity through an inspired person. Was this apparent parallel so similar to canonical Israelite prophecy as to rob the latter of its claim to uniqueness? The data make it clear beyond doubt that in terms of mechanism canonical Old Testament prophecy was not unique. In Israel itself, the mechanism was identical in what we know as 'false prophecy', so that contemporaries had no means of distinguishing between what subsequently came to be accepted as on the one hand false and on the other hand true prophecy. This is quite clear from Deut. 13:1–5, which deals with the problem of distinguishing true from false prophecy. According to this, the fulfilment of a prophet's words was in itself no authentication: even if a prophet's words came true, if he said 'Let us go after other gods and let us serve them' (13:2 RSV), he was to be put to death. That is to say, the ultimate touchstone, and the only infallible test, was whether or not the prophet was a thorough-going supporter of official Yahwism. Thus it was not claimed that there was anything distinctive about the mechanism of the 'true' prophet in Israel. Furthermore, such limited evidence as we have on prophecy at Mari shows that, despite some differences of detail, the Mari mechanism was so close to that of Israel that it is not proper to claim that, as a technique for ascertaining the divine will, Israelite prophecy stood alone.

Yet although uniqueness cannot be claimed on grounds of mechanism, when we come to look at the nature of the message, it may be possible to see a significant difference. One must, how-ever, first discount apparent differences which may have a sub-jective origin in the religio-cultural associations of modern scholars with a biblical background. Thus a prophecy relating to the fate of Hezekiah might at first sight appear different in kind from a prophecy relating to a king of Mari or Assyria, because from our modern religious point of view Hezekiah was not merely a Judaean king but a person who stood at a particular point within the history of the Judaeo-Christian religious tradition, so that for the modern Jewish or Christian scholar a prophecy relating to Hezekiah might have a universal relevance. But, even with such subjective differences discounted, a real difference does remain. The difference is that, unlike the message of many Israelite prophecies, the message in the reports in the Mari letters, or the oracles of later Assyria, is always bounded. What is meant here by 'bounded' can be indicated quite simply by quoting an observation that has been made on Israelite prophecy. This is to the effect that

with the lone exception of the most legendary sections of the Elijah-Elisha cycles, there is not one single indication of a prophetic oracle being delivered to anyone outside of the royal court prior to the time of Amos. Nor is there any indication that any of the pre-classical prophets uttered even one oracle against the whole nation or individual non-royal groups within the nation.[83]

But, the author quoted points out, in the case of prophets from the eighth century onwards, with the exception of Isaiah of Jerusalem, there is 'a dramatic shift of the primary object of the prophetic address away from the ruling houses of the twin kingdoms and to the people of Israel as a whole'.[84]

The Mesopotamian counterparts of Israelite prophecies were bounded in the same sense that the pre-canonical Israelite oracles were; that is, they had their points of application contained within certain restricted limits of time, subject-matter, and personalia. In terms of time, the application was always to events in the near future, not eschatological time. Like the messages of pre-classical Old Testament prophecy, the Mesopotamian oracles always related wholly or predominantly to royal affairs. Above all, the subject-matter, even at its least trite, concerned only the will or intention of the god for a particular person in particular circumstances.

It might be argued here that the last point made does not exemplify a difference between Mesopotamian oracles and classical Old Testament prophecy, in that the canonical Israelite prophets also delivered their messages to, or with relevance to, a particular social or ethnic group in a particular historical context.

That Israelite prophecies were delivered in specific settings is true, but this does not necessarily make them bounded. Many of the prophetic messages, although delivered in a particular context, were general universal statements about the nature of God or the demands of God upon man, transcending the immediate context. It is necessary, however, to distinguish between those messages where it was possible to find a general universal element by later extrapolation from the sense of the particular message to the immediate context, and those in which the universal application was inherent, even if only latent and not necessarily explicit in the mind of the prophet himself. Messages of the latter type were unbounded in essence, not merely in subjective later interpretation. A few obvious and well known examples which illustrate this may be offered. Thus: 'I am Yahweh, there is no other' (Isa. 45:6); 'Am I a god only near at hand, not far away? Can a man hide in any secret place and I not see him? Do I not fill heaven and earth? This is the very word of Yahweh' (Jer. 23:23–4); 'As I live, says Yahweh God, I have no desire for the death of the wicked. I would rather that a wicked man should mend his ways and live. Give up your evil ways, give them up; O Israelites, why should you die?' (Ezek. 33:11). The first two passages are explicitly unbounded, the last latently so. Whilst the final passage mentions its application to Israelites, the statement about God's attitude to the wicked cannot be taken as implying a limitation to the case of the Israelites. To take it as inherently intended in that limited sense would give the absurdity of implying either that no one except Israelites could be wicked, or that except in the case of Israelites Ezekiel supposed that God did desire the death of the wicked.

It is in this sense that it is argued that Mesopotamian oracles were bounded in a way that Israelite prophetic messages were not. Never in any circumstances did the message of the Mesopotamian ecstatic break through these bounds to give a message not to a man but to Man, not merely about the behaviour demanded from a particular man in a particular situation but about the behaviour demanded from mankind, not about the intentions of the gods for the immediate circumstance but about God's very nature. The canonical prophets of Israel did burst these bounds, and in doing so burst through the limitations not only of ancient Near Eastern religions but also of traditional Yahwism itself.

Universalism

The jacket to the excellent English translation of Mowinckel's
The Psalms in Israel's Worship[1] depicts a number of severe-looking
gentlemen in oriental head-dress, scantily bearded and open-
mouthed. These figures are evidently intended to represent
Israelites chanting, as P. G. Wodehouse once put it, 'one of the
song-hits from the psalms'. This well epitomizes the popular view
that for the ancient Israelites religion was the principal element in
life, a view that many theologians, and some religious historians,
would probably share. In relation to the people of ancient Mesopotamia views have been less consistent. Whilst some scholars
have stated, or written as though they assumed, that religion was
one of the main drives in ancient Mesopotamia, A. L. Oppenheim
has, on the contrary, pressed the view that Mesopotamian religion
made minimal demands on the common man:

The influence of religion on the individual, as well as on the community
as a whole, was unimportant in Mesopotamia. . . The individual's . . .
body, his time, and his valuables were in no serious way affected by
religious demands. . . The participation of the individual in the cult of
the city deity was restricted in the extreme; he was simply an onlooker
in certain public ceremonies of rejoicing or communal mourning.[2]

In the final sentence of the passage quoted, Oppenheim is not
only stating a religio-historical conclusion but also offering an
assessment of a point of historical fact. Yet as an historical fact, it
is by no means certain that the ordinary man was no more than an
onlooker in public religious ceremonies. An indication to the
contrary is given by a passage in the Gilgamesh Epic, which speaks
of the Flood hero giving his workmen abundant food and wine
'that they might feast as on New Year's Day'.[3] This indicates that
feasting was an accepted feature of the New Year Festival, implying widespread communal participation in at least that religious

occasion. Furthermore, it is a subjective judgement that, even when feasting was not involved, onlookers in Mesopotamia took no part in public religious ceremonies. If we possessed only the texts for the relevant liturgies, corresponding but wrong conclusions could be drawn for the non-involvement of Christians at the Mass, or for Shi'ite Muslims at the Muharram Passion-play. For ancient Mesopotamia there remains the possibility, disregarded by Oppenheim, that the onlookers in public ceremonies may have been involved by ritual cries, chanting the name or epithets of the deity, groans, prostrations, hand-raising, chest-beating or many other manifestations of emotional response. Even in modern secular societies, a state parade on a day of royal or national significance (such as the funeral of Churchill) can evoke the most deep-seated emotional response and psychological involvement from vast crowds, even though in physical terms they are mere onlookers. At the level of mere sporting events, supposedly passive onlookers may become so involved emotionally that rioting ensues.

Yet, although Oppenheim overstates his case in reducing religion for the ordinary man in Mesopotamia to a matter in which he was a mere uninvolved onlooker, there is the possibility that religion dominated the life of the common man less there than within some other religious cultures. Despite the abundance of textual material directly relating to Assyro-Babylonian religion, it is not an easy matter to make a confident assessment on this. Such text categories as hymns and prayers, in which religious concepts are inevitably dominant, must be used with caution, since though they give considerable information on some aspects of Mesopotamian religion, this has reference mainly to the concepts and attitudes of what Eliade has called the elitist group, in the official cultus: they do not necessarily reflect attitudes and emphases which were substantially those of the common man. The same situation is true of some other classes of documents where, although the religious aspect is less overtly marked, religious concepts from the official cultus lie at the basis of the category; royal annals are a case in point. On the other hand, text categories of these kinds, though

they do not give a complete picture, may not be wholly disregarded in relation to popular religion, since even though the
official cultus to which such texts belonged centred on the king,
account must be taken of the tendency for religious concepts
originally involving only an elitist circle to be diffused into a wider
sphere: a striking example of this is found in Egyptian religion in
the assimilation of the dead king to Osiris, a concept which was
ultimately extended to embrace every individual at death.[4]

There is one method by which it may be to some extent
possible to arrive at an assessment of the part played by religion in
the life of the ordinary man of ancient Mesopotamia. This is to
attempt to compare attitudes found in texts linked to the official
cultus with attitudes reflected in texts unrelated to the cultus. The
principal extensive classes of document falling into the latter
category are letters and (largely) business documents. Business
documents are, however, in a highly stereotyped form which
offers few opportunities for revealing personal attitudes. In letters,
on the other hand, the contents are, except for the stylized introduction, determined far less by tradition or convention than by the
need to describe, discuss, question, or criticize a particular situation
which has currently arisen. This potentially permits the writer to
reveal his own attitudes and values in a more positive manner
than is ever possible in royal inscriptions or religious or literary
texts.

It is thus significant that across the whole span of Assyro-
Babylonian civilization letters give less prominence to religious
concepts than one might have expected on the basis of contemporary documents (or documents of other periods on the same
kind of subject) of many classes.

Some illustrations of this may be given from Assyrian letters of
around 700 B.C.[5] Amongst such letters, there are some specifically
related to the official cultus, which contain information from cult
functionaries on such cultic matters as the significance of state
omens, and details of rituals to be performed:[6] these may properly
be excluded from consideration in the attempt to arrive at the
place of religion in life outside the cult. Of Assyrian letters not

directly related to cultic affairs, the greatest number were written to the king by provincial administrators, across a wide range of topics. Of these topics, some provide little opportunity for religious allusion; but a substantial number of topics are discussed which also find mention in texts related to the official cultus, and a comparison of the treatment of such topics in the different classes of texts displays instructive differences of attitude.

An example of this occurs in connection with agriculture. In a cultic setting national well-being, including good crop yields, was considered to be related to the king. This is expressed in a celebrated passage in the Annals of Ashurbanipal:

After [the gods] had kindly made me sit upon the throne of the father who begot me, Adad released his rains, Ea loosed his fountains, the grain grew five cubits high in its furrow, . . . [there were] favourable harvests and prosperous crops, the grasslands continually gave abundance. . .[7]

In letters, the state of the harvest is recorded in quite different terms. Whilst there are a number of references in letters to plentiful rains resulting in agricultural prosperity, these are usually reported without any allusion to the activity of the gods. Thus one official reports:

On the night of the twenty seventh until dawn, the whole of the day of the twenty seventh, the whole of the night of the twenty eighth, very much rain poured down. . . The harvest prospect is very favourable.[8]

The whole implication is that the rain was accepted as a natural phenomenon rather than (as in the royal inscription quoted earlier) a mark of divine favour. It is almost invariable in the Assyrian royal letters that references to crop prospects, whether favourable or unfavourable, attributed the situation directly to the presence or absence of suitable rain or flooding: normally there is no mention of the interposition of the gods in such matters.[9] It is not suggested that there is to be seen here any implicit denial of the ultimate responsibility of the divine powers for fertility, but the absence of

any specific mention of the gods does suggest that the activity of
the gods was not as much in the foreground of ancient Mesopotamian thought as texts more directly connected with the cult
might indicate.

The way in which unusual phenomena are mentioned in letters
is also significant. Since omens were frequently drawn from unusual occurrences, one might have expected any abnormal happening to have been regarded as relevant to the activity of the divine
powers. However, in letters occurrences in this category often
appear to have been recorded without eliciting any comment in
the sphere of religion or superstition. Thus, in a letter in which an
earthquake was reported there is no comment as to its ominous
significance: the only matter of interest appears to have been the
practical one of the extent of the damage.[10]

Another indication of limitation in the importance of the cultic
sphere is that sometimes less respect was paid to the right of
deities than one might have anticipated. Thus, when the king of
Elam sent a present of white horses to the goddess Ishtar of Erech,
the administrator did not hesitate to withhold them from the
goddess until he had received instructions about the matter from
the king of Assyria.[11]

Elsewhere in an Assyrian letter it was reported that a man had
been adversely affected (perhaps drowned) by a river.[12] This
recalls a passage in the Laws of Hammurabi, in which it is said of
a man who drowned when put to the river ordeal, that 'the River-
god seized him'.[13] But whereas in the Laws of Hammurabi the
river is thought of as a deity, in the Assyrian letter the statement
simply has the form 'the river has "touched" him', with the term
for river not marked by the god determinative. Clearly, in the
thought of the man writing the letter, the river was a mere
natural force, not a deity.

A frequent topic both of royal inscriptions and of letters was
military affairs, but there was a marked difference in the manner
in which they were described. Whereas royal inscriptions designated Assyrian armies as the armies of the gods and their victories
as the gods' victories, in the letters, such an attitude, although not

wholly lacking, was far less marked. There are many instances of military successes being referred to without any mention of the gods. Even where the gods are mentioned in such a connection, the reference sometimes has a political rather than a theological basis. Such is the case, for example, in a letter in which the people of Kishik, near Ur, tell the king: 'Sin and Ningal your gods have delivered your enemy into your hands.'[14] These particular deities are mentioned because the city of Kishik, which had favoured the king's cause, was a cult centre of this divine pair;[15] thus the report was in substance not so much a theological statement as a political claim on behalf of the city.

There are first millennium letters from the archives of Babylonian temples which may also be taken into account.[16] Typically these documents represent correspondence between temple administrators (most commonly not cult functionaries) in temples in Erech and the authorities in Babylon. Such letters show that the approach of the writers, except those who were actually cult functionaries, were not basically cult-orientated, even when matters concerning the cult were under discussion from the administrative point of view. Reports and comments in these letters are typically on the human rather than the mythological or cultic plane. Thus, although in one letter we find an official being reproached for negligence in the matter of providing cattle for cult festivals, the wording contains no implication that the delinquent risked anything beyond ordinary human sanctions.[17] In other letters, an official had been detected in embezzling grain or cattle intended for the temple; but there is nowhere in the correspondence any suggestion that either the writer or the addressee regarded the defrauded deity as so immediately involved with the ordinary man that he would wreak personal vengeance on the offender.[18]

Evidence such as the foregoing does not necessitate acceptance of Oppenheim's extreme view that religion held a minimal importance for the ordinary non-royal individual in ancient Mesopotamia. It does, however, establish beyond dispute that, at least in the case of ancient Mesopotamia, the idea sometimes expressed that ancient man's life was dominated by religion is quite without basis.

For ancient Israel, there is much less scope for making a significant comparison between attitudes found in documents relating to the official cult and those outside. All the biblical documents have passed through the screen of religiously-orientated editors; and non-biblical texts from pre-exilic Israel are markedly exiguous, comprising little more than the Siloam inscription, the Arad and Lachish letters, the Gezer calendar (not certainly Israelite), and a handful of miscellaneous inscriptions.[19]

The Siloam inscription is of potential importance in this connection, in that it gives an account of an event also mentioned in the Bible, the cutting at Hezekiah's orders of a tunnel to bring water from the Gihon spring to a reservoir inside the walls of Jerusalem. In the extant part of the Siloam inscription there is no religious allusion at all; however, this proves nothing about a difference of attitude in the writer, since both the biblical passages (2 Kgs. 20:20 and 2 Chron. 32:30) which mention Hezekiah's engineering operation are equally devoid of religious allusion at this immediate point.

In view of the usefulness of letters in investigating the Mesopotamian situation, the Arad and Lachish letters (both groups written in Judah at the time of Nebuchadrezzar's attacks) might appear to hold promise. However, compared with the number of letters available from Mesopotamia they are extremely scanty, the total number of substantially intelligible Hebrew letters not exceeding two dozen, some of them very slight. The extant intelligible parts of these letters give little that is so closely parallel to situations in biblical texts that we can make a significant comparison of attitudes. Yahweh is, it is true, mentioned in greetings and in an oath,[20] but these are mere matters of conventional literary form, not of personal piety. A letter from the late seventh century from another site makes it clear that it was taken as a matter of course that work was not done on the Sabbath;[21] but this was related to social custom and cannot in itself be taken as evidence of a marked piety or religiosity in the writer. Throughout these letters there is no situation where one might have expected the writer to show a different attitude had he been obsessed with religion.

None of the other ancient non-biblical Israelite inscriptions seems to contain anything of which one could say either that it is evidence of religion being deeply felt in non-cultic matters of everyday life, or on the contrary that the attitude differs from that which one would expect of a person whose life was permeated with religion.

Thus extra-biblical material seems to provide no evidence on the matter under consideration, and any judgement on the question will need to be based wholly on the Old Testament texts. As already pointed out, these texts are not raw material but have all been edited by pious Jews who are likely to have orientated the texts in keeping with their own religious concepts, making it *prima facie* difficult to distinguish within them between texts worded in accordance with cultic concepts and texts displaying the attitudes of non-cultic everyday life. Yet in the Old Testament texts we possess something which has no counterpart in Mesopotamian literature, in the form of explicit criticism, by prophets and biblical editors, of the attitudes and practices of ordinary people; and these criticisms themselves may serve to test the general implication of Old Testament writings that Israelites as a whole were dominated by the demands and concepts of religion. We are not now asking whether or not the mass of Israelites were always good Yahwists, from the point of view of rigid official Yahwism, which they plainly were not; but practices for which the commonalty were condemned by official Yahwism—such as rituals at high places or offering cakes to the Queen of Heaven[22]—may themselves have been marks of an intense (if, from the biblical editors' point of view, misguided) religious devotion. Lack of devotion to traditional Yahwism did not necessarily imply apathy towards religion. For example, Elijah is represented as complaining that he alone was left of those jealous for Yahweh God of Hosts (1 Kgs. 19:10), but this does not necessarily establish (even if the claim was substantially true) that the mass of Israelites were apathetic to religion, but only that they were not attached to the form of Mosaic Yahwism practised by Elijah. One contemporary of Elijah equally fanatical with himself about religion was his arch-enemy Jezebel. Jezebel was—although this point seems usually to have been disregarded—an aggressive monotheist, intolerant of other cults, and making an exclusive claim in much the same way, though in the service of a different god, as Elijah or Jehu.[23] Thus mere accusations of apostasy from Yahweh establish nothing about attitudes to religion. What is required is to investigate whether or not indications are at all common in the Old Testament of a criticism of Israelites not for wrong religious attitudes, but rather for apathy towards religion as a whole.

Some such indications can be found. Thus Amos speaks of merchants who find the New Moon festival and the Sabbath a troublesome interruption of commercial business (8:5): much later, Trito-Isaiah implies that it was a common attitude that Sabbaths and other holy days were regarded as an imposition rather than a delight (Isa. 56:2; 58:13). In Zephaniah we have a reference to people who say: 'Yahweh will do nothing, good or bad' (1:12), apparently indicating that they regarded Yahweh as otiose and religious practices as pointless. Jeremiah gives a similar indication in 5:12, regardless of whether the crucial words are to be taken with RSV as '[Yahweh] will do nothing' or with NEB as '[Yahweh] does not exist'.[24] However, a passage in Ezekiel, mentioning people who say 'The way of Yahweh is not just' (33:17 RSV) cannot legitimately be adduced to support this point, since the questioning of the justice of God in a particular context may well imply a keen concern for living religion rather than apathy. There are occasional adverse references to people who rely upon the protection of foreign powers rather than upon Yahweh (Isa. 30:2, 31:1), and Jeremiah pronounces

A curse on the man who trusts in man and leans for support on human kind, while his heart is far from Yahweh! (Jer. 17:5.)

King Jehoiakim was not afraid to burn the scroll on which Jeremiah's prophecies were written (Jer. 36:23-4), but this can hardly be taken as proof of any general attitude of indifference to religion, since it may have been a matter of non-acceptance of Jeremiah's prophetic credentials rather than of contempt for a prophecy accepted as coming from Yahweh; moreover, Jehoiakim was an exceptionally bold man, and there were others present who were horrified at what was happening (Jer. 36:25). At an earlier period Michal, Saul's daughter and David's wife, criticized David for having (in her view) disgraced himself by taking part in a cultic dance (2 Sam. 6:20), and this might be taken to establish that Michal regarded religious observance as secondary to personal dignity. But it is equally possible that that particular cultic dance was a custom confined to the southern tribes and that it had no religious significance for Michal, from the tribe of Benjamin; if so, from her point of view her comment could have been not on participation in a religious custom but on the propriety of the king of all Israel personally engaging in a wild tribal dance.

One could glean a few other passages which might be interpreted as demonstrating instances of Israelite lukewarmness towards religion, but compared with the criticisms of Israelites for wrong religious observances such passages are rare. The provisional conclusion must be that indications of Israelite apathy towards religion (not necessarily limited to what the Deuteronomists and prophets thought of as true religion) are very slight, and that the conventional picture of Israelite life as religion-dominated—almost, indeed, religion-bloated—is not basically a distortion of the real situation.

Any evidence showing lack of awe towards holy things is also relevant here. Some small items of such evidence are available, and although not very extensive do permit us to make an impressionistic comparison between the two cultural areas. From cuneiform sources there are references to thefts from temples, even from the statue of a great god himself, as when the sun-disk was stolen from the breast of the statue of Ashur by burglars in the early second millennium.[25] The only thing remotely comparable to this in Israelite literature is the use by David and his men, in an emergency, of the sacred bread placed before Yahweh (1 Sam. 21:4-6);

but according to the existing record there were certain mitigating factors which obviated or lessened the element of sacrilege. On the other hand, we do know of two instances in Israel of disaster overwhelming a person from too near approach to the holy things of the deity. One involved the unfortunate Uzzah, who put out his hand to steady the Ark when the cart on which it was being transported swayed, and was immediately struck dead (2 Sam. 6:6–7). The other case was that of King Uzziah, who ventured to attempt to usurp the prerogatives claimed by the Aaronic priest-hood at the incense altar (2 Chron. 26:16–20). Though the form of the latter narrative was certainly related to priestly manipulation of a situation, it was because of the horror generally evoked by improper meddling with holy things that it could be so used. A further difference that may be noticed in this area is that whilst in Mesopotamia there were laws against sacrilegious theft,[26] there seem to have been none in Israel. This suggests that in Israel the possibility was unthinkable.[27] It may also be remembered that in Jewish legend incorporated in the Book of Daniel, the beginning of the end for Belshazzar of Babylon came when at a banquet he desecrated the sacred vessels taken by Nebuchadrezzar from the Temple in Jerusalem (Dan. 5:1–5).

This evidence, though certainly not conclusive, does further impressionistically support other indications that the attitudes of the common man were more religion-dominated in Israel than in Mesopotamia.

In both Israelite and Mesopotamian religion one finds taken for granted the possibility of man's personal relationship with God or the gods. There seems nothing striking about this to the average Western reader, but this is only so because his own religious environment has familiarized him with the concept from the Old Testament through the New and through Judaism. In terms of religion generally there is no inevitableness in a man being able to enter into a personal relationship with deity: in some forms of Gnosticism, for example, the possibility of a human normally being able to know the Supreme Being is specifically denied.

The reflection of the possibility of personal relationship with the divine may be seen in both Israel and Mesopotamia in the mythology of the creation of man. In both areas explanations are given of the purpose of man's creation. These explanations seem to assume from the beginning that man was acting in the world on behalf of the divine beings, with the corollary of a necessary personal relationship through which the gods could control their stewards or servants.

The reasons given for the creation of man seem simple and straightforward, although on examination they give rise to further problems. In Israel man was *prima facie* created either to have dominion over the earth and all living things[28] or to look after the Garden of Eden.[29] In Mesopotamia, the basic reason for the creation of man was to relieve the gods of certain chores.[30]

The alleged circumstances of the creation of man in Mesopotamia, referred to in a number of places, are most explicit in the myth *Atrahasis*. This begins with the words

> When the gods like men
> Bore work and suffered toil[31]

which sets the scene. Already there is a hierarchy, with Anu supreme in heaven, Enki in the waters, and Enlil on earth. The gods outside the courts of the hierarchs seem to have been working at irrigation to make the land fertile. It is not explained why they needed to; the underlying assumption is that irrigation and fertility were activities essential in themselves—in fact, that they were part of a world order which did not depend upon the will of the gods. Eventually they complained about the excessive toil and organized a militant strike. In response, the god Ea (Enki) proposed that the Birth-goddess should create Lullu (an obscure name for man) to bear the toil of the gods: this was put in hand by killing a god and mixing his blood with clay.[32] Assisted by Enki, the birth-goddess then pinched off fourteen pieces of clay, which, with the help of midwives, became seven pairs of humans, male and female.[33]

A significant point is, that once humans are made, the interest of the myth in its present form turns right away from the original problem of removing toil from the gods, and runs on to refer to customs at childbirth.[34] It is also to be noted, that before there is any mention of the matter of pinching off pieces of clay to become humans, the Birth-goddess has already told the gods 'I have removed your heavy work, I have imposed your toil on man', and been acclaimed for this.[35] This suggests that the details about the fourteen pieces of clay are an addition (though an early one) to the original creation story,[36] and that the present form of the myth is aetiological in purpose, to explain certain details of birth-customs (and marriage customs).[37] The myth may not then be assumed to have had the purpose of giving theological teaching about the origin and nature of man.

This has a bearing upon how one is to understand the slaughtering of a god to provide blood to mix with the clay. It would be tempting to conclude that this detail was the vehicle for the theological doctrine that the constitution of man includes a spark of the divine. Yet there are objections to such a view, and reasons for taking the details given as directed to establishing something quite different. The editors of the text translate the relevant passage:

> From [the god's] flesh and blood
> Let Nintu mix clay,
> That god and man
> May be thoroughly mixed in the clay,
> So that we may hear the drum for the rest of time
> Let there be a spirit from the god's flesh.
> Let it proclaim living (man) [*balṭa*] as its sign [*ittu*],
> So that this be not forgotten let there be a spirit.[38]

This passage is obscure, but it must mean something other than simply that created man was the memorial to a dead god. It would be absurd to assume the circular situation that on the one hand the god was killed in order that man might be created, and on the other that man was created in order that a killed god might have a memorial; quite apart from the fact that a different purpose for creating man has already been explicitly stated. The word translated 'spirit' is *eṭemmu*, but this means 'spirit' only in the sense of 'spirit of the dead' or 'ghost'; by extension it sometimes comes to be used for the image of a dead person, but it certainly never means 'spirit' in the sense 'vitality'.[39] Thus the rendering 'Let it [the *eṭemmu*] proclaim living (man) as its sign' is hardly valid, since it is difficult to understand how a man can be a sign of a ghost or spectre. Furthermore, *balṭu* need not specifically mean 'living (man)' but can mean 'living (thing)'. I would therefore suggest that what the penultimate line quoted means is: 'May it [the *eṭemmu*] make known its sign (in the form of) a living thing', that is, let the characteristic of a ghost be that it creates the deception of being a living human. It is then not man as such who is a memorial to the dead god, but the ghost, which may have been thought of as existing as a kind of invisible double of man (perhaps analogous to the Egyptian Ba in some aspects), which after the man's death was enabled to appear in human shape. This might help to explain the enigmatic mention of the drum. In the *Gilgamesh Epic*, there is mention of a drum (not denoted by the same Akkadian word) in connection with the underworld,[40] whilst elsewhere the Sumerian term 'the man with the b a l a g - drum' is equated in Akkadian with 'he who makes the ghosts of the dead emerge'.[41] One wonders if perhaps a drum was beaten as a man died, to signal (or assist) the passing of his ghost to the underworld; there are many instances, from various parts of the world, of the sounding of bells, drums, gongs and other sources of noise on the occasion of death.[42]

The god slaughtered in *Atrahasis* was said to possess *ṭēmu*, a term which, as the editors of the myth point out, is used elsewhere in parallel to the word for 'self'. The paronomasia on *eṭemmu* and *ṭēmu* was noted by the editors. Taking this with the considerations earlier noted, we see the possibility that the purpose of the details at this point in the myth was aetiological and not theological, purporting to explain the supposed existence of the ghost (or Doppelgänger) of a human being, a specious rationale being given by linkage with a folk-etymology for the term denoting 'ghost'.

There are other Mesopotamian accounts of, or references to, the creation of man, without any mention of ghosts. In the Baby-lonian myth of creation it is Tiamat's defeated champion Qingu who is slain, and his blood used to create man to relieve the gods of their chores. Here again, the function of the blood of the slain god was to give life to the clay; there is no implication that its presence bestowed upon man a divine quality. Indeed, if this point were pursued, one would have to consider the theological con-sequences of the fact that the blood used in man's constitution came from a god who had not only been defeated but who was the epitome of opposition to the existing pantheon. There is the possibility that this point was indeed later taken account of and the myth modified, since Berossos in the third century B.C. appears to make it Marduk himself, the champion of the gods, who was decapitated by his own decision. There is, however, no trace of this in cuneiform literature, and if the view of Berossos has been accurately transmitted and understood, it may represent a modifi-cation of the original myth under the influence of Hellenistic ideas.[43]

There is also a Sumerian version of the creation of man which has him created from clay, to relieve the gods of the trouble of producing their own sustenance,[44] but here there is nothing in the extant portions of the text which mentions the killing of a god or the use of the blood of a god; the humans in this Sumerian myth seem to have been animated simply by their destinies being decreed. In this example of the myth of creation we find the further elaboration that Enki and the creatrix-goddess also create a number of types of human regarded in Mesopotamian society as anomalous, such as the sterile woman or the natural eunuch.

There is yet another Sumerian myth of the creation of man which employs quite a different concept. Man grew out of the ground—or, as one text puts it, 'broke through the earth like grass'[45]—at the place where heaven and earth had been separated in the cosmic creation, the god Enlil assisting by splitting the crust of the earth with a pickaxe.[46] (It is theoretically possible that this myth is not in conflict with the idea of the creation of man from clay by Enki and a goddess, on the assumption that the moulding from clay took place previously in the Apsu beneath the earth, and that humans so formed were simply waiting there under the earth's crust to be let out; however, there is nothing positively to suggest this and certain facts are against it.[47])

The principal difference between the Sumerian and the Babylonian forms of the myths of the creation of man is clearly that the reference to the blood of the slain god occurs only in the Babylonian forms. It is likely, as already pointed out by W. G. Lambert,[48] that this detail is due to the ancient concept of the life being in the blood, as well attested in the Old Testament. This again is against the interpretation that the use of the god's blood implied that man's nature included a divine quality.

The foregoing considerations all appear to favour the view that the creation stories in Mesopotamia are aetiological only, that is, that they are intended to explain the existence of man himself, ghosts, and various customs of birth and death and other features of human society; they do not represent theological doctrine, intended to convey teaching about the nature of man.

A corresponding conclusion is probably also applicable to the main theme, concerning the creation of mankind to act as servants to the gods. This does not necessarily enshrine some profound theological comment on the nature of man, but rather reflects a pattern of society. The form of society in question is that which was predominant in the Sumerian city-state of the first half of the third millennium and which continued to influence the Babylonian way of life as long as it endured. In the Sumerian city-state, although it is now known that part of the population was outside the temple-estate economic system,[49] the characteristic and most significant organization was the temple-estate, in which thousands of people co-operated in works of irrigation and agriculture in a politico-economic system centred on the temple, with all these people thought of as the servants of the god. The myth of the creation of man, therefore, was not basically a comment on the nature of man but an explanation of a particular social system, heavily dependent upon communal irrigation and agriculture, for which the gods' estates were primary foci of administration.

When we turn to the Israelite traditions, we find that the myth of the creation of man in the J source also gives rise to problems. It might be suggested that God's setting man in the Garden of Eden to till it is to be seen as a parallel to the Mesopotamian creation of man in order to relieve the gods of their chores, but this would ignore some significant differences. Man was not created for the service of the Garden, but rather the Garden was formed after Adam's creation as a pleasant abode for him. There is no suggestion of the Garden's producing food for God's benefit, nor of Adam's introduction there relieving God of any task. Nor, though tillage of the Garden is indeed mentioned, is there any indication that the tillage involved actual labour for Adam: it was God who produced the trees; and it was without any intervention on the part of Adam that those trees bore fruit, and that (originally) the ground produced food plants. The painful toil of agriculture did eventually arrive but it was not, as in Mesopotamia, an inherent part of the world order which had to be undertaken by someone, and thus by the gods themselves until man was created. Toil was not inevitable, and came into existence only because of Adam's behaviour. Thus, in no sense was man in Israel created as God's servant. Nor can such an idea be derived from the P story, in which man was created to exercise dominion over the whole earth: man was, perhaps, God's steward or agent, but not a menial servant.

This matter can be looked at from the existential as well as from the mythological side. Did the ordinary man in Mesopotamia act as though his relationship towards the divine powers was a mere matter of his attending to irrigation and agriculture on their behalf? In Israel, did he act as though the purpose of his existence was satisfied by exercising dominion over the earth on behalf of God? There is good evidence for both cultural areas that the relationship between the divine and man was not bounded by the performance of such functions.

In Mesopotamia, the concept of mankind being the servants of the gods was certainly present, and was not limited to myths; but this concept did not necessarily imply that the relationship between man and the divine beings had no other dimension than that of man's obligation to engage in toil on behalf of the gods. In the first place, there was, as F. R. Kraus has pointed out,[50] the reverse side of this. If men had to labour to support the gods, this had the corollary that the gods were dependent upon men. In the last resort, man was lord of all: the proper functioning of the universe itself depended upon man's maintaining agriculture, supporting the temples, and providing the gods with their sustenance. This is explicitly recognized in a cynical epigram in the Wisdom literature:

> Don't perform sacrifice, . . . don't perform sacrifice!
> If you train a god, he'll trot behind you like a dog.[51]

There are other texts which contribute to making it clear that the slave-master nexus was not a complete and sufficient definition of the relationship between men and gods. Thus in one incantation we find the following fragment of myth, which depicts a situation where the attitude of deities to men was quite other than that of master to slave:

> The sum of human kind was reduced,
> Belet-ili looked on them, weeping over them,
> Belet-ili went into the presence of Ea, the king:
> 'Ea, mankind was created by your spell,
> . . .
> By your great command you determined their state.'[52]

Here there is an unambiguous implication that because Ea had created mankind, he had a responsibility to them. Mankind was more than an expendable labour force. The goddess Belet-ili herself shows a compassion, which is not explicable from the master-slave relationship. The same divine compassion is known from other passages, for example, from the Flood story in the *Gilgamesh Epic*, where Belet-ili laments the fate of mankind:

> I give birth to my people,
> They fill the sea like fish fry.[53]

Here the terminology of relationship is specifically that of parent to child, not of master to slave, and the grief of the goddess extended to the other great gods, the Anunnaki, who wept with her.

Also relevant is the fact that a man is frequently referred to, particularly in rituals and incantations, as 'the son of his god'. The usage is shown in the following typical excerpt from a ritual:

> Take water from the junction of two streams,
> Cast your pure exorcism upon that water,
> Make it ritually pure by your spell,
> And sprinkle with that water the man, the son of his god.[54]

Here the god in the final phrase is the sufferer's personal deity, who would rarely be one of the great gods.[55] The use of the term 'son' does not therefore reflect the idea that the human owes his existence to a creator deity, who is his parent in that sense. Rather it implies that between a man and his personal god there exists a relationship which is analogous to that between a man and his parents in human society.[56] Terminology speaking of a deity as like father or mother (or both at once) to a human is common, and although some instances could be special cases as being used in relation to kings, this is not true of all of them.[57] Thus in a ritual a sufferer has to say: 'On my right stands Shamash the judge, father of the black-headed'[58] [that is, father of the people of Mesopotamia]. The same god is called 'upright judge, father of destitute women'.[59] Since Shamash, though indeed sometimes given the title 'Creator', was not properly a creator-god but primarily the divine judge, his paternal relationship to humans related not to creation but to the benevolent care—patronage in the original sense—which he exercised in his dealings towards them.

Gods could also be described as loving humans, and not only kings, as in the phrase '[the gods] who love mankind'.[60] Correspondingly, humans could not only reverence but could also love gods, though here most passages indicating this relate to the king[61]. Of more general reference, probably, is the incipit of a song:

> Give honour to the god, love the god.[62]

However, these statements need to be qualified by pointing out that evidence for the god's love (as distinct from compassion) for humans is neither widespread nor prominent. Furthermore, despite the advice just quoted to 'love the god', it does not appear that the gods actively sought the love of humans. This is a point at which a difference of emphasis can be seen from that in Israel, where (at least in the Deuteronomic theology) there is the express command: 'You must love Yahweh your God with all your heart and soul and strength' (Deut. 6:5). In Israel this love was reciprocal, since it is said that Yahweh chose Israel because he loved her (Deut. 7:7-8).[63]

It seems obvious that the particular way in which man sought to approach the divine was necessarily affected by the type of relationship envisaged. If this relationship was, indeed, seen in terms of child to parent, possibly embracing an element of love, one might expect to find evidence of a quest for immediate personal communication with the divine. Examination of this matter is often coloured by assumptions based on modern Protestant Christianity, in which there is a tendency to see cultic prayer as lacking the intimate personal involvement found in private prayer.

The relevance which cultic prayers or hymns in ancient Mesopotamia had to the matter of intimate personal communication with the divine has been very differently estimated by different people. Francis Brown, senior editor of BDB (the *Hebrew Lexicon* of Brown, Driver and Briggs), was so impressed by the apparent spirituality of certain hymns in Babylonian religious literature that he was moved to write:

In these penitential hymns of Babylonia there is something even more profound—self-abasement, and self-abandonment, and humble appeal to the divine grace. Must not any man who wrote such a hymn out of his own soul, or who used it, . . . have followed the divine leading? Must not 'Ishtar', 'Shamash', and 'Merodach' have been for him a stammering way of pronouncing 'God'? In appealing to their mercy, and laying hold of their hands, must he not have appealed, in truth, to the God of gods, and laid hold of the sceptre of the King of kings?[64]

A. L. Oppenheim, at the other extreme, would have firmly answered 'No!' to all these rhetorical questions. He discounted almost any element of personal religious involvement in prayers as found in Mesopotamian literature, expressing the view that such prayers 'contain no indication of an emotion-charged preference for a specific central topic such as . . . the problem of immediate contact with the divine'.[65]

Oppenheim's argument relates to cultic prayer, but evidence does exist (adduced elsewhere by Oppenheim himself) for the occurrence of prayer in Mesopotamia, outside the cult, which certainly sought immediate contact with the divine. Admittedly such evidence is rare, but this by no means proves that personal prayer was a rare phenomenon. On the contrary, what is surprising is that there should be any evidence at all, in view of the lack of occasion for committing to permanent written form prayer direct from the heart.

The evidence in question comes from a fascinating little omen. The omen predicts that if such-and-such happens,

The wife of the man will become pregnant by another man and she will constantly be praying to Ishtar, saying, while looking at the face of her husband: 'I want to make my child to be born look like him'.[66]

Quite clearly, the situation envisaged is that the unfortunate erring woman was praying not in a cultic setting but in her own home, and not openly but in her own heart. She was reaching out directly for help, in solitary secrecy, to the great goddess.

We may recall that evidence for private non-cultic prayer by a woman also exists for an early period in Israel, in the story of Hannah praying for a child:

Hannah rose in deep distress, and stood before Yahweh and prayed to him, weeping bitterly. Meanwhile Eli the priest was sitting on his seat beside the door of the temple of Yahweh. . . For a long time she went on praying before Yahweh, while Eli watched her lips. Hannah was praying silently; but, although her voice could not be heard, her lips were moving and Eli took her for a drunken woman. (1 Sam. 1:10, 12–13.)

Though Hannah's prayer was at the cult place it was neither in nor through the cult. That no cult ceremony was in progress is clear from the fact that the priest Eli was merely watching the pilgrims. If there was an accepted posture for cultic prayer at the time, it does not appear that Hannah had adopted it, since had she done so Eli's mistaken conclusion about her being drunk would hardly have arisen.[67]

This very limited but unequivocal evidence of a personal seeking after contact with the divine may in the case of Meso-potamia be supplemented by data from other classes of texts. Thus, despite the categorical denial by Oppenheim, it is possible that even in hymns and prayers there may be some indications of a personal—as distinct from cultic—piety and a quest for personal approach to the deity. A possible example may be seen in a hymn to the goddess Gula, who is asked:

Have pity on the slave who fears your divinity.
Attend to what his mouth utters, stand present at the raising of his hands.
Accept his prayers, hear his words.[68]

It must be conceded, however, that though this technically represents personal piety, it does not give the impression of an intense yearning for contact with the deity; and though not strictly a cultic document, it could be a literary composition intended to be presented by a private person at the temple, so that it might ultimately have been destined for a cultic setting. A similar qualification may need to be made in our understanding of possibly relevant documents of another class—letters to the gods, of which some two dozen are extant.[69]

The majority of letters to the gods are literary compositions rather than personal letters, and in a substantial number of them the authors were kings; but there are known at least two docu-ments addressed to gods, which in terms of form, style and con-tents may be considered genuine letters.[70] In these the writers, non-royal individuals, directed to the deity complaints and appeals about personal circumstances. How far these represented personal piety, as distinct from a religious means of seeking to obtain a personal advantage, is not clear. It could, however, be argued that though such documents may well have been presented to the god through the cult, in the same way that Hezekiah placed a letter before Yahweh in the Temple (2 Kgs. 19:14), their motivation was not as such participation in the cult but a personal approach to the deity. This would help to establish the possibility of an individual seeking an immediate personal approach to the deity, even if in these particular cases the approach was coloured by the seeking of personal advantage.

Indisputable evidence of a more intimate kind of personal approach to a deity is provided by certain personal names. Some personal names are recognized as deriving from a cry of the mother during childbirth, and such a name as Ahulap-Ishtar[71]— 'How long, O Ishtar!'—indicates that a woman in the anguish of labour could spontaneously cry out for the compassion and help of a deity. Here plainly is an example of the emotion-charged relationship between man and the divine which Oppenheim was unable to find.

If the divine powers were assumed to be concerned for man, and to be willing, or even desirous, for man to approach them, there was inherent in this the question of the extent of the human group to which this applied. This occasioned less problem in a polytheism than in a monotheism. With polytheistic peoples there was no difficulty in accepting that other peoples had their gods, who stood in the same relationship to their worshippers as their own gods to themselves. There is some possible evidence that this idea was also present in an early stage of Israelite religion. This arises from part of the Song of Moses:

When the Most High parcelled out the nations, when he dispersed all
    mankind,
. . .
Yahweh's share was his own people,
Jacob was his allotted portion. (Deut. 32:8–9.)

If one follows Eissfeldt in seeing 'the Most High' (Elyon) as here a High God distinct from Yahweh,[72] the principle is perfectly clear: the High God had put each nation in the charge of some divine being. But even if one rejects Eissfeldt's interpretation and sees Elyon as here simply an epithet of Yahweh, it is clear that Yahweh himself must have handed over other nations to the care of subordinate divine beings.

A monotheism precludes such a view, and it eventually becomes necessary to define the relationship of the Sole God to other peoples. Then, unless the view is taken that God has divided mankind into two species, the elect and the non-elect (a solution represented in Calvinism), the conclusion can only be that the Sole God cares for all mankind, and that the national group earlier taken as his elect simply represents a channel through which God mediates his care for all mankind. Hence develops a doctrine of religious universalism.

The general problem of universalism in Israelite religion has received abundant attention in works on Old Testament religion and theology, and reference to the matter in the following pages will therefore be limited to a summary of the general concensus, with special relationship to the comparative aspects.

It is now generally accepted that, apart from any traces that may be seen within the traditions attached to patriarchal religion, there are clear indications of religious universalism in the Israelite prophets from the mid-eighth century. Thus Ringgren speaks of Amos as seeing 'Yahweh as the universal God who controls the history of the nations':[73]

Are not you Israelites like Cushites to me? says Yahweh.
Did I not bring Israel up from Egypt,
the Philistines from Caphtor, the Aramaeans from Kir? (Amos 9:7.)

For Amos, past history neither gave nor implied any special status for Israel. Fohrer even goes so far as to conclude that Amos specifically rejected the old doctrine of election (in its crude form), though this depends upon taking Amos 3:2 in an ironical sense:

Indeed, you are my 'chosen people' upon earth.
Therefore—I will punish you for all your iniquities.[74]

Fohrer sums up what he takes as the prophetic attitude in general by saying that 'the prophets . . . surmounted the approach of religious nationalism, breaking down its nationalistic barriers. . . Yahweh's exclusive association with Israel was surmounted.'[75]

Explicit universalistic teaching arrives with Deutero-Isaiah, though, as Ringgren points out, Israel continues to hold a privileged position, and the teaching of Deutero-Isaiah on universalism is subject to the 'important restriction . . . [that] Israel is the dominant nation, and the Gentiles will serve Israel and its God'.[76] The markedly universalistic Book of Jonah, on the other hand, sees the special status of Israel as involving service rather than privilege. As Ringgren puts it, in the Book of Jonah 'Yahweh is the God of all nations, and is concerned for them all. God's revelation is valid for all nations, and the Jews must not evade the task of making it known to the others'.[77]

Whilst Amos and Jonah quite specifically deny the relevance of the old belief that Israel had special privileges because of Yahweh's earlier relationship with her, Deutero-Isaiah does not. Instead, he brings the old doctrine into relationship with his new recognition that Yahweh is creator of the whole earth and therefore lord of all history, of which Israelite history is a part.

With minor differences of emphasis there is general agreement that religious universalism did develop within Israelite religion, even though within emergent Judaism it was stifled by the work of Ezra and Nehemiah. Where the possibility of a wide divergence appears is in the question of whether religious universalism was, in the ancient world, unique to Israel, or whether what is seen in Israel was only one aspect of a widespread trend. The Dutch theologian Vriezen had no doubt about the matter. In his view, 'within the eastern world only the Old Testament arrived at a truly religious universalism'.[78]

The validity of this statement depends very much upon how one defines 'truly religious universalism'. Vriezen's understanding of it is indicated by the following quotation:

In contrast with the Creation-narratives of other ancient peoples the Old Testament does not hold that towns and temples (i.e. the original states) . . . were created. The nations all form one great family; their dispersal was the punishment for their sins (Gen. 11), but they are all looked upon as having sprung from only one ancestor: Noah (Gen. 10). . . The Old Testament is the only ancient Eastern work in which we find this universal outlook.[79]

Despite Vriezen's claim, there is little trace of this supposed universal outlook throughout much of the Pentateuch, with the exception of some passages (already noted) linked to the Abraham tradition. Thus, despite Ham's being a brother of Shem, it was felt proper that Egypt should suffer bereavement in every family in the interests of Israel, and that Canaan should be (if possible) exterminated to provide Lebensraum. Nor, on the other side, was a comparable basis for a universal outlook lacking from the primeval history of Mesopotamia; in the myth *Enki and the World Order*, the god Enki is concerned to bestow certain gifts upon lands and peoples other than those of Mesopotamia.[80] In fact, the difference of presentation of early history as between Israel and Mesopotamia is probably based not on theological considerations, as Vriezen assumed, but upon sociological factors. An entirely settled society, such as the populations of the urban complexes of south Mesopotamia from the middle of the third millennium onwards, has no need of genealogical traditions. Israel, on the other hand, was, during the crucial period when its traditions were crystallizing, in a state of flux, when line of descent was likely to be emphasized to preserve stability of group membership in time of social change.[81] It may have been for this reason, rather than in pursuit of any supposed theological aim of emphasizing the unity of all nations under Yahweh, that Israelite traditions took a genealogical form, whereas those of Mesopotamia predominantly did not.

In the matter of religious universalism there is one indisputable distinction between Israel and Mesopotamia. This is that in the Mesopotamian world there is no evidence of any teacher proclaiming, as a matter which he had a compulsion to make known, that God, or the gods, cared for all men. But this does not prove that the view that the gods cared for all men was not known in

Mesopotamia. It certainly was held, as we see from the following lines from an Assyrian royal inscription:

Peoples of the four regions, of foreign tongue and diverse speech, living in mountains and plains, as many as the Light of the gods, the Lord of all, shepherded, at the command of Ashur my lord ... I took captive.[82]

Here is the plain statement, by a contemporary of Isaiah of Jerusalem, that a member of the Assyrian pantheon was concerned with people of all regions of the earth, of all languages, mountaineers and plainsmen. It is true that this is not blazoned forth as a piece of theological teaching,[83] as in the Israelite prophets, but in this connection the circumstances which (in human terms) required the Israelite prophets to make their view of universalism explicit need to be considered. This prophetic proclamation was in part a reaction to the older (and in many quarters still current) belief in God's exclusive concern for Israel. Once God was recognized as creator of mankind, even before the theological consequences of this were developed by Jeremiah and Deutero-Isaiah, the idea that God, creator of all men, was concerned only with one people, gave a tension. This tension demanded for its resolution an explicit denial of the old exclusivism. In Mesopotamian polytheism the problem would not present itself in the same way. Anu or Enlil or Ea or Marduk or Ashur might be claimed as Creator, and might at the same time be regarded as specifically concerned with Mesopotamia.[84] But with the extensive Mesopotamian pantheon, in which certain gods were identified with the gods of other peoples or even directly introduced from the pantheons of other peoples,[85] there was no difficulty in accepting that the gods of other peoples were acting either on behalf of, or in consort with, the great gods of Mesopotamia in guiding and controlling their people.

If religious universalism is taken as the belief that the gods are concerned about all mankind, and not merely the proclamation of theological teaching to that effect, there is a good deal of evidence that can be adduced to establish the existence of religious universalism in ancient Mesopotamia, contrary to the view of Vriezen.

Religious universalism, in the sense that the gods were concerned about all mankind and not merely the favoured in-group, was implicit in Sumer from early times. The Mesopotamian gods did not exclude from their concern mankind living outside the river plains. Thus, in the myth *Enki and the World Order*, the nomadic Martu of the Syrian desert, 'who have no city, who have no house', have the gift of cattle bestowed upon them by Enki.[86] Elsewhere the goddess Nisaba is described as 'providing the k u r with plenty', in a context indicating that here k u r probably meant the foreign mountain-land, as distinguished from Sumer.[87] The epic *Enmerkar and the Lord of Aratta*,[88] a Sumerian composition from the beginning of the second millennium though probably representing ideas of half a millennium earlier, provides another example. This epic deals with commercial relations between the city-state of Erech and Kullab in the plain of the lower Euphrates, and Aratta, far away in Iran over seven mountain ranges.[89] The tutelary goddess of Erech also knew and cared for Aratta, though it is said that she preferred the lord of Kullab to the lord of Aratta.[90] However, this preference seems to have been a mere whim of the same kind as Yahweh's preference for Abel over Cain, and does not affect the indication of the whole tenor of the story, that the goddess was concerned for both states. It may be added that the same epic contains a passage referring to a primeval era when all lands gave praise to the god Enlil in unison.[91] Whether or not this also reflects (as has been suggested) a belief in an original single language, it seems clear that at the least it postulates a time when all peoples acknowledged Enlil, implying that in an ideal world Enlil would be the focus of the cult of all mankind.

Not perhaps unexpectedly, the Sun-god in particular is thought of as caring for all peoples, and this is plainly stated in a hymn:

> You care for the people of the lands, all of them;
> What Ea . . . has created is wholly entrusted to you.
> Whatever has breath you shepherd impartially;
> . . .
> . . . you direct all the affairs of inhabited regions.[92]

In addition to the foregoing rather general indications of the existence of the principle of universalism in Mesopotamian religion, there is some quite specific evidence. At least some Mesopotamian deities must have been thought of as both able and willing to take beneficent action on behalf of people who were neither in the cultural group of worshippers of the Mesopotamian pantheon, nor residents within Mesopotamia. We find an example of this in correspondence between the Assyrian and the Egyptian royal courts in the half-century after 1400 B.C., where there is a reference to an Assyrian goddess, given the epithet 'Lady of the lands', who had earlier been conveyed to Egypt to assist the Pharaoh in some way:

Thus says Ishtar of Nineveh, Lady of all lands: 'I will go and return to Egypt, the land that I love'. I have now sent her. . . In the time of my father, . . . [she] went to that land. . . May my brother [*i.e.* the king of Egypt] honour her and send her back in gladness.[93]

Assyrian kings specifically claimed for their gods authority over all the peoples of the earth, as did New Babylonian rulers.[94] That the great gods of Mesopotamia were considered to be universal as well as eternal is shown by such a group of epithets for Enlil as

the eternal king, . . . the glorious potentate whose lordship will not be challenged as long as the gods endure, . . . the lord over the spread of the firmament.[95]

The foregoing is only a small representative selection from evidence available to support the view that there existed in Mesopotamia, at least as early as in Israel, the idea that the gods were concerned with all mankind. In the light of the evidence adduced, it would appear that no difference of principle can be substantiated between the religions of Israel and of Mesopotamia in relation to the belief that the concern of God or the gods was not limited to a closed group but extended to all mankind. With religious universalism, as with creation, the divine control of history, and the problem of evil, whilst there are abundant differences of detail and developments, no fundamental differences of principle are discernible, sufficient to set Israelite and Meso-potamian religions apart as two distinct systems. This conclusion is drawn in the face of attempts by various scholars to define just such differences of principle in relation to creation, to the divine control of history, to the problem of evil, or to the development of religious universalism. In both Mesopotamia and Israel the divine as a principle (not necessarily particular manifestations of the divine) was recognized as pre-existent and creator of the physical universe, as governing both history and nature, as having decreed some aspects of the framework of life within primeval times and as operating a continuing plan within certain areas of history, as allowing man freewill to choose whether or not to conform to the divine plan (though at his own peril if he declined), as responsible (in some ill-defined way) for evil as well as good, as having created man and as caring for all men, and as permitting all men to know the divine.

This interpretation of the evidence is in no way dependent upon the so-called 'Ritual Pattern' theory of ancient Near Eastern religions, nor necessarily in support of it, since that theory operates primarily with myths and rituals, whereas the present study has attempted to take account also of concepts. There is the possibility that superficially similar rituals might convey quite different con-cepts (as, for example, in the case of the Roman Catholic Mass and the Nonconformist Lord's Supper), or that superficially very different rituals might reflect similar concepts (as, for example, between a Quaker and a Pentacostal prayer meeting, where both —but one in dignified silence and the other with exuberant noise— seek the coming of the Holy Spirit).

The factors which differentiate between Israelite and Meso-potamian religion within the area surveyed must therefore be sought in details and points of emphasis, and the divergent ways in which basically similar concepts developed in the course of time, and not in basic principles. It may prove useful to attempt to relate such factors to general differences between the two cultures as a whole.

An obvious and indisputable difference between the cultures of

Mesopotamia and Israel, when we look at them in the first half of the first millennium, when Israelite religion had emerged from the obscurity of its origins and before it had evolved into Judaism, lies in their age. Except for a relatively few traditions going back to the Patriarchs, Israelite history began only within the century before the Settlement in Palestine. At the time of the Settlement, there were very few specifically Israelite institutions. There was a tribal structure, of diminishing importance after the Settlement; there was the Ark, important until the building of the Temple in Jerusalem but eventually lost sight of; whilst the main other institutions were the pastoral festival which became the Passover (or one element in the Passover), the nucleus of the Sinai Law (of very recent origin), and some religious traditions associated with patriarchal numina and El-worship. The institutions which gave shape to later Israelite society—such as kingship, professional priesthood (except the old tribal Levitical priesthood[96]), an extended corpus of law, cult places in general and a house for the god, rituals appropriate to a settled people, and agriculture—still had to be acquired. In contrast to this, Mesopotamia had a history going back a millennium and a half before the time of the Israelite Settlement, and many institutions long regarded as being divinely ordained.

Israel, at her appearance in Palestine in the late thirteenth century, was, by contrast with Mesopotamian civilization, virtually culturally naked, and had to garb herself in institutions appropriate for the new situation. However the traditions of the Settlement process are interpreted in detail, it is clear that Israel was under considerable pressure—whether social, political, or military—and was not in a situation where she would be likely automatically to assimilate in all details to the society already existing in Palestine. The tension between the necessity of adopting new institutions, and the hostile reaction to the existing society in Palestine, led to a critical selectivity, which could involve conscious and violent rejection as well as adoption of institutions.[97]

The situation in this respect was very different in Mesopotamia. A feature of Mesopotamian civilization, with its very long history, was its conservatism. This must not be exaggerated: conservatism does not necessarily imply stasis, and new developments both in religious concepts and in technology could and did arise in Mesopotamia in the first millennium. But Mesopotamian conservatism had the consequence that the new did not lead to rejection of the old; rather, the old continued to exist alongside the new. A striking example of this is found in connection with eclipses of the moon. At some very early period there had been the belief, reflected in a fragment of myth earlier adduced,[98] that an eclipse was due to an attack upon the moon by demons. At the onset of an eclipse, therefore, a ritual drum was set up in the temple courtyard and beaten to assist in driving off the demons. By the fourth century Babylonian mathematics had reached such a stage that lunar eclipses could be accurately predicted in advance, on the basis of the periodic movements of the sun and moon; clearly, by that time it was known that a lunar eclipse was not an indication of the moon being under attack. Yet still, in the Seleucid period, the text of the ritual drum ceremony for a lunar eclipse was copied out, and presumably the old ritual still practised, irrelevant though it had become in the current state of knowledge.[99]

A similar, though less glaring, situation, of the old and new existing together in passive contradiction of each other, is found in relation to divination. As earlier shown, the old non-deistic view was that there was a mechanistic relationship between certain present events and certain future events. By at least the beginning of the second millennium there had developed the idea that the future depended upon the will of a deity, who could be supplicated or cajoled to direct the future nearer to the heart's desire. But the old non-deistic techniques continued not only in use, but predominant, no more than superficially brought within the framework of belief in anthropomorphic gods.

Changes in Mesopotamian religion did come about, but they were neither presented nor seen as changes. An early innovation, successfully contrived, was the identification of Ishtar with Inanna by Sargon of Agade in the third millennium.[100] But Sargon was not superseding Inanna; he was leaving Inanna with all her old properties and adding an identification. Similarly later, there were approaches towards monotheism, but the existence of other gods than the god adored by the particular worshipper was not bluntly denied; the other gods were made hypostases or aspects of the one great god. A new concept could be added, if it did not involve an explicit attack upon the existing system. But any proposed innovation which involved a rejection of something already existing did provoke a violent reaction: the examples of the attempt by Shalmaneser V to alter the cult in the city of Ashur, and of Nabonidus the cult in Babylon, have already been adduced.

The antecedents of Israel gave Israelites less reverence for tradition, and they could, more readily than the people of Mesopotamia, reject the old in the course of accepting the new. This does not mean that everything which ceased to be relevant was immediately discarded; for example, the scapegoat ritual, incorporating very primitive ideas, continued to be practised well after the underlying ideas had ceased to be effectively held. But the scapegoat ritual was *sui generis*, and conflicted with nothing else. What the Israelite situation ultimately meant was that Israelites could accept what was relevant to the particular religious circumstances of the time and reject anything in conflict with current concepts. Thus Hezekiah was able to throw out the old snake-image Nehushtan; he could do this, despite its venerable association with Moses, because it was being treated as a distinct manifestation of the divine and having sacrifices burnt to it.

Thus, although there is no static difference of basic principle between Mesopotamian and Israelite religion, there can be seen a dynamic difference in the way in which religious concepts could develop. The difference was that whilst the traditions of Mesopotamian society tended to permit an accretion of religious concepts, even though logically non-compatible, Israelite society was, because of the forces which had moulded it, much readier to reject, and, because of the pressures upon Israel threatening her very existence in her early stages, Israelite society was, both for good and for bad, basically less tolerant than Mesopotamian. One can see how this operated in relation to the development of mono-theism. In Mesopotamia, it is likely that each of the original Sumerian city-states had a single city god. As the city-states came into political relationship, they brought their gods into corre-sponding relationship, creating a pantheon. Later, as the Baby-lonian kingdom or Assyrian empire came into contact with other peoples, they admitted the gods of those other peoples into the pantheon. With the Israelites, the development was quite different. The pre-settlement group of Israelites associated with Moses began, like any Sumerian city-state, with one god, possibly the god of some Kenite tribe. Other Israelite groups had other gods, the patriarchal numina. These were not placed alongside the Mosaic god in a pantheon,[101] but identified with him, avoiding a clash of claims. Other tribal groups, contemporary with early Israel, had yet other gods, and the Israelites showed their dis-tinctive reaction to these. Instead of following the accretive principle of Mesopotamian civilization, they exercised selectivity and rejection. They first ignored those other gods, and later denied their very existence. Thus, what began as monolatry in both Sumerian city-states and Israel developed on one side into polytheism and on the other into monotheism.

With the Israelite negative element of rejection as well as the positive element of assertion, it became possible in Israelite religious thought not only to question, but also to challenge and deny, in a way which is not found to any significant extent in Mesopotamia. Certainly in Mesopotamia questioning is found in one particular area (the problem of suffering) in one particular literary category (Wisdom literature). But the application of this to society as a whole was very limited: it was the work of a literary elite, intended—as shown by the acrostic structure in some cases and the erudite language in all—for a literary elite. It never came to be addressed, as came the utterances of the canonical prophets of Israel, as a challenge to the nation as a whole.

To this point the statement of differences in the dynamics of the two religions has been in terms of social and literary considerations. When one goes beyond this, one enters into an area where value judgements become involved, and the following observations are offered with recognition that they are conditioned by the writer's own religious background.

We have already seen that the canonical prophets, though employing a deistic mechanism known elsewhere in the ancient Near East, in their use and application of it gave it a unique breadth. It was within this mechanism that the prophets developed the possibility of questioning, challenging and denying, which had become possible because of the general socio-historical background of Israel. The manner in which Israelite society had originated made possible the direct challenge to older concepts which much of the prophetic message involved, and that challenge in turn made Israelite religion a dynamic religion, able to face the problems of a changing society, as Mesopotamian religion was not. If one is seeking a single facet of Israelite religion to which to apply the description 'unique', it is in canonical prophecy that it is to be found.

But there was another dimension to the Israelite use of rejection alongside assertion. Rejection in certain areas closed the door upon some possible theological developments. With the Mesopotamian concept of the multiplicity of forms of the divine, there was no difficulty in accepting that the divine could be both transcendent and immanent. But with the Israelite insistence upon the unity of God, it followed that if he was transcendent, he could not also be immanent within the physical world. This latter statement might well be challenged, and requires amplification to preclude misunderstanding. It is quite true that Yahweh was 'close to those whose courage is broken' (Ps. 34:18), and 'very near . . . to those who call to him' (Ps. 145:18), that the Israelite worshipper could say 'Where can I flee from thy presence? . . . If I take my flight to the frontiers of the morning or dwell at the limit of the western sea, even there thy hand will meet me' (Ps. 139:7, 9–10). Likewise, Yahweh was so near that he might be represented as saying 'I, Yahweh, search the mind and test the heart' (Jer. 17:10). All this is sometimes loosely referred to as evidence of a doctrine of immanence; in fact, such passages relate not to immanence in the technical sense of 'indwelling', but rather to the omnipresence of God.

In primitive Yahwism, indeed, Yahweh probably was in some circumstances regarded as immanent, notably in connection with the Ark; that is, he was present there (as in the Uzzah episode in 2 Sam. 6:6–7) though not identified with it, in much the same way that Dumuzi was present in but not identifiable with milk (see page 90 above). But after a long struggle, official Yahwism succeeded in eliminating all such concepts, the prohibition against all images and representations of the divine being a part of the process. This closed off theological developments in one direction.

Eliade has made the point: if a god can assume a human nature, why should he not assume a wooden or stone nature?[102] This has a converse: if the possibility of god being present through an image is denied, how is it possible that he should be present through the form of a man? This is a point at which the theologies of Christianity, Israelite religion and Mesopotamian religion, though not in agreement, touch. The Christian claim of the incarnation of God was for orthodox Jews of the first century a blasphemy, but for pagans in the Mesopotamian tradition, who could already accept that the divine could be experienced through a body of stone or wood, the claim could be intelligible and significant. Without taking for the present argument any view as to whether or not the claim of the Christian gospels is true, one may see that Mesopotamian religion and related paganisms provided one path to acceptance of that claim. The comparative religionist may regard both Mesopotamian religion, and Israelite religion and its descendants, as (in Radcliffe-Brown's words) 'bodies of erroneous beliefs and illusory practices'.[103] But the believing liberal Jew or liberal Christian is free to look at the evidence in another way: Mesopotamian religion may also, with Israelite religion and those religions to which it has given birth, have been one vehicle by which came knowledge of a finite part of the infinity of the divine.

NOTES

1. A. R. Radcliffe-Brown, 'Religion and Society', *Journal of the Royal Anthropological Institute* 75 (1945), 33.
2. A. B. Davidson, *The Theology of the Old Testament*, 1.
3. See N. W. Porteous, 'Old Testament Theology', 319 in H. H. Rowley (ed.), *The Old Testament and Modern Study*.
4. N. W. Porteous, op. cit., 328.
5. G. E. Wright and R. H. Fuller, *The Book of the Acts of God*, 14.
6. Bright, HI, 102.
7. Bright, HI, 35.
8. Bright, HI, 164.
9. It may be noted that one judgement made here by J. Bright in the religio-historical area is plainly contrary to the facts, and further illustrates the 'we'– 'they' dichotomy. He speaks of Sumerians making, 'as is the case in all paganisms', 'little distinction between moral and purely ritual offenses'. This implies a basic essential difference between 'paganism' (exemplified by Sumerian religion) and Israelite religion. But one need look no further than Ezek. 18:5–9 (see also 22:10) to find clear evidence that even as late as the sixth century the Israelites also made 'little distinction between moral and purely ritual offenses', sexual approach to a menstruating woman being grouped with adultery and robbery. See also Ezek. 33:25–6, where eating meat not ritually drained of the blood is mentioned as an offence comparable with idolatry, murder and adultery.
10. G. E. Wright, *God who acts*, 20–1.
11. See page 15.
12. See, e.g., N. H. Snaith, *The distinctive ideas of the Old Testament*, 9 and 11–20, and G. E. Wright, 'How did early Israel differ from her neighbours?', BA 6 (1943), 1–10, 13–20.
13. W. G. Lambert, 'Destiny and divine intervention in Babylon and Israel', OTS 17 (1972), 65.
14. One of the minority of Old Testament scholars to adopt this methodology rigorously is Morton Smith; see, e.g., his 'The common theology of the ancient Near East', JBL 71 (1952), 135–47 and *Palestinian Parties and Politics that shaped the Old Testament* (New York, 1971). See also idem, 'The present state of Old Testament studies', JBL 88 (1969), 19–35.
15. E. T. Clark, *The small sects in America*, passim.
16. AM, 172. For a criticism of this view (as expressed in an earlier work by Oppenheim) see J. Nougayrol, 'Recherches nouvelles sur la religion Babylonienne', *Semitica* 13 (1963), 5–20. F. R. Kraus expresses agreement with

Oppenheim in *Vom mesop. Menschen* 135 [331], with a dry comment that Oppenheim has not thereafter adhered to 'this well-founded view'.

17. AM, 173.

18. On the argument that the Mandaeans originated in south Mesopotamia see E. M. Yamauchi, *Gnostic Ethics and Mandaean origins*, 71–89.

19. 2 Kgs. 10:18–27.

20. AM. 173. Oppenheim himself used the phrase only of the gulf between Mesopotamian religion and modern man; examination of this concept in relation to mutual understanding between Mesopotamian and Israelite religion is an extension due to the present writer.

21. It is immaterial for the present argument whether the proclamation represented the actual words of the Assyrian officer or whether they were a creation of the Judaean editor, since on the one view they would represent the actual attitude of an Assyrian officer, and on the other an attitude which a Yahwist contemporary of the Assyrians regarded as conceivable for such a person.

22. Isa. 45:1–5.

23. ANET³, 316.

24. C. Bigg, *The Christian Platonists of Alexandria*, 48.

25. E. F. Weidner, 'Der Tag des Stadtgottes', AfO 14 (1944), 341–2.

26. Quoted from M. L. W. Laistner, *Christianity and pagan culture in the later Roman Empire*, 61.

27. See W. W. Baudissin, *Adonis und Esmun* (Hinrichs, Leipzig, 1911), 95; the Syriac text has not been available to me. On the late-surviving pre-Christian paganism at Harran see D. Chwolsohn, *Ssabier*, passim, especially vol. I, Cap. VII, 'Allgemeine Characteristik der Harrânier und deren Religion'.

28. Greek text Δαχὴν καὶ Δαχόν by corruption from Λαχὴν καὶ Λαχόν.

29. I. P. Cory, *Ancient Fragments*, 318.

30. W. W. Hallo, 'Individual prayer in Sumerian: the continuity of a tradition', JAOS 88 (1968), 72.

31. The basic work is H. Gunkel, 'Die Israelitische Literatur' (= P. Hinneberg (ed.), *Die Kultur der Gegenwart* 1/7, Berlin and Leipzig, 1925), 51–102. For a criticism of the work of Gunkel (not in relation to the point made here) see J. W. Rogerson, *Myth in Old Testament interpretation* (= BZAW 134, 1974), 57–65. For some criticisms of terminology in Old Testament form criticism, see R. M. Hals, 'Legend: a case study in OT form-critical terminology', CBQ 34 (1972), 166–76. For an assessment of the value of form criticism in a particular case, note a comment by G. Fohrer, HIR, 243: 'Form-critical study does not furnish any extensive insights for our understanding of Amos. The mere use of certain rhetorical forms proves very little, since they can always take on a function totally different from that corresponding to their original *Sitz im Leben*'. Note also the comment of K. Koch, *The growth of the biblical tradition*.

NOTES 191

The form-critical method, ix, that 'on many points we are still far from having achieved convincing results, and indeed there are many parts of the Bible which have not as yet been studied from the form-critical point of view'.

32. Note the very pertinent comments by M. Eliade, *The Quest*, 59: 'It is necessary above all to renounce the easy excuse that not all the documents have been conveniently collected and interpreted... Besides, it is necessary to free oneself from the superstition that analysis represents the *true* scientific work and that one ought to propose a synthesis or a generalization only rather late in life. One does not know any example of a science or a humanist discipline whose representatives are devoted exclusively to analysis without attempting to advance a working hypothesis or to draft a generalization. The human mind works in this compartmented manner only at the price of its own creativity'.

33. So, e.g., K.-H. Bernhardt, *Das Problem der altorientalischen Königsideologie im Alten Testament*, 66.

34. See Paul Radin, 'The religious and the non-religious man' in J. Waardenburg (ed.), *Classical approaches to the study of religion; 1: introduction and anthology*, 582–6.

35. AM, 175.

36. S. Mowinckel, ' "Psalm criticism between 1900 and 1935" (Ugarit and Psalm exegesis)', VT 5 (1955), 16–17.

37. Isa. 40:22, 12, 15; 44:9–20; 40:18–20; 41:6–7. The satire on idolatry in Jer. 10:3–10 is probably a later elaboration of a Deutero-Isaiah oracle; see O. Eissfeldt, OTI, 359.

38. His account implies that a tree-trunk might pass immediately from sculptor to worshipper; a person with the detailed knowledge of the processes involved, which Deutero-Isaiah's descriptions of image-making show he possessed, could hardly not have known that this was not the case.

39. B. Landsberger, 'Die Eigenbegrifflichkeit der babylonischen Welt', *Islamica* 2 (1926), 369–70, also made this point, in a form worth quoting: 'Probably the Babylonian scholar, whose deity ruled simply by means of the institution of the world order, would have laughed in the same superior way at the God of the Israelites, always mechanically intervening, as the Jewish prophet mocked at the Babylonian images'.

40. Exod. 37:1–9; Num. 10:33–6; 1 Sam. 4:3–5; 5:2–4; 1 Kgs. 8:11; Ps. 132:8; etc.

41. *En. El.* I: 93–4.

42. KAR, I, 46, Nr. 25, obv. Col. II, line 16.

43. W. G. Lambert, 'The Gula hymn of Bulluṭsa-rabi', OrNS 36 (1967), 124, lines 133–4. Similarly, Enki was so vast that his shadow covered heaven and earth; see C. Benito, *Enki*, 85, line 6.

44. Letter of Jeremiah 6:10–11.

45. Wisd. 13:11–14:1.

46. Wisd. 14:15–16.

47. For a summary of the *Apology* of Aristides see P. Carrington, *The Early Christian Church*, II, 96. For the Syriac text see J. R. Harris and A. Robinson, *The Apology of Aristides.*

48. Tertullian offers some comments on the history of idols which make him a precursor of Th. Jacobsen (see *Tammuz*, 339, n. 27) in postulating a pre-anthropomorphic stage of religion. 'Idols in ancient times there were none. Before the artificers of this monstrosity had bubbled into being, temples stood solitary and shrines empty, just as to the present day in some places traces of the ancient practice remain permanently' (Ante-Nicene Christian Library, ed. by A. Roberts and J. Donaldson, vol. XI, *The writings of Tertullian*, vol. 1 (1869), 143–4).

49. See, e.g. Robert Burton (1577–1640), *The Anatomy of Melancholy*, passim.

50. Layard Papers 38977, 45–6, published in H. W. F. Saggs (ed.), abridged edition of Henry Austen Layard, *Nineveh and its remains* (Routledge & Kegan Paul, London, 1970), 52.

51. Th. C. Vriezen, 'The study of the Old Testament and the History of Religion', VTSup 17 (1968), 1–24.

52. One writer has pointedly remarked that 'one of the most interesting pursuits of the biblical scholar is the search for allusions in the Bible to Canaanite and to Mesopotamian mythology' (E. M. Yamauchi, 'Tammuz and the Bible', JBL 84 (1965), 283). For an interesting recent example see I. M. Kikawada, 'Two notes on Eve', JBL 91 (1972), 33–7; the author wishes to make Eve a demythologized creatrix-goddess, on the grounds that Eve's epithet 'mother of all living' is a counterpart of 'mistress of all the gods' applied to Mami in *Atrahasis*. The present writer is unable to accept that part of the argument which he is able to follow.

53. OTI, 5.

54. 'Canonical' in this context refers to the literary form, not to the religious authority, though in practice the latter follows closely in the wake of the former.

55. W. von Soden, 'Religiöse Unsicherheit Säkularisierungstendenzen und Aberglaube zur Zeit der Sargoniden', *Studia Biblica et Orientalia III: Oriens Antiquus* (= AnBi 12, Rome, 1959), 360. Similarly, it has been established (on the basis of personal names) that Adad had an increasing importance in Assyria from the fifteenth to the twelfth centuries, associated with growing cosmopolitanism (H. A. Fine, 'Studies in Middle-Assyrian chronology and religion', part II, HUCA 25 (1954), 116ff.

56. *Gilg.*, VI, lines 22–79.

57. AM, 178–9.

58. On Bethel see G. von Rad, OTT, I, 58. On Aaron see op. cit., I, 295–6. Another instance is the Shiloh tradition, on which see M. Haran, 'Shiloh and

Jerusalem: the origin of the Priestly tradition in the Pentateuch', JBL 81 (1962), 14–24.

59. See W. von Soden, 'Gibt es ein Zeugnis dafür, dass die Babylonier an die Wiederaufstehung Marduks geglaubt haben?', ZA 51 (1955), 130–66. For another example see I. M. Diakonoff, 'A Babylonian political pamphlet from about 700 B.C.', AS 16 (= *Studies in Honor of B. Landsberger*, Chicago U.P., 1965), 343–9. Diakonoff shows that the 'warnings' of a text commonly called *Der babylonische Fürstenspiegel* constitute, under the guise of an omen text, a political pamphlet addressed to Sennacherib in his early years, or possibly to his son as sub-king in Babylon.

60. W. W. Hallo and J. J. A. Van Dijk, *The exaltation of Inanna*, 9–10.

61. E. Reiner, 'The etiological myth of the "Seven Sages" ', Or. NS 30 (1961), 11.

62. A. L. Oppenheim, 'Analysis of an Assyrian ritual (KAR 139)', HR 5 (1966), 255. It has even been suggested (J. B. Curtis, HUCA 28 (1957), 164) that there were salvation-cults with a belief in the possibility of resurrection; against this see E. M. Yamauchi, 'Additional notes on Tammuz', JSS 11 (1966), 12–13.

63. For bibliographical details and convenient translation see ANET³, 312–15. The lines quoted in the succeeding paragraph (BHT, pl. V, lines 20–3; pl. VI, obv. col. II, lines 2–3; pl. X, lines 12 and 24) have been re-translated by the present writer.

64. See H. W. F. Saggs, 'Historical texts and fragments of Sargon II of Assyria: I. The "Aššur Charter" ', *Iraq* 37 (1975), 15, lines 30–5, and 16–20, notes on lines 3–4, 8, 37.

65. OIP, II, 83, line 48.

66. *Assurbanipal*, 54, lines 62–9.

67. Even H. Ringgren, who usually achieves an admirably objective statement of the data of Israelite religion, does not wholly escape this risk. E.g., IR, 100: 'even if such hypostases [of "justice", "righteousness", etc.] occasionally developed into independent divinities, this was unable to take place within the domain of the genuine [sic] religion of Yahweh'. On the possibility of a cult of a god Ṣedeq ['Righteousness'[in Jerusalem, see R. A. Rosenberg, 'The God Ṣedeq', HUCA 36 (1965), 161–77.

68. 2 Kgs. 23:7.

69. 2 Kgs. 12:3; 15:4, 35; 18:22; 23:8; 2 Chron. 15:17.

70. 2 Kgs. 10:29.

71. 2 Kgs. 13:6.

72. 2 Kgs. 13:14–19.

73. 2 Kgs. 14:13.

74. C. J. Gadd, 'Inscribed prisms of Sargon II from Nimrud', *Iraq* 16 (1954), 179, line 32.

75. 2 Kgs. 18:4 ('Asherah' is rendered 'sacred pole' in NEB). On the Asherah

cult see R. Patai, 'The goddess Asherah', JNES 24 (1965), 37–52. For the suggestion that the Asherah was not introduced into the Temple until the time of Manasseh see M. Haran, 'The disappearance of the Ark', IEJ 13 (1963), 46–58. But even if Haran is correct, it still remains that an Asherah image was closely associated with the Temple, even if not actually inside it, at the time of Hezekiah.

76. 2 Kgs. 18:4. On the pagan associations of the bronze serpent (of which specimens have been found in pre-Israelite Palestinian towns) see K. R. Joines, 'The bronze serpent in the Israelite cult', JBL 87 (1968), 245–56.

77. 2 Kgs. 17:12, 15–16.

78. 2 Kgs. 10:21; 11:18.

79. 2 Kgs. 23:24. See also Isa. 30:22; Jer. 7:30.

80. Jer. 7:31; 19:5. For human sacrifice in Israel see also Hos. 13:2; Mic. 6:7.

81. *Gilg.*, XI, line 161.

82. See W. von Soden, loc. cit. in note 55 above.

83. A. R. Radcliffe-Brown, 'Religion and Society', *Journal of the Royal Anthropological Institute* 75 (1945), 34.

84. OTT, I, 105.

85. M. Eliade, *Patterns*, 7. F. Heiler, without any denigratory intention, designates the religion of the uneducated masses as 'naive religion'; see F. Heiler, 'Prayer' 466 in J. Waardenburg (ed.), *Classical approaches to the study of religion; 1: introduction and anthology*, 461–71.

86. In the Old Testament it is often possible to see in a single narrative both the popular and the elitist levels of understanding. A good example is Gen. 32:24–30, on which see G. von Rad, *Genesis Comm.*, 319–26.

87. J. J. M. Roberts, *The earliest Semitic pantheon*, 1.

88. See E. Ullendorff, 'What is a Semitic language?', OrNS 28 (1959), 75. Since both Sumerian and Akkadian were used in Mesopotamian religion, even if this argument is valid in principle, it is irrelevant to the study of Mesopotamian religion.

89. As possibly the idea of life being in the blood, possibly introduced into Mesopotamia by speakers of a Semitic language; see below, 168.

90. See I. J. Gelb, 'Sumerians and Akkadians in their ethno-linguistic relationship', *Genava* 8 (1960), 261–4.

91. E.g. Josiah in 2 Kgs. 23:15–20.

92. A. L. Oppenheim, 'Assyro-Babylonian religion', 66 in V. Ferm (ed.), *Forgotten religions*.

93. A. L. Oppenheim, op. cit., 78.

CHAPTER II

1. OTT, I, 136. For a more recent statement of this view see R. Martin-Achard, 'Remarques sur la signification théologique de la création selon l'Ancien Testament', *Revue d'Histoire et de Philosophie Religieuses* 52 (1972), 3–11.

2. OTT, I, 106.

3. OTT, I, 106. Von Rad also claims that the Salvation History concept is 'present [in some Psalms] by implication', and argues that 'where it is actually absent, as for example in the Book of Job and Ecclesiastes, this very lack is closely connected with the grave affliction which is the theme of both these works'. It seems an over-simple, and indeed glib, solution of the universal problem raised by Job to attribute its existence to failure to conform to a Salvation History approach.

4. G. von Rad, *Genesis Comm.*, 45–6. Ringgren, IR, 104, has dealt with the argument that the idea of creation was late and played no role in the early history of Israel.

5. OTT, I, 136. Relevant here is also a Hebrew graffito of c. 700 B.C. from a burial cave near Lachish, saying: 'Yahweh (is) the God of the whole earth; the mountains of Judah belong to him, to the God of Jerusalem': see J. Naveh, 'Old Hebrew inscriptions in a burial cave', IEJ 13 (1963), 84. F. M. Cross, CMHE, 72 and 69, in seeking for early references to Yahweh as creator, adduces Gen. 49:25 and Deut. 32:6. It is difficult to follow the argument for Gen. 49:25, since although El and Shaddai (or by emendation El Shaddai) are mentioned, Yahweh is not; indeed, there is only one mention of Yahweh in the whole of Jacob's Blessing, and that is in verse 18, which may be intrusive. Furthermore, Gen. 49:25 says nothing about creation, and merely mentions the blessings of heaven, the deep, the breasts and the womb—i.e. fertility. The Deut. passage adduced speaks only of Yahweh as 'father who formed you', which at the most relates to the creation of man and not to cosmic creation.

6. For an explicit statement of the distinction see OTT, I, 136–40. A division of categories which is both more objective and more useful than that made by von Rad between 'older belief' and 'theological doctrine' is inherent in a statement by J. Fontenrose, *The ritual theory of myth*, 58: 'In advanced societies ideology tends to take the expository form of belief statements rather than the narrative form of myth'.

7. OTT, I, 136.

8. A. Alt, *Der Gott der Väter* (= BWANT, III. Folge, Heft 12, Stuttgart, 1929), translated into English as 'The God of the Fathers' in A. Alt, *Essays on Old Testament history and religion*, 3–77. For references to the more important derived literature up to 1964 see H. Seebass, *Der Erzvater Israel* (= BZAW 98, Berlin, 1966), 49–55.

9. W. F. Albright attempted to establish the meaning 'kinsman' for *paḥad*,

and this has been widely accepted. Its invalidity has, however, been demonstrated by D. R. Hillers, JBL 91 (1972), 90–2.

10. Some scholars have divided El Elyon into two gods originally distinct in the Canaano-Phoenician pantheon; for references and discussion see N. C. Habel, JBL 91 (1972), 321–4. But even if El and Elyon were originally distinct, the two occurrences in the Old Testament in which they had certainly been fused show that at some stage in Israelite thought there was the concept of a deity El Elyon.

11. CMHE, 71.

12. Cross, CMHE, 69, reconstructs for *'hyh 'šr 'hyh* the 'original' formula *yahwī ḏū yahwī*. He then notes that his hypothetical reconstructed *ḏū yahwī* is precisely parallel to formulae in Ugaritic, but fails to note that this form and usage of the relative pronoun are probably not specifically early North-West Semitic but proto-Semitic. A corresponding usage occurs also in Arabic; see W. Wright, GAL, I, 272,B, C, Rem. *e* وَبِئْرِي ذُو حَفَرْتُ وَدُرْ طَوَيْتُ 'and my well which I dug and which I lined'. Wright does not ad. loc. cite an example of ذُو with prefixing verbal form, but in GAL, II, 318,A, أَلْمَلِكُ ٱلَّذِي يَعْدِلُ 'the king who is just', adduces an example of a prefixing verbal form introduced by ٱلَّذِي in syntax exactly corresponding with *ḏū yahwī*. Furthermore, Akkadian *ša*, regularly used to introduce prefixing verbal forms in relative clauses, is in origin a declined form of *šu* (GAG, §46b), which (see I. J. Gelb, MAD, No. 2, 136) may be connected with ذُو in origin; note also examples of the determinative-relative *šu* introducing a prefixing verbal form (Gelb, op. cit., 133). Thus the reconstructed hypothetical clause *ḏū yahwī*, even if accepted, need not be taken as establishing a cultic parallel with the corresponding formula in Ugaritic literature. Furthermore, the 'Midianite League' used as part of Cross's argument (op. cit., 71) is hypothetical, and there is no proof that even if such a league did exist that its High God was El. Finally, had 'Yahweh' been simply an epithet of El, it would be difficult to understand why, when Yahweh was introduced into the Exodus situation, he should be specifically presented as a hitherto unknown deity.

13. Had that identification been Mosaic, it would have been unnecessary to introduce Yahweh into the deliverance from Egypt at all; the god of Jacob, who led Israel into Egypt (Gen. 46:4), could equally well have led the Israelites out again.

14. For a recent balanced discussion, rejecting the Kenite-Midianite hypothesis, see R. de Vaux, HAI 313–21.

15. Exod. 5:3; 13:21; 7:10–12; 8:17–19; 9:23; 10:19.

16. Exod. 10:21–3.

17. Exod. 7:4–5.

18. Exod. 11:7; 12:23.

19. See Alt, *God of the Fathers*, 62: 'the gods of the Fathers were the παιαγωγοί leading to the greater God, who later replaced them completely.'

20. Exod. 3:4-6.

21. M. H. Segal, JQR 52 (1961), 41.

22. Gen. 12:3; 26:4; 28:14.

23. Gen. 16:7-12; 21:14-20.

24. Gen. 12:15-17.

25. Exod. 11: 4-5; Gen. 18:32.

26. Gen. 22:12.

27. Exod. 11:3.

28. For a summary of the arguments in favour of this interpretation, and an attempted rebuttal of counter-arguments, see F. M. Cross, CMHE, 60-6. Against this view see Fohrer, HIR, 77.

29. See especially W. von Soden, 'Jahwe "Er ist, Er erweist sich" ', WO 3 (1966), 177-87, whose argument on this F. M. Cross attempts to counter in CMHE, 63, n. 68.

30. See J. P. Hyatt, 'Was Yahweh originally a creator deity?', JBL 86 (1967), 369-77.

31. Gen. 19:24 (J).

32. Gen. 24:3, 7.

33. The evidence is summarized in F. M. Cross, CMHE, 13-15.

34. See CMHE, 50-2.

35. Gen. 33:20.

36. O. Eissfeldt, 'El and Yahweh', JSS 1 (1956), 25-37.

37. See also Num. 23:21-2 and 24:13, 16.

38. This raises the question, which does not appear to have been previously discussed, of whether El may not have continued to be venerated under that name in some parts of the Israelite cultural area after the introduction of Yahweh. L. R. Bailey, 'The Golden Calf', HUCA 17 (1971), 97-115, has (see especially 100-3) given arguments for the view that in the northern kingdom there was a cult of a god other than Yahweh, associated with a bull; he argues for this other god being the Mesopotamian Sin. (It may be noted that a similar hypothesis was propounded nearly a century ago; see T. K. Cheyne, *Founders of Old Testament Criticism*, 218, n. 2, who refers to 'Schrader's Assyriological explanations of names of deities in Amos 5:26' as proving that 'the northern Israelites in the time of Amos worshipped Assyrian deities'. If one proposes to put a name other than Yahweh or El to an Israelite god with a bull-symbol, the West-Semitic Adad [Hadad] would seem more probable than the Mesopotamian Sin; for the bull as a symbol of Adad see MDP, 2, pl. 17, IV, line 17, *būru ekdu ša Adad*.) The arguments for Bailey's (or Schrader's) particular identification are not compelling, but the argument for there having been some god not in all respects

identical with Yahweh as worshipped in the southern kingdom seems much stronger. Since El of the Ugaritic texts also bore the title 'bull', the possibility may be considered that the deity continued to be venerated in the old form El in some parts of the northern kingdom, the reason for acceptance of this in some Yahwistic circles being the recognized identification of El with Yahweh, and the cause of offence in others being the tendency to assimilate the old general Semitic High God El to the particular form of El as a bull which was venerated in the Ugaritic-Canaanite context. S. Terrien, VT 20 (1970), 326ff., has drawn attention to the fact that there were differences between the cult at Jerusalem and that of the northern kingdom, not all of them (on modern value judgement) in Jerusalem's favour.

39. Isa. 46:9.

40. Eissfeldt, JSS 1 (1956), 28–30.

41. OTT, II, 244.

42. Jer. 27:8.

43. Isa. 10:5–6.

44. Isa. 10:16–23, which in NEB translation concludes by saying that Yahweh 'will bring final destruction upon all the earth' is not part of the oracle against Assyria; see Eissfeldt, OTI, 308, 312. As part of an oracle against Judah, the concluding words of verse 23, *kl h'rṣ*, may simply mean 'all the land [of Judah]' rather than 'all the earth'.

45. OTT, I, 328.

46. 2 Kgs. 6:17–18.

47. G. von Rad, *Der heilige Kriege im alten Israel*, 68, points out that 'Deuteronomy is by far the richest source in the Old Testament for the conception of . . . holy war.'

48. Botta, MN, IV, pl. 75, line 5.

49. OIP, II, 169, col. II, lines 45–6.

50. Botta, MN, IV, pl. 109, lines 5–6.

51. Botta, MN, IV, pl. 81, line 8. For another example from Sargon II see Lie, *Sargon*, 62, line 5: 'the mighty hosts of Ashur took countless plunder for three days and nights'.

52. OIP, II, 177–8, col. IV, lines 54–5.

53. *Asarhaddon*, 43, lines 59–62.

54. *Assurbanipal*, 48, lines 100–1.

55. See K. Tallqvist, *Götterepitheta*, 266.

56. See W. von Soden, 'Gibt es ein Zeugnis dafür, dass die Babylonier an die Wiederauferstehung Marduks geglaubt haben?', ZA 51 (1955), 130–66.

57. Op. cit., 138, line 54. See also W. von Soden, 'Aus einem Hymnus Assurbanipals an Aschschur (Anschar)', SAHG, 254–6 and 384.

58. On the identification of Ashur with Anshar, see also J. J. M. Roberts, 'The Davidic origin of the Zion tradition', JBL 92 (1973), 342.

59. Jer. 39:11–14; 40:2–5.

60. On the impact of Nebuchadrezzar on Syria and Palestine see also M. Lambert, 'Le destin d'Ur et les routes commerciales', RSO 39 (1964), 91–4.

61. W. von Soden, 'Religiöse Unsicherheit Säkularisierungstendenzen und Aberglaube zur Zeit der Sargoniden', AnBi 12 (1959), 367, points out the marked difference between the attitudes to religion displayed by the Chaldaean kings and by the Assyrian kings, which he summarizes in terms of the latter alone showing a 'secularizing tendency'.

62. Nabopolassar does make a brief reference to Nabu and Marduk ordering him to attack Subarum (= Assyria) (VAB, IV, 60, Nr. I, col. I, lines 23–31), and alludes passim to his defeat of Assyria. He also mentions Shamash (VAB, IV, 66, Nr. 3, col. I, lines 21–3) and Marduk (op. cit., 68, Nr. 4, line 13) going at his side. But the latter reference is part of a longer passage (op. cit., 66–8, Nr. 4, lines 8–21) of which the whole presupposition is that Marduk began with a plan to exalt Nabopolassar to rulership. The warfare which followed was an incidental consequence of the plan: it was not Marduk's war as such.

63. For references see RLA, III, 576, nos. 13, 16, 20, 23, 24.

64. E.g., VAB, IV, 84, Nr. 5, col. II, lines 21–9.

65. See, e.g. VAB, IV, 78, Nr. 1, lines 48–9, Nr. 2, lines 41–4; 80, Nr. 3, col. II, lines 27–9; 84, Nr. 5, col. II, lines 26–9; these may be compared with *Asarhaddon* 27, lines IX 6–13 and 75, lines 34–5 and *Assurbanipal*, 302, line 23.

66. VAB, IV, 120, lines 36–8 and (with minor variants) passim. See also VAB, IV, 100, Nr. 12, Col. I, lines 17–20; 104, Nr. 13, Col. I, lines 22–5; 112, Nr. 14, Col. I, lines 13–17.

67. VAB, IV, 94, Col. III, lines 18–20.

68. OTT, I, 138.

69. On the increase of Babylonian influence upon Jewish religious thought during the Exile see 1–2 et passim in J. Koenig, 'Tradition iahviste et influence babylonienne a l'aurore du judaïsme', RHR 173 (1968), 1–42 and 133–72.

70. Gen. 14:19, 22; F. M. Cross, CMHE, 16, 50–1, 60.

71. Isa. 43:11–13 is related to the challenge to the nations in 43:9 and 45:22 to that in 45:21. The third identification of Yahweh with El, in 46:9, immediately follows a passage on the futility of the Babylonian gods.

72. See C. Stuhlmueller, 'The creation theology of Second Isaias', CBQ 21 (1959), 429–67. See also N. C. Habel, 'He who stretches out the heavens', CBQ 34 (1972), 417–30, with the suggestion that the phrase of the title, used by Deutero-Isaiah seven times, was a motif related to an ancient tradition of a celestial tent for the creator-god El.

73. H. D. Preuss, *Verspottung fremder Religionen im Alten Testament* (= BWANT, 5. Folge, Heft 12, 1971), 178–82. The anti-mythological tendency was also noted in F. M. Th. de Liagre Böhl, 'Babel und Bibel (1)', JEOL 16 (1959–62), 106.

74. Preuss, op. cit., 180, notes a parallel in Hesiod, but argues that this is too remote to be relevant to the present issue.

75. R. Pettazzoni, *The all-knowing God. Researches into early religion and culture,* 9.

76. *Schöpfung,* respectively 29–90, 91–111, 111–14.

77. *Schöpfung,* 111.

78. *Schöpfung,* 113.

79. Ps. 74:13ff. and 89:9ff., adduced in *Schöpfung,* 84.

80. See, e.g. M. K. Wakeman, 'The biblical earth monster in the cosmogonic combat myth', JBL 88 (1969), 313–15, with references in notes 3, 7, 8a. See also L. I. J. Stadelmann, *HebCW,* 19–27. Note, however, the view of W. H. Schmidt, *Alttestamentlicher Glaube und seine Umwelt,* 154–6, that in such passages as Ps. 77:17–20; Ps. 93; Isa. 27:1; Nah. 1:3f, Hab. 3:8, the mythical Drachenkampf had lost its original meaning and served to illustrate the Red Sea crossing, taken as an historical event.

81. H. Ringgren, IR, 107.

82. D. J. McCarthy, ' "Creation" motifs in Hebrew poetry', CBQ 29 (1967), 394.

83. For recent re-examinations of the passages concerned see L. I. J. Stadelmann, *HebCW,* 10–36, and M. K. Wakeman, *God's battle with the Monster,* 56–136.

84. M. K. Wakeman, op. cit., 67.

85. W. G. Lambert, 'A new look at the Babylonian background of Genesis', JTS 16 (1965), 291.

86. That Tiamat was not always thought of as evil is shown by the occurrence of personal names compounded with the element *tiāmat;* e.g. H. Hirsch, *Untersuchungen,* 34, *Puzur$_4$-tiāmtim.*

87. TuL, 32, Nr. 7, line 19 = KAR, II, 252, Nr. 307, obv. line 19.

88. M. Eliade, *Patterns,* 81, n. 2, notes the difference between Ea's magical victory over Apsu and Marduk's heroic combat. The taming of the primeval waters did not necessarily presuppose combat even in Mesopotamia, so that there is no need to require the beginning of Gen. 1 to be a demythologized version of an early combat theme.

89. S. G. F. Brandon, 'The propaganda factor in some Ancient Near Eastern cosmogonies', 29 in F. F. Bruce (ed.), *Promise and Fulfilment; Essays presented to Professor S. H. Hooke.*

90. For the myth, see S. N. Kramer, MAW, 105–6; Th. Jacobsen, 'Sumerian mythology: a review article', JNES 5 (1946), 146–7(= *Tammuz,* 124–5); S. N. Kramer, *Sumerians,* 151–3.

91. See S. N. Kramer, *Sumerians,* 151–2.

92. For bibliography, and translation of the myth, see ANET³, 111–13 and

514–17. The present writer has ready for publication a new edition of the myth, on the basis of a newly discovered text.

93. For the existence of the pantheon, see ANET³, 111, Tablet 2, lines 4–8. For the existence of light see op. cit., 113, ii, line 25, where 'brilliance' represents *namurratu* 'a numinous splendour of light', etymologically connected with *nawāru* 'to be bright'.

94. W. G. Lambert, 'The Gula hymn of Bulluṭsa-rabi', OrNS 36 (1967), 124, line 149. Note also that another primeval monster slain in a theomachy, the Labbu (see M. K. Wakeman, *God's battle with the Monster*, 13–14), had been terrorizing men and gods, showing that creation had already occurred before the fight; see A. Heidel, BG, 141–3. Even in *Enuma Eliš*, kingship was not the result of the primeval combat but its antecedent, both Qingu and Marduk having been made supreme before the fight.

95. Kramer, SM, 37–8; Jacobsen, *Tammuz*, 111, 114–18. Kramer sees a subsequent struggle involving a supposed monster Kur, but even if this is accepted (see, *contra*, Jacobsen, op. cit., 121–3) it cannot be seen as a combat of which creation was a concomitant or consequence.

96. *Rit. Acc.*, 46, line 24.

97. *En. El.* I, lines 133, 136, 140–2.

98. BWL 128, line 38. For other references to Lahmu in a corresponding sense see CAD, L, 41b.

99. I. Bernhardt and S. N. Kramer, 'Enki und die Weltordnung', *Wissenschaftliche Zeitschrift der Friedrich-Schiller-Universität Jena* 9 (1959/60), 235, line 184; re-edited in Benito, *Enki*, 95, line 186.

100. C. H. Gordon, 'Leviathan: Symbol of Evil', 1–9 in A. Altmann (ed.), *Biblical Motifs. Origins and transformations* (see also C. H. Gordon, 'Near East seals in Princeton and Philadelphia', OrNS 22 (1953), 243–4) has argued that the interpretation of the Leviathan passages as fragments of a myth of a primordial struggle (a view which he accepts) makes Hebrew monotheism philosophically a dualism, in which there are accepted two independent principles, Leviathan representing evil in opposition to God, the principle of the good. The only specific evidence offered in substantiation of the view that Leviathan represented evil is the interpretation of the adjective applied to Leviathan in Isa. 27:1 and in a parallel Ugaritic passage. But the adjective concerned (*brḥ* in both languages, taken by C. H. Gordon OrNS 22 (1953), 243 as meaning 'evil' *tout court*), though certainly obscure in meaning, in Hebrew is related to a root with a number of occurrences which do not fit into the semantic area 'evil' (see references in BDB, 137b–138a; note also that the adjective itself occurs in Isa. 43:14 in a sense which though uncertain can hardly in the context be 'evil'). In Ugaritic *brḥ* occurs three times (see references in Aistleitner, WUS, 58, no. 577), twice in a context in which a meaning 'evil' is not appropriate, and once as applied to Leviathan, where the meaning 'evil' is a mere guess. Whilst in both Hebrew and

Ugaritic a word used in parallel to *brḥ* is '*qltn*, meaning 'twisted' or 'crooked', there is nothing to suggest that the latter has any application to moral crookedness, and thus obliquely to evil. A further suggestion, that Leviathan was associated with darkness which was evil, does nothing to establish an original dualism in Hebrew thought, since the darkness itself was controlled by God (Gen. 1:3-5, 16-18; Ps. 104:20; 105:28).

101. HIR, 171.

102. W. G. Lambert, 'History and the gods; a review article', OrNS 39 (1970), 171.

103. *En. El.* I 1-2.

104. *En. El.* I 12-17.

105. *En. El.* I 92.

106. *En. El.* I 85.

107. Elsewhere (not in *Enūma Eliš*) Marduk is brought into relationship with Lahmu; see G. Meier, 'Ein Commentar zu einer Selbstprädikation des Marduk aus Assur', ZA 47 (1942), 242, lines 1, 3, where ᵈ*asari-lú-ḫi ša nam-ri-ir lit-bu-šú* is interpreted as meaning that Asarluhi [= Marduk] 'is clothed in/as Lahmu' (ᵈ*laḫ-mu il-lab-bi-šú*). Note also that one of the names of Marduk is ᵈ*Mu-um-mu ba-an šamê̂ᵉ erṣeti^ti*, 'Mummu, creator of heaven and earth'; W. von Soden, 'Neue Bruchstücke zur sechsten und siebenten Tafel des Weltschöpfungsepos Enūma eliš', ZA 47 (1942), 12, line 86.

108. For references, and translations of the relevant texts, see Heidel, BG, 72-4.

109. BMS, 126, no. 61, lines 7-8.

CHAPTER III

1. OTT, II, 368. On the unbalance of such a view see J. Barr, *Old and new in interpretation*, chapters 1 and 3. See also N. W. Porteous, 'Magnalia Dei', 417-27 in H. W. Wolff (ed.), *Probleme biblischer Theologie, Gerhard von Rad zum 70. Geburtstag*. Von Rad's 'Salvation History' views in relation to the prophets have been examined, on a literary-critical basis and strictly inside the Israelite context, by J. Vollmer, *Geschichtliche Rückblicke und Motive in der Prophetie des Amos, Hosea und Jesaja*(= BZAW 119; de Gruyter, Berlin, 1971). Vollmer rejects von Rad's view that the prophets looked on past Israelite history as an unfolding of a divine plan of salvation. Rather the prophets referred to history to point out the past guilt of the Israelites and the penalty this entailed in terms of divine judgement.

2. S. G. F. Brandon, 'The ritual technique of salvation in the Ancient Near East', 17-18 in S. G. F. Brandon (ed.), *The Saviour God*, offers a definition of the

concept of salvation: 'Even if kept within the context of religion, its application ranges from the idea of safety from disease and misfortune, engendered by demoniac agency, to that of deliverance from some form of eternal damnation'. On the translation 'salvation history' for the German 'Heilsgeschichte', see Translator's Preface, 17 in Oscar Cullmann, *Salvation in History*. On the difficulty of arriving at the precise meaning of 'Heilsgeschichte' for von Rad, see D. G. Spriggs, *Two Old Testament Theologies* (SCM Press, London, 1974), 34–8; Spriggs concludes (38) 'we are left with the uncomfortable feeling that ['Heilsgeschichte' in von Rad's *Theology*] does not have any clear or uniform meaning'. Some scholars (not von Rad) have attempted to define 'salvation' in the O.T. context by reference to the semantic spread of the root *yš'*, but the inappropriateness of this is sufficiently made evident by the nonsense which results; e.g., 'David gained salvation when he reduced the surrounding peoples to obedience (2 Sam. 8:14)' (F. J. Taylor, 219 in A. Richardson (ed.), *A Theological Word Book of the Bible*, SCM, London, 1950). For *tešû'āh*, often translated 'salvation', as denoting 'victory', see A. R. Johnson, *Cultic Prophets*[2], 40, n. 1. R. J. Sklba, 'The Redeemer of Israel', CBQ 34 (1972), 1–18, makes (see especially 13–17) an attempt to explain what he understands by salvation concepts.

3. OTT, II, 368.

4. OTT, I, 178.

5. OTT, I, 183.

6. OTT, I, 191.

7. OTT, I, 193–4.

8. J. Muilenburg, 233 in 'A liturgy on the triumphs of Yahweh' (W. C. van Unnik and A. S. van der Woude (edd.), *Studia Biblica et Semitica Theodoro Christiano Vriezen . . . Dedicata*, 233–51) regards Exod. 15:1–18 'the most primitive of the old credos (Deut. 26:8; 6:21–3; Josh. 24:6–7; 1 Sam. 12:6)'. On Deut. 26:5–10, note also that literary analysis leaves only the beginning of v. 5 and v. 10 as primitive (see R. de Vaux, HAI, 161 and references in n. 12).

9. OTT, I, 122.

10. It might be argued that God preserved Israel in order to transmit a particular revelation of him (a view which—as a theological judgement—the present writer would accept). If so, there are two possibilities for the nature of the transmitted revelation (which could overlap). The postulated revelation could relate to the nature of God and man, or it could be teaching about what God had done in history. If, as von Rad implies, it was overwhelmingly the latter, then one reaches the conclusion that in the Israelite view it was not to ensure the continuance of Israel as a religio-ethnic unit that God intervened in history, but rather, in order to provide striking deeds, the records of which Israel might transmit. If this was the case, God was in effect thought of as undertaking spectacular interventions in history for no better ultimate end than publicity. This would be not Salvation History but Advertisement History.

Fohrer is certainly correct in saying (HIR, 182) that 'the view that Yahweh acts in or through history is one-sided, and comprehends only a single aspect of the totality and fullness of Yahwism'.

11. It is to be noted that Amos met, and rejected, the idea that Yahweh made interventions in history affecting Israel of a different kind from those affecting other nations; see Amos 9:7. Doubts as to the originality of the verse have no more substantial basis than *a priori* assumptions as to the kind of ideas appropriate to Amos.

12. OTT, I, 112.

13. The Gibeonites were alleged to have entered the Israelite community (albeit as second-class members) by political treaty, without reference by either party to religious belief; Josh. 9:3–23. For cutting off from the community (in some cases by death, in others perhaps only by excommunication, but in all cases for wrong actions and not for false beliefs) see Exod. 12:15, 19; 30:33, 38; 31:14; Lev. 7:20, 21, 25, 27; 17:4, 9–10; etc.

14. Von Rad's importation of the Christian concept of Credo into his treatment of the Old Testament data is made explicit in his further comment on Deut. 26:5–9. 'As in the Apostles' Creed, there is no reference at all to promulgated revelations, promises, or teaching, and still less any consideration of the attitude which Israel on her side took towards this history with God.' (OTT, I, 122). The conclusions von Rad appears to wish to draw from this comparison are invalidated by the circumstance that the statement about the Apostles' Creed is factually inaccurate. It does contain 'reference . . . to promulgated revelations, promises, [and] teaching': what else than this is the epithet 'Maker of heaven and earth' applied to God the Father, or the statement 'from thence he shall come to judge the quick and the dead' applied to God the Son, or the specific mention of the doctrines of the forgiveness of sins and the resurrection? The Apostles' Creed cannot, moreover, be compared with the Deuteronomy passage on form-critical grounds; its *Sitz im Leben* is quite different. On von Rad's argument, the Deuteronomy Credo is a very early document, standing near the beginning of the Israelite religious tradition. But the Apostles' Creed is, within the Christian tradition, a relatively late compilation, having been formulated in the eighth century as a definitive statement of Christian belief, to which a man must consciously subscribe if he wishes to be regarded as a Christian. It was not a formative element in Christian faith, but rather a summary of Christian faith, arrived at after the great controversies on the Trinity, the Incarnation, and the Atonement. Thus the Apostles' Creed cannot be invoked in aid of arguments concerning the Deuteronomy Credo: the one stood at the end of a period of intense theological discussion; the other was itself a starting point.

15. Quoted from Albrektson, HG, 11. The original work was not available to the present writer.

16. HIR, 182.
17. *History and the Gods* (Gleerup, Lund, 1967), adduced as HG.
18. HG, 8.
19. HG, 27.
20. HG, 96.
21. For references to reviews see KSB 30 [OrNS 38 (1969)], 59*, no. 635; KSB 31 [OrNS 39 (1970)], 64*, nos. 736, 747; KSB 32 [OrNS 40 (1971)], 68*, no. 945; KSB 33 [OrNS 41 (1972)], 57*, no. 828.
22. HG, 7.
23. W. G. Lambert, OTS 17 (1972), 65.
24. W. G. Lambert, 'Destiny and divine intervention in Babylon and Israel', OTS 17 (1972), 65–72.
25. Op. cit., 65.
26. Ibid.
27. Op. cit., 66.
28. On m e see G. Farber-Flügge, *Inanna und Enki*, 116–26.
29. See S. N. Kramer, *Sumerians*, 116, and G. Farber-Flügge, *Inanna und Enki*, 97–115.
30. G. Farber-Flügge, op. cit., 113, nos. (79)–(81), and 58, lines II vi 4–6.
31. This is not a complete list. It may be noted that extant complete lists do not include some of the essential bases of Sumerian civilization, such as irrigation. The origin of the latter is, however, reflected in a myth; see C. J. Gadd in *Cambridge Ancient History* (third edition, 1971), vol. I, part 2, 125.
32. B. Landsberger, 'Die Eigenbegrifflichkeit der babylonischen Welt', *Islamica* 2 (1926), 369.
33. W. G. Lambert, OTS 17 (1972), 67.
34. S. N. Kramer, 'Keš and its fate; laments, blessings, omens', *Gratz College Anniversary Volume* (Gratz College, Philadelphia, 1971), 165–75.
35. S. N. Kramer, 'The death of Ur-Nammu and his descent to the Netherworld', JCS 21 (1967), 112, lines 8–9.
36. W. G. Lambert, OTS 17 (1972), 69.
37. Benito, *Enki*, 97, lines 210–18. The translation is slightly modified from that given in op. cit., 124–5.
38. W. G. Lambert, OTS 17 (1972), 70.
39. Ibid.
40. E. Evans (ed.), *Tertullian adversus Marcionem* (Clarendon Press, Oxford, 1972), Book I, 3 : 'Parentum cadavera cum pecudibus caesa convivio convorant.'
41. SKL, 76, lines 40–1.
42. TCL, III, 2, lines 6–7.
43. W. G. Lambert, OTS 17 (1972), 67.
44. See S. N. Kramer, *Sumerians*, 46–9, and E. Sollberger, 'The Tummal inscription', JCS 16 (1962), 40–7.

45. AM, 150.
46. For edition of the text see H.-G. Güterbock, 'Die historische Tradition und ihre literarische Gestaltung bei Babyloniern und Hethitern bis 1200', ZA 42 (1934), 47–57. For the attempt to establish a Deuteronomic view of history therein see E. Osswald, 'Altorientalische Parallelen zur deuteronomistischen Geschichtsbetrachtung', MIOF 15 (1969), 286–96.
47. For a reference to an article by B. Albrektson (not available to the present writer) taking 'the Oriental cyclic view of woe and prosperity [as] unproved', see KSB 33 [OrNS 41 (1972)], 58*, no. 829.
48. W. G. Lambert, OTS 17 (1972), 72.
49. T. C. G. Thornton, 'Charismatic Kingship in Israel and Judah', JTS 14 (1963), 1–11, denies (against Alt) the existence of any distinctive type of 'charismatic' ideal of kingship in northern Israel that was not present in Judah.
50. E.g., Amos 9:7.
51. A. L. Oppenheim, 'Analysis of an Assyrian ritual (KAR 139)', HR 5 (1966), 255.
52. H. W. F. Saggs, Iraq 37 (1975), 14, lines 13–15.
53. Ibid., line 30.
54. Ibid., lines 31–2.
55. Ibid., line 34.
56. Ibid., lines 34–5.
57. AKA, 31, lines 24–7.
58. Asarhaddon, 43, lines 58–60.
59. Op. cit., 3–5, lines III 16 to V 40.
60. Op. cit., 4, lines 33–40.
61. Op. cit., 46, lines 29–31.
62. Op. cit., 97, lines Rs. 16–17.
63. OIP, II, 139, lines 59–60.
64. Ibid., lines 60–72.
65. For these epithets see K. Tallqvist, Götterepitheta, 267, 'Aššur als Krieger und Kriegsherr', and alphabetically in 1–244.
66. TCL, III, 20, line 118.
67. Ibid., lines 119–20.
68. W. von Soden, 'Aufstieg und Untergang der Grossreiche des Zweistromgebietes (Sumerer, Babylonier, Assyrer)', 53, in W. F. Mueller (ed.), Aufstieg und Untergang der Grossreiche des Altertums.
69. Botta, MN, IV, pl. 71, lines 2, 10; pl. 73, lines 3–4.
70. P. Schnabel, Berossos, 253, III. De Oanne, lines 27–37.
71. OIP, II, 94–5, lines 64, 68, 69.
72. Op. cit., 99, lines 46–9.
73. Op. cit., 108, lines 57–64. New sources of massive timber were also

discovered; see op. cit., 107, lines 49–53. Ashur opened new springs in historical times for an Assyrian king of the early second millennium; see IAK, 6–8, IV, Nr. 2, col. 1, lines 27–30 (for *a-ga-am* read *a-bi-iḫ* = Mt. Epih).

74. Op. cit., 109, lines VI 89 to VII 19. The succeeding translation is of ibid., lines VII 1–8.

75. E.g., the *bīt ḫilāni*; for references see CAD, Ḫ, 184b–185a. See also A. L. Oppenheim, 'On royal gardens in Mesopotamia', JNES 24 (1965), 328–33.

76. For other Yahwistic claims that Yahweh was active in the sphere of nature see Amos 4:7–13; Hos. 10:12; Isa. 5:6; Jer. 14:22.

77. See, e.g., HIR, 176ff.

78. J. L. Crenshaw, *Prophetic Conflict*, 81–2.

79. *Tammuz*, 3.

80. Benito, *Enki*, 107, lines 374–5; and I. Bernhardt and S. N. Kramer, 'Enki und die Weltordnung', *Wissenschaftliche Zeitschrift der Friedrich-Schiller-Universität Jena* 9 (1959/60), 238, lines 373–4.

81. Benito, *Enki*, 107, lines 376–7; Bernhardt and Kramer, op. cit., 238, lines 375–6.

82. *Tammuz*, 337, n. 16. Jacobsen mentions a differing older version of the text, published in RA 8, a volume to which the present writer has not had access.

83. SAHG, 82–3.

84. Op. cit., 82.

85. Ps. 104:3.

86. H. Ringgren, IR, 97–8.

87. Op. cit., 63.

88. 1 Kgs. 19:11–12. *qôl*, qualified by *dᵉmāmāh* 'silent', is taken as related to Akkadian *qūlu*, on which see AHw 927b. See also G. Farber-Flügge, *Inanna und Enki*, 119, adducing A. Falkenstein, ZA 57 (1966), 87 for n ì. m e . g a r = *qūlu* 'ehrfurchtsvolle Scheu'.

CHAPTER IV

1. On Azazel see Kluger, *Satan*, 47, where the view is taken that 'Azazel, originally probably an ancient demonic deity, . . . is now nothing more than a concept. . . He is no more than a symbol of the desert.' For a different view see note 94 below.

2. For some references see CAD, K, 179a, *kapāru* A, 3a; 179b, *kapāru* A, d2', d3'.

3. E. Reiner, 'Lipšur Litanies', JNES 15 (1956), 136–8, lines 98–103; 140–2, lines 7'–37'.

4. For some examples see *Maqlû*, 7, Tafel I, lines 15–18; 14–15, Tafel II, lines 31–68; et passim.

5. Van der Leeuw, *Religion*, 139.

6. RLA, II, 107a.

7. Van der Leeuw, *Religion*, 135.

8. The element of the irrational and arbitrary in the activity of demons is reflected in the ancient terminology, where demons are said not to know *tašimtu* (DES, I, 74, line 9). Such a noun form is typically associated with a sense of 'that in which the activity denoted by the verb is seen in operation'; see H. W. F. Saggs, JSS 3 (1958), 173. One might thus expect *tašimtu* (from *šiāmu* 'to determine, to fix') to mean 'a course of action which is the result of, or in accordance with, a settled plan', *i.e.*, the opposite of arbitrary action. For a usage conforming to this sense see TCL, III, 14, line 81.

9. DES, I, 32, lines 32–9.

10. DES, I, 32, lines 26–9. For interpretation and translation of these lines see CAD, E, 162a–b, '*emūtu* in *bît emūti*', lexical section. The kind of behaviour envisaged suggests that child-marriage was in question.

11. UDUG. HUL. A. MEŠ and AZÁG. GIG. GA. MEŠ (for references see A. Falkenstein, *Haupttypen*, 12–14); SAG. GIG. GA. MEŠ (CT 17, pl. 12–26); *Lamaštu* (D. W. Myhrman, 'Die Labartu-Texte. Babylonische Beschwörungs-formeln nebst Zauberverfahren gegen die Dämonin Labartu', ZA 16 (1902), 141–200; F. Thureau-Dangin, 'Rituel et amulettes contre Labartu', RA 18 (1921), 161–71.

12. See C. Frank, *Lamaštu, Pazuzu und andere Damonen* (MAOG 14/2, 1941), and E. Unger, RLA II, 113–15, 'Dämonenbilder'.

13. DES, I, 6, lines 40–1; II, 20, lines 29–30.

14. F. Köcher and A. L. Oppenheim, 'The Old Babylonian Omen text VAT 7525', AfO 18 (1957–8), 67, iii, line 30.

15. *Religion*, 139.

16. DES, I, 90, 92, 94, lines 48–51, 70–4, 98–9.

17. DES, I, 30, line 21.

18. DES, I, 188–90, lines 68–79. Lines 64–5 were misunderstood by R. C. Thompson in the translation ad loc.; see CAD, K, 446b, *kišādu*, lexical section.

19. DES, I, 62, 64, lines 13–28. The repeated use of 'seven' for the various categories is clearly not to be taken cumulatively, but as different descriptions of the one group of beings.

20. KAH, I, 4*, text 2, Col. VI, lines 19–21: a curse calls upon the god Sin to become an evil *rābiṣu* to an offender. A great god could also be asked to be a good *šēdu* or *lamassu* (on these terms see W. von Soden, 'Die Schutzgenien Lamassu und Schedu in der babylonisch-assyrischen Literatur', *Baghdader Mitteilungen* 3 (1964), 148–56) to accompany a man; DES, I, 28, lines 284–7. A street name gives the statement 'Ishtar (is) the *lamassu* of his (! sic) people';

O. R. Gurney, 'The fifth tablet of "The Topography of Babylon"'. *Iraq* 36 (1974), 44, line 70.

21. In Akkadian *utukku, alû, eṭemmu, gallû, ilu, rābiṣu*.

22. E.g., KAR, I, 62, Nr. 34, lines 8–9 (bilingually), *eṭemmi dumqi* to be ever present at a man's side as a favourable circumstance; for edition of text see O. Schroeder, ZA 30 (1922), 89–91. For good and evil *rābiṣu* see CAD, E, 260b.

23. Either triad can occur without the other, but the members of each triad are closely related; in one triad Sumerograms are inter-related, and in the other the Akkadian names, suggesting different periods or circumstances of origin.

24. *Lamaštu* (= DÌM.ME), *Labaṣu* (= DÌM.ME.A), *Aḫḫāzu* (= DÌM.ME. LAGAB); DES, I, 160, line 37; et passim. *Lilû, Lilītu, Ardat Lilî*; DES, II, 118, line 20; et passim.

25. DES, I, 16, line 156 (*Mūtum* included in a list of demons); ibid., (*Namtaru lemnu* similarly); DES, II, 120, lines 21–2 (*Namtaru lemnu* and *Asakku* following the *Lamaštu* and *Lilû* groups); et passim.

26. E. Ebeling, RLA, II, 107–8.

27. DES, I, 76, lines 37–8. See also H. and J. Lewy, HUCA 17 (1942–3), 38.

28. DES, I, 190, lines 96–7. The *Utukku* and *Alû* could also be said to have no name; DES, I, 152, line 189.

29. DES, I, 190, lines 94–5.

30. H. and J. Lewy, 'The origin of the week and the oldest West Asiatic calendar', HUCA 17 (1942–3), 17–28.

31. DES, I, 58, line 23.

32. ABRT, II, 13, K.48, Reverse, lines 1–8, translated by W. von Soden, SAHG, 345, text 71, 'An Enmescharra'.

33. For references for the defeat of Enmesharra see RLA, II, 396b.

34. DES, II, 130, lines 1–3: 'The bound gods have come forth from the grave'. Cf. TuL, 38, text 8, line 5.

35. H. and J. Lewy, HUCA 17 (1942–3), 37–40.

36. See D. O. Edzard, WdM, I/1, 124–5, 'Sebettu'.

37. Or, according to Th. Jacobsen, *Tammuz*, 116, 'Lord modus operandi of the universe'; the slightly different interpretation does not affect the point made.

38. W. G. Lambert, RLA, III, 470.

39. H. and J. Lewy, HUCA 17 (1942–3), 21, n. 82.

40. The corresponding goddess Ninmesharra (see Th. Jacobsen, *Tammuz*, 116) had no independent significance.

41. See H. and J. Lewy, op. cit., 27–8. The chthonic aspect of Enmesharra need only reflect the fact that the totality of numinous powers comprehended the underworld and fertility; it does not establish that Enmesharra was an old chthonic deity.

42. By a later development, the sons of Enmesharra became separately identified with specific great gods; see H. and J. Lewy, op. cit., 37–9.

43. Other deities certainly deriving from an abstraction were the pair Duri Dari 'Ever and Ever'; see E. Ebeling, RLA, II, 244a, 'Duri', and W. G. Lambert, RLA, III, 470a.

44. DES, I, 62, col. III, lines 1ff.; see H. and J. Lewy, op. cit., 17–18.

45. W. G. Lambert, RLA III, 470a.

46. *Tammuz*, 22, 32–3.

47. On the possibility of seeing traces of animism in ancient Mesopotamia see Ebeling, RLA, I, 108b, 'Animismus', and 'Kultische Texte aus Assur', OrNS 23 (1954), 116–18; in the latter text not only named gods but also images, doors and temple rooms were invited to a ritual meal.

48. W. G. Lambert, RLA, III, 469–70. Corresponding syzygies, also manifestly the product of scribal speculation rather than of religious traditions from earliest times, occur in the theogony of Anu, who is traced back to 'Ever and Ever', eternal time.

49. The etymology of her Akkadian name, or of the Sumerian form DÌM. ME, is uncertain, though the equations DÌM.MA = $šir$-ru ['small child'] and DÌM.ME = $ú$-$lál$-ti ['weakling'?] (Deimel, ŠL, II, 150[8,10]) may be noted. The other two demons with whom Lamashtu was commonly linked (see n. 24 above) had virtually no separate existence and probably represented particular symptoms within the syndrome covered by Lamashtu.

50. W. von Soden, 'Eine altassyrische Beschwörung gegen die Dämonin Lamaštum', OrNS 25 (1956), 141–8, and W. von Soden, 'Eine altbabylonische Beschwörung gegen die Dämonin Lamaštum', OrNS 23 (1954), 337–44. Formally one might argue that the term 'daughter of Anu' in the Old Assyrian text does not necessarily denote Lamashtu, but the equation is explicitly made in the Old Babylonian texts, probably within a century of the Old Assyrian example.

51. The parallel which immediately suggests itself here is Hillel ben Shahar, 'Day Star, son of Dawn', of Isa. 14:12–16 (RSV). The latter passage appears to be a vestige of an ancient Canaanite myth, applied to the king of Babylon, but it clearly knew, as did the Old Assyrian text, of a divine being cast out of heaven for presumptuousness. Here, however, the parallel ends. Whilst Lamashtu became one of the commonest and most feared demons in Mesopotamia, there is no indication of Hillel having become a demon in Israel.

52. W. von Soden, OrNS 25 (1956), 143, lines 22–3. Lamashtu could also be considered as acting against men, but that this was secondary is suggested by the giving of a different name to the demon in such a context; see IV R², Additions and Corrections, 10, addition to Plate 56 [63], Col. I, from K. 3377 + K. 7087, lines 4–5.

53. *Atrahasis*, 102, vii, line 3. For *pāšittu* as an epithet of Lamashtu see references in AHw 845a. The term apparently meant 'the female being who snuffs out (life)'.

54. *Atrahasis*, 62, lines 15–19.
55. See references in CAD, D, 165b, *di'u* a.
56. DES, II, 86, lines 5, 9–10.
57. DES, I, 128, lines 18–19.
58. DES, II, 124, lines 78–9.
59. DES, I, 148, lines 137–8.
60. CAD, I/J, 55b, K.166:12ff.; DES, II, 130, lines 4–10; DES, I, 124, lines 17–20 and 31–2.
61. KAR, I, 228, Nr. 142, obv. II lines 8–9.
62. See references in CAD, A/2, 326a, *asakku* A a.
63. *Pantheon*, 166, no. 1917; 181, no. 2165. These hypostases of Nergal do not appear to be mentioned in Weiher, *Nergal*, although the passage establishing the connection of Muhra with Nergal (CT 24, pl. 36, lines 51–62) is adduced, 69–70. Another named Asakku was ^{d}Equ (CAD, A/2, 326a, a); since *ēqu* seems to have denoted a cult object in the innermost shrine of a temple (see CAD, E, 253b–4a, *ēqu* 2), this suggests the hypostatization of a cult object into a deity, with its classification as an Asakku resulting from conflation of Asakku used of demons and *asakku* in *bīt asakki* ('tabooed place', CAD, A/2, 327b), which would have been an apt description of the *bīt ēqi* or innermost shrine. The deity Muhra could have arisen by a similar process from the term *muḫru* 'cult offering' (references in AHw 669a).
64. Geller, *Lugale*, 280, rev. line 5; 282, rev. line 37; 315, line 25.
65. E.g., for demons of sickness thought of as under the control of Shamash, to whose hold they were conjured to return, see A. Goetze, 'An incantation against diseases', JCS 9 (1955), 11, (B), lines 28–31.
66. DES, I, 4, lines 26–7.
67. DES, I, 62, col. III, lines 9–10.
68. DES, I, 74, lines 16–17.
69. Paul Volz, *Das Dämonische in Jahwe*, adduced hereafter as DJ. See also J. L. Crenshaw, *Prophetic Conflict*, 77–9; H. Ringgren, IR, 73. Ringgren appears to find the term 'demonic' unsatisfactory, in that he comments: 'This does not mean, of course, that Yahweh is somehow connected with demons; it means rather that there is something unfathomable and sinister about him.'
70. DJ, 4.
71. Ibid.
72. DJ, 17, 15.
73. DJ, 5.
74. DJ, 27–8.
75. DJ, 29.
76. Ibid.
77. DJ, 30.
78. DJ, 31.

79. There would appear to be an element of self-contradiction here, since elsewhere (DJ, 29) Volz has already suggested that Yahweh may have become identified with an old local demon known as 'the fear of Isaac'.

80. DJ, 33.

81. DJ, 5.

82. Crenshaw, *Prophetic Conflict*, 78.

83. Oppenheim, *Dreams*, 233, speaks of the 'demonic nature of the Dream-god'.

84. E.g., Crenshaw, *Prophetic Conflict*, 81. It may be noted that in places Crenshaw supplies the demonic element where it is not explicit; e.g., op. cit., 84, in discussion of 1 Kgs. 22:1–40, he states 'to divert the death angel to [presumably a misprint for 'from'] Jehoshaphat, a stray arrow is guided by Yahweh to an unprotected area of Ahab's chest'. Where a 'death angel' is to be found in the original passage is not evident.

85. Already used by Crenshaw, *Prophetic Conflict*, 78.

86. Crenshaw, ibid.

87. Von Rad, *Genesis Comm.*, 322–3.

88. BDB 925a.

89. 1 Sam. 16:14–15; 19:9.

90. Ringgren, IR, 94.

91. Kluger, *Satan*, 151–62.

92. W. F. Stinespring, annotation to 1 Chron. 21:1 in *Oxford Annotated Bible RSV* (1962).

93. Kluger, *Satan*, 155.

94. No attempt has been made to mention all Old Testament passages which may bear reference to demons. Other demons may have been mentioned in terms translated 'wild beasts', 'satyrs' and 'hyenas', foretold in Isa. 13:21ff. as prowling around devastated Babylon (Ringgren, IR, 101); there are other allusions to 'satyrs' as aspects of paganism in Lev. 17:7 and 2 Chron. 11:15. A number of possible references to demons in Psalms (see inter alios Ringgren, IR, 181) must be used with caution for comparative purposes, as many of the supposed instances have been recognized (or invented?) on the basis of Meso-potamian material, so that in some instances the recognition of a demon is the consequence of interpreting a biblical phrase through Mesopotamian rather than Israelite eyes. Lilith (RSV 'night hag', NEB improbably 'nightjar') is mentioned in Isa. 34:14, but since she was certainly of Babylonian origin this tells nothing of Israelite beliefs but at the most of syncretistic tendencies. The same could be said of the *šēdîm* (RSV 'demons', NEB 'foreign demons') in Deut. 32:17 and Ps. 106:37; the Deuteronomy passage, in which the *šēdîm* are equated with, or at the least placed in parallel with, 'new gods that had come in of late' (RSV; NEB 'new gods from their neighbours'), emphasizes their non-Israelite origin. Azazel, to whom a goat was sent in Lev. 16:7–10, 20–2, is usually taken as a

desert demon (but see G. R. Driver, JSS 1 (1956), 97–8, for the suggestion that *azāzel* meant 'jagged rocks, precipice'; some Hittite evidence giving an important contribution to the understanding of the Azazel ritual was adduced by Professor O. R. Gurney in his 1976 Schweich Lectures.) Another possible demon is in Gen. 4:7, where sin is enigmatically said to be 'couching at the door' (RSV). 'The destroyer' of Exod. 12:23 was certainly a demon, although one specifically under the control of Yahweh; there may be an allusion to the same demon of death in the term 'mountain of the destroyer' (so MT; RSV 'mount of corruption', NEB 'Mount of Olives') in 2 Kgs. 23:13. A suggested demon 'great wrath' (J. Boehmer, 'Zorn', ZAW 44 (1926), 321–2) seems improbable.

95. S. N. Kramer, 'The death of Ur-Nammu and his descent to the Netherworld', JCS 21 (1967), 112, lines 8–9.

96. Op. cit., 115, lines 155–7, 159, 161.

97. S. N. Kramer, *Sumerians*, 127–9.

98. Op. cit., 126.

99. W. von Soden, 'Das Fragen nach der Gerichtigkeit Gottes im Alten Orient', MDOG 96 (1965), 46.

100. S. N. Kramer, *Sumerians*, 127.

101. Op. cit., 128.

102. W. von Soden, 'Das Fragen nach der Gerichtigkeit Gottes im Alten Orient', MDOG 96 (1965), 41–59.

103. Op. cit., 42–4.

104. Op. cit., 46.

105. Edited by E. Reiner, *Šurpu; a collection of Sumerian and Akkadian incantations* (= AfO, Beiheft 11, Graz, 1958).

106. See, e.g., MSL, VI, 23ff., and A. Salonen, *Türen*, passim.

107. W. von Soden, MDOG 96 (1965), 48.

108. Ibid.

109. Op. cit., 49.

110. Edited by W. G. Lambert, BWL, 32–61.

111. BWL, 38, 40, lines 12–30.

112. BWL, 50, lines 57–60.

113. BWL, 40, lines 34–6, 38.

114. A. Guillaume, *Prophecy and divination among the Hebrews and other Semites*, 372, n. 1.

115. BWL, 67. W. von Soden, MDOG 96 (1965), 51–2, dates it two centuries later.

116. Edited by W. G. Lambert, BWL, 70–89.

117. BWL, 74, 76, lines 70–2, 75, 77.

118. BWL, 86, lines 267–8, 271–2.

119. See 115 above.

120. BWL, 88, line 280.

121. W. von Soden, MDOG 96 (1965), 52.

122. BWL, 88, lines 295-7.

123. OTI, 211.

124. It would be tempting at this point to divagate into a discussion of what is meant by 'just' and 'justice' in the Old Testament, but this would be an unprofitable exercise for the immediate purpose, since it is quite clear in the context of Gen. 18:25 that 'just' in regard to action by Yahweh means rewarding the good and punishing the bad.

125. Childe Rowland XIV.

126. S. Mowinckel, *Psalms*, I, 207.

127. In Israel, God did not desert man because of sin, but rather, because of the nature of God, sin—the product of man's will—cut a man off from him. God could use punishment to restore communication:

> Purge me with hyssop, and I shall be clean;
> Wash me, and I shall be whiter than snow.
>
> . . .
>
> Hide thy face from my sins,
> and blot out all my iniquities. (Ps. 51:7, 9 RSV).

128. 2 Sam. 12:15.

129. MDOG 96 (1965), 55.

CHAPTER V

1. For a mention (in the Christian era) of a belief that all events are a matter of chance, see H. J. W. Drijvers, *The book of the laws of countries. Dialogue on Fate of Bardaisan of Edessa*, 29.

2. E.g. Ebeling, *Handerhebung*, 48, line 110, where Shamash is told: 'You inscribe the oracle on the inside of the sheep.' See also TCL, III, 48, line 319.

3. P. Artzi and A. Malamat, 'The correspondence of Šibtu, Queen of Mari in ARM X', OrNS 40 (1971), 82, on no. 11, lines 15-17.

4. On the 'substitute king' see references in Oppenheim, AM, 358, n. 25.

5. Note the specific statement that 'Bel and Nabu are able to avert the portent and will avert it for the king', ABL no. 51, rev. lines 3-6. Here the portents are clearly not the result of the gods' will but of non-deistic origin.

6. See A. R. Johnson, *Cultic Prophets*[2], 44, and G. Fohrer, HIR, 233.

7. A. R. Johnson, op. cit., 40.

8. See Dan., passim; Strabo, *Geography*, Book 16, section I.6 (= edition by H. L. Jones, Loeb Classical Library, 1966, vol. VII, 202-3); Pliny, *Natural History*, Book 6, section xxx. 123 (= edition by H. Rackman, Loeb Classical

Library, 1942, 430, section 123). See also the comments of Bardaiṣan on Chaldaean astrology, H. J. W. Drijvers, *The book of the laws of countries. Dialogue on Fate of Bardaiṣan of Edessa*, 27.

9. CT 20, pl. 44, lines 59–61, adduced by C. J. Gadd, *Divination*, 26.

10. AM, 213–14.

11. *Contra* see J. Nougayrol, *Divination*, 14.

12. See reference in Oppenheim, AM, 366, n. 33.

13. B. Landsberger and H. Tadmor, 'Fragments of clay liver models from Hazor', IEJ 14 (1964), 201–18.

14. Ezek. 21:21.

15. See CAD, E, 335a, (c). An omen could also fall into the intermediate category of being technically specific, but actually so general as to give virtually only an indication 'favourable' or 'unfavourable'; e.g. 'If the top of the gall bladder is like a hammer head, success!', YOS, 10, pl. XLI, no. 28, line 3.

16. See n. 2 above.

17. A. L. Oppenheim, *Divination*, 39.

18. For the Babylonian group see W. G. Lambert, 'The "Tamītu" Texts', *Divination*, 119–23.

19. Knudtzon, *Gebete*, I, pl. 1, text 1, lines obv. 1–6.

20. It may be noted that the requested answer 'yes' is not necessarily to be taken literally but rather means an answer in accordance with the enquirer's wishes, which—in the example quoted—would actually have been in the negative, supplying the assurance that the various enemies mentioned would not take action against Assyria.

21. One exception is known; see J. Aro, *Divination*, 110.

22. E.g., O. R. Gurney, 'The Sultantepe Tablets, IV: The Cuthaean Legend of Naram-Sin', AnSt 5 (1955), 102, lines 79ff. See also comments by A. L. Oppenheim, AM, 227 and further references in his footnotes 72–4 in op. cit., 369. For other instances of scepticism about omens see A. L. Oppenheim, 'Divination and celestial observation', *Centaurus* 14 (1969), 119–20.

23. W. G. Lambert, JCS 21 (1967), 132, ii, lines 1–12.

24. For the date of the Flood as Early Dynastic I, see M. E. L. Mallowan, 'Noah's Flood reconsidered', *Iraq* 26 (1964), 69. dIM (later, but not at that period, equated with Adad) appears in the Fara texts (Early Dynastic III), Adad possibly in the Old Akkadian texts at earliest (D. O. Edzard, 'Wettergott' WdM, I/1, 135–6). For a corresponding secondary linking of Babylon with earlier traditions see W. G. Lambert, JCS, 21 (1965), 127.

25. The basic work on these is A. L. Oppenheim's important monograph *The interpretation of dreams in the ancient Near East* (1956), hereafter abbreviated as *Dreams*.

26. *Dreams*, 197–206.

27. *Dreams*, 256–344.

28. Sometimes the general omen is a little more specific. E.g., when a forth-coming death is mentioned, it may be specified as through the collapse of a wall, a falling roof-beam, or by influenza (*Dreams*, 328, lines 82–5). This, however, still leaves the prognostications within the same general range of health, wealth, life and happiness, or the reverse.

29. *Dreams*, 308, obv. col. i, line 16.

30. *Dreams*, 308, obv. col. i, lines 11–15.

31. See Oppenheim, *Dreams*, 232–7.

32. *Dreams*, 232.

33. Ibid.

34. See KAR, II, 192, 197, Nr. 252, obv. col. 1, line 51 and rev. col. 3, lines 41–4, translated by Oppenheim, *Dreams*, 302.

35. See Oppenheim, *Dreams*, 301–2.

36. See examples given by Oppenheim, *Dreams*, 300.

37. *Dreams*, 301.

38. This was equally true of evil portents by other techniques. See, e.g., R. I. Caplice, 'Participants in the Namburbi rituals', CBQ 29 (1967), 40 [346], on n a m . b ú r . b i rituals.

39. *Šumma ālu ina mēlē šakin*, published in CT 38–40, edited by F. Nötscher in OrAF, 31 (1928), 39–42 (1929), 51–4 (1930).

40. OrAF, 31, 16, Tafel 15, line 1; op. cit., 20, Tafel 20, line 1; OrAF 51–4, 29, Tafel 42(?), line 1.

41. OrAF, 51–4, 46–8, Tafel 45, lines 55–68.

42. OrAF, 31, 24, lines 46–51.

43. F. Köcher and A. L. Oppenheim, 'The Old Babylonian Omen Text VAT 7525', AfO 18 (1957–8), 66, iii, line 11.

44. E.g., *Asarhaddon*, 2, lines 31–8 (if Borger's restoration d*Sin* u d*Šamaš* (line 31) is correct; but in the succeeding passage other heavenly bodies are referred to as planets, not as deities); 16–17, Episode 12–13 in text A.

45. ABL, no. 519, lines rev. 3–7.

46. ABL, no. 565, lines obv. 10–13.

47. J. Nougayrol, *Divination*, 15–16.

48. M. L. W. Laistner, *Christianity and pagan culture in the later Roman Empire*, 4–5. Note that Christian teachers had to warn their converts against divinatory practices (op. cit., 6–7, adducing Theodore of Mopsuestia in A. Mingana, *Woodbridge Studies* VI (Cambridge U.P., 1933), 41–3).

49. The evidence for divination (amongst other forms of superstition) in mediaeval Christianity is abundant though scattered; instances will be found adduced *passim* in almost any serious work on mediaeval Christianity. For some specific contemporary references to belief in divination as widespread in the mediaeval period see F. J. Furnivall (ed.), *Robert of Brunne's 'Handlyng Synne'*, *A.D. 1303* . . ., Part I (= Early English Text Society, Original Series, no. 119;

London, 1901), 13–18, lines 339–500, with references to necromancy (line 340), sacrificing to the devil (lines 341–2), and (lines 357–60) those many who

> belevyn yn the pye [= magpie]
> whan she comyth lowe or hye
> Cheteryng, and hath no reste,
> than sey they we shul have geste.

Robert also counselled (line 379)

> Belevë nought moche yn no dremys

implying that many people did; he himself accepted of dreams that (lines 397–8)

> sum beyn goddys pryvyte
> that he shewyth to warnë thee.

[The spelling in quotations has been slightly modernized.]

50. See Oppenheim, *Dreams*, 186–206 and 245–50.

51. For translation see Oppenheim, *Dreams*, 249, No. 8.

52. For translation see ibid., No. 9.

53. IV R², pl. 61 [68].

54. For ⊢𝕏𝕏𝕏 = *meḫû* see Deimel, ŠL, II/1, 93, no. 49*, C3. For idiom *meḫû ritkusu*, see AHw, sub vv.

55. *a-ta-ṣa-ak-ka*, taken as from *naṣṣ, with AHw 757b, B.2. For a denial of the existence of a verb *naṣṣ, see S. Parpola, *Monographic Journals of the Near East*, *Assur* 1/1 (May 1974), 1–10.

56. Reading *i-di-ba-kan-ni* as CAD, A/1, 232b, d 1′, but taking the verbal stem as *dêpu* (with presumed variant *dêbu*), on which see H. W. F. Saggs, *Iraq* 37 (1975), 17, note on line 10.

57. IV R², pl. 61 [68], col. II, lines 16–39.

58. So commonly written in New Assyrian; it is not clear whether the form is basically morphologically *rāgintu* or *raggimtu* (see AHw 942a) written defectively; the meaning is unaffected; see GAG, §55, forms 18b III and 20b II.

59. ABL, no. 149, lines rev. 7–11. For another example see ABL, no. 437, lines rev. 1–5. The meaning of the latter is obscure, but it looks as if the *ragintu* had given an unfavourable oracle and n a m . b ú r . b i rituals had to be resorted to.

60. H. W. F. Saggs, 'The Tell al Rimah tablets, 1965', *Iraq* 30 (1968), 161, TR. 2031, line 6.

61. E.g. IV R², pl. 61 [68], col. II, line 14, *al*da-ra-a-ḫu-u-ia, which is mentioned nowhere else; see S. Parpola, *Neo-Assyrian toponyms* (Butzon & Bercker, Neukirchen-Vluyn, 1970), 99, entry DARĀḪŪJA.

62. See F. Ellermeier, *Prophetie in Mari und Israel*; A. Malamat, 'Prophetic

revelations in new documents from Mari and the Bible', VTSup 15 (1966), 207-27; J.-G. Heintz, 'Oracles prophétiques et "guerre sainte" selon les archives royales de Mari et l'Ancien Testament', VTSup 17 (1969), 112-38 [114-15 contains a good bibliography of Mari material up to 1969]; W. L. Moran, 'New evidence from Mari on the history of Prophecy', *Bib.* 50 (1969), 15-56.

63. ARM, X, no. 7, no. 8, no. 50, no. 81 (the text does not establish that this instance occurred in a temple but does not preclude it); ARM XIII, no. 23; A455, translated by G. Dossin, *Divination*, 79-80.

64. ARM, XIII, no. 114, lines 8-11.

65. ARM, III, no. 40, lines 7-23.

66. See W. L. Moran, 'New evidence from Mari on the history of Prophecy', *Bib.* 50 (1969), 21-3. Authentication was also in some cases ensured by cutting off and sending the hem of the diviner's garment and a lock of his or her hair; for references see Moran, op. cit., 19-21; A. Malamat, VTSup 15 (1966), 225 (where ARM VI 45 is to be read for ARM VI 40); ARM X, no. 8, lines 21-8, no. 50, lines 29-33, no. 81, lines 16-21.

67. Another category of texts which might appear to be relevant to Old Testament prophecy is that misleadingly called 'Akkadian prophecies'. For translations and bibliography see ANET³, 451-2, 606-7; and for another text in this category and further references and discussion see H. Hunger and S. A. Kaufman, 'A new Akkadian Prophecy text', JAOS 95 (1975), 371-5. See also the important discussion in A. K. Grayson, *Babylonian Historical-Literary Texts* (Toronto U.P., 1975), 13-22.

68. For a useful discussion of some aspects of this matter see Burke O. Long, 'The effect of divination upon Israelite literature', JBL 92 (1973), 489-97.

69. E. Robertson, 'The 'Urim and Tummim', VT 14 (1964), 67-74.

70. Established by 1 Sam. 14:40-2.

71. Jacob: Gen. 28:11-17.
    Joseph: Gen. 37:5-11; 40:5-23; 41:1-36.
    Solomon: 1 Kgs. 3:5-15.
Even in the New Testament God-sent dreams form a significant theme in Mat. (1:20-4; 2:12, 13, 19, 22; 27:19).

72. Deut. 18:10-11 (on which see Lindblom, *Prophecy*, 87); Lev. 19:31; 20:6, 27.

73. ABL, no. 614, lines rev. 1, 3-7. There may be another instance of Assyrian necromancy in a text of Ashurbanipal, which refers to a message of consolation given by 'a *zaqīqu* from before Nabu' (*Assurbanipal*, 346, line 23). It is not, however, certain that the latter implied necromancy; *zaqīqu* was not the usual word for 'ghost', although it certainly denoted some kind of spirit manifestation. It is not excluded that the idea of the '*zaqīqu* from before Nabu' was comparable to that of *mal'āk Yahweh* ('messenger of Yahweh'), which in some instances (see Ringgren, IR, 89) was an emanation of Yahweh himself. On

mal'āk Yahweh see A. Ohler, *Mythologische Elemente im Alten Testament*, 195–9.

74. For the most balanced discussion of cultic prophets, see A. R. Johnson, *Cultic Prophets*².

75. 1 Sam. 10:5–6; 19:23–4.

76. The common use of the term 'priests' for the cult-functionaries of the various cultures contributes to confusion, with its implicit assumption that the cult-functionaries so designated were in substantial measure analogous. The careful distinction which it is necessary in some contexts to make between 'priests' (*kohením*), 'priests' (*kemārîm* 2 Kgs. 23:5, etc.), RSV 'idolatrous priests'), and 'Levites' in Israel is a warning against the too easy use of 'priest' as a general term for cult-functionary. Not merely one, but at least two, priesthoods existed in Israel, of distinct origin and function, even though they may have merged; there was a Jerusalem priesthood linked to Aaron and an old tribal priesthood linked to Levi. A third priesthood, possibly originally distinct, was that of Zadok. See Sabourin, *Priesthood*, 127, 130. For a division of Mesopotamian 'priests' into three groups see J. Renger, 'Untersuchungen zum Priestertum in der altbabylonischen Zeit, I. Teil', ZA 58 (1967), 112.

77. W. G. Lambert, JCS 21 (1967), 132, lines 23, 27–8.

78. For an instance of the *ad hoc* seeking of an oracle see 2 Kgs. 22:13, where the required prophecy was supplied by the (cultic) prophetess Huldah. The acceptance of activating processes did not imply that an answer from Yahweh could be compelled; e.g., in the case of Saul, 1 Sam. 28:6, no answer was forthcoming from any of the available activating techniques.

79. It may be noted that there is some evidence of the compulsion to speak in connection with oracles in Mesopotamia. A letter to the king contains a passage in which the writer reports someone as saying: 'The god has spoken thus: "If you do not speak, you shall die"' (ABL, no. 656, lines rev. 6–7).

80. OTT, II, 4. Von Rad somewhat modifies these views later in the volume.

81. See W. von Soden, 'Religiöse Unsicherheit Säkularisierungstendenzen und Aberglaube zur Zeit der Sargoniden', *AnBi* 12 (1959), 356–67.

82. 2 Kgs. 18:4.

83. J. S. Holladay, Jr., 'Assyrian statecraft and the prophets of Israel', HTR 63 (1970), 35.

84. Ibid.

CHAPTER VI

1. S. Mowinckel, *The Psalms in Israel's worship*, translated by D. R. Ap-Thomas, 2 vols.

2. AM, 176. Elsewhere ('Assyro-Babylonian religion', 78, in V. Ferm (ed.),

Forgotten religions, Oppenheim contrasts 'the Religion of the Common Man without cult, priests or temples' with 'the Royal Religion with one adherent, the King, . . . enjoying unique privileges in his relation to the deity'.

3. *Gilg.*, XI, lines 70–4. For indications of joy being associated with the *Akitu* festival see also M. Civil, 'The "Message of LÚ.DINGIR.RA to his mother" and a group of Akkado-Hittite proverbs', JNES 23 (1964), 4, lines 41–2.

4. See WdM, I/3, 370.

5. For the principal collections of these letters see R. F. Harper, ABL, edited in L. Waterman, *Royal correspondence of the Assyrian Empire*, vols. I–IV; and H. W. F. Saggs, 'The Nimrud Letters, 1952', *Iraq* 17 (1955), 18 (1956), 20 (1958), 21 (1959), 25 (1963), 27 (1965), 28 (1966), 36 (1974).

6. See, e.g. E. Behrens, *Assyrisch-babylonische Briefe kultischen Inhalts*.

7. V R, pl. 1, lines 41–6, 48–9.

8. H. W. F. Saggs, 'The Nimrud Letters, 1952', *Iraq* 21 (1959), 166, LVI, lines 2'–8', 13'–14'.

9. See, e.g., ABL no. 128, rev. lines 10–16; No. 157, rev. lines 8–12.

10. ABL no. 191, lines 7-rev. 5.

11. ABL no. 268, lines 13-rev. 5.

12. ND 2698+2702 (unpublished), lines 5–7.

13. CH, §2, lines 42–3.

14. ABL no. 210, lines 22-rev. 2.

15. ABL no. 1000, line 19.

16. The principal collections are edited in E. Ebeling, NBBU, and R. C. Thompson, *Late Babylonian Letters* (London, 1906).

17. NBBU, C25.

18. NBBU, C40, C63.

19. For bibliographical details see ANET[3], 320–2, 568–9. See also N. Avigad, 'A seal of "Manasseh son of the king" ', IEJ 13 (1963), 133–6 (dealing with a seal inscribed *lmnšh bn hmlk* with astral symbols showing Assyrian influence), and H. Torczyner, 'A Hebrew incantation against night-demons from biblical times', JNES 6 (1947), 18–29.

20. Arad letter A (ANET[3], 569); Lachish letter III (ANET[3], 322).

21. ANET[3], 568, 'A letter from the time of Josiah'.

22. Jer. 7:18; 44:19.

23. 1 Kgs. 18:4, 13, 19.

24. Zeph. 1:12 and Jer. 5:12 might be taken as indications that in some strata of Israelite society Yahweh was becoming otiose, as the sky-gods Anu and El elsewhere before him; on otiose sky-gods see Eliade, *Patterns*, 46.

25. H. Hirsch, *Untersuchungen*, 14, *Bab.* 6 p. 191 (Nr. 7). It is true that the incident quoted occurred in the Assyrian merchant colony in Cappadocia, so that the sacrilege could have been perpetrated by natives of Anatolia outside the

Mesopotamian cultural tradition. But the cuneiform document gives no indication of regarding the crime as of exceptional impiety, suggesting that it was accepted as falling within the pattern of life conceivable in the Mesopotamian cultural area. Also relevant here is the commonness in the ancient Near East of tomb-robbers, who were apparently not deterred from their nefarious deeds by dread of the supernatural. On tomb-robbers, see A. Parrot, *Malédictions et violations de Tombes*, 14–16.

26. CH, §6.

27. 'You shall not revile God' (Exod. 22:28 NEB) does not necessarily show that an Israelite might deliberately curse God. The usage of the verb *qillel* in Lev. 24:15–16 and elsewhere suggests that it denoted something not as positive and deliberate as 'to revile' but rather 'to make trifling, of small account', either by improperly using the divine name or more generally (1 Sam. 3:13) by unworthy actions in the name of Yahweh. See also Lev. 24:11.

28. Gen. 1:28.

29. Gen. 2:15.

30. For a useful presentation and discussion of the material see G. Pettinato, *Das altorientalische Menschenbild und die sumerischen und akkadischen Schöpfungsmythen*.

31. *Atrahasis*, 42, lines 1–2. For discussion of these lines see W. von Soden, ' "Als die Götter (auch noch) Mensch waren"; einige Grundgedanken des altbabylonischen Atramḫasīs-Mythus', OrNS 38 (1969), 415–32; W. G. Lambert, 'New evidence for the first line of Atra-ḫasīs', OrNS 38 (1969), 533–8; W. von Soden, OrNS 39 (1970), 311–14; W. G. Lambert, OrNS 40 (1971), 95–8; W. von Soden, OrNS 40 (1971), 99–101.

32. *Atrahasis*, 54–8. Ruth Amiran, 'Myths of the creation of man and the Jericho statues', BASOR 167 (Oct. 1962), 23–5, has drawn attention to human figures moulded in clay in primitive realistic style found at Jericho, and has sought to draw parallels with the creation of man from clay in the Mesopotamian myths and in Gen. 2:7. It is difficult to see that this proves anything of significance, except that to ancient Near Easterners the obvious material for moulding a human body, whether mythically or practically, was the plastic material most readily available—clay.

33. *Atrahasis*, 60, line 256,—62, line 14.

34. *Atrahasis*, 62, line 15,—64, line 295.

35. *Atrahasis*, 58–60, lines 240–7.

36. Note in addition that whilst the previous discussion has referred to the creature made as either *lullu* or *awīlum*, the 14 humans created as a group are referred to either as *zikarī* and *sinnišāti* or as *nišī*.

37. *Atrahasis*, 64, lines 299–304.

38. *Atrahasis*, 58, lines 210–17.

39. See examples of usage adduced s.v. in CAD, E, 397a–401a. Various

animals are said to be the *eṭemmu* of Enlil, Anu, Tiamat; see KAR, II, 254, Nr. 307, rev. 11, 13.

40. For references see AHw 878a, *pukku(m)*.

41. See Oppenheim, *Dreams*, 223. The relevant part of the lexical series LÚ=*ša* adduced by Oppenheim is edited in MSL 13, 208, line 234; MSL, 12, 120, line 27'.

42. For some references see Sir J. G. Frazer, *Folk-lore in the Old Testament*, 420–1, 431.

43. See Schnabel, *Berossos*, 253. See also S. G. F. Brandon, *Creation legends of the ancient Near East*, 107, with further references to sources and discussions.

44. Kramer, SM, 70.

45. SAHG, 133, Nr. 31. For publication and edition see op. cit., 372.

46. Jacobsen, *Tammuz*, 112–13.

47. The 'pickaxe' story is specifically linked to Enlil and his cult city Nippur, whilst the Enki story has no such affinity.

48. *Atrahasis*, 22.

49. See I. M. D'yakonov, *Vestnik Drevnei Istorii* 4 (1955), 10–40.

50. F. R. Kraus, 'Altmesopotamisches Lebensgefühl', JNES 19 (1960), 117–32.

51. BWL, 146, 148, lines 59–60. CAD, L, 58b, *lamādu* 7b2', gives a translation offering a slightly different sense.

52. W. G. Lambert, 'Fire incantations', AfO 23 (1970), 43, lines 22–5 and 27.

53. *Gilg.*, XI, lines 122–3.

54. CT 17, pl. 26, lines 65–70 (= DES, II, 94, lines 65–70).

55. G. Widengren, *Acc. and Heb. Ps.*, 79, stresses the possibility and seems to regard it as not inordinately rare; but even on Widengren's view it would still be the exception for a personal god to be one of the great gods. On the personal god, see most recently H. Vorländer, *Mein Gott. Die Vorstellungen vom persönlichen Gott im Alten Orient und im Alten Testament* (Neukirchen-Vluyn, 1975), to be evaluated in the light of the review by W. G. Lambert in Society for Old Testament Study *Book List 1976*, 78.

56. This relationship, expressed in terms of human society, was discussed long ago by W. Robertson Smith; see his *Religion of the Semites*, 59 et passim.

57. See references in CAD, A/1, 69b, *abu* 1b.

58. KAR, II, 40, Nr. 184, lines rev.! 43, edited in TuL, 86, Nr. 21, line 43.

59. ZA 43 (1936), 306, line 12.

60. R. Caplice, 'Namburbi texts in the British Museum, II', OrNS 36 (1967), 14, line 17; KAR, II, 297, Nr. 355, line 13.

61. H. Waschow, *Babylonische Briefe aus der Kassitenzeit* (MAOG X/1, 1936), 20, BE5, lines 21–3, 'Ishtaran [see W. G. Lambert ZA 59 (1969), 100–3] who loves you and whom the king loves'.

62. KAR, I, 268, Nr. 158, obv.? col. 2, line 42, edited in E. Ebeling, 'Ein

Hymnen-Katalog aus Assur', *Berliner Beiträge zur Keilschriftforschung* I/3 (1923), 14.

63. See also Hos. 6:6; 11:8; 14:3; Mic. 6:8; 7:20; Jer. 9:24. For an argument that the very name Yahweh implied love see S. D. Goitein, '*Yhwh* the passionate. The monotheistic meaning and origin of the name *Yhwh*', VT 6 (1956), 1–9.

64. Francis Brown, 'The religious poets of Babylonia', *The Presbyterian Review* 9 (1888), 86.

65. AM, 175.

66. Adduced by A. L. Oppenheim in *Divination*, 38.

67. On the Hannah incident see D. R. Ap-Thomas, 'Notes on some terms relating to prayer', VT 6 (1956), 227–8.

68. W. G. Lambert, 'The Gula hymn of Bulluṭsa-rabi', OrNS 36 (1967), 128, lines 189–91.

69. See R. Borger, 'Gottesbrief', RLA, III, 575–6, with criticisms by F. R. Kraus, RA 65 (1971), 35–6.

70. See F. R. Kraus, 'Ein Altbabylonischer Privatbrief an eine Gottheit', RA 65 (1971), 27–36, and J. J. A. Van Dijk, *La Sagesse Suméro-Accadienne*, 13–14. For a more detailed discussion of Sumerian 'letter-prayers' see W. W. Hallo, 'Individual prayer in Sumerian: the continuity of a tradition', JAOS 88 (1968), 71–89.

71. For this and other names of the same type see CAD, A/1, 213b–15a, *aḫulap*. On Ahulap-^{d}Šamaš (also Ahulap-^{d}Sin, Admat-ili 'How long, my god?', and other names incorporating a cry to the deity), see J. J. Stamm, *Namengebung*, 162–4 and 17–19.

72. O. Eissfeldt, JSS 1 (1956), 29–30.

73. H. Ringgren, IR, 265.

74. HIR, 185–6.

75. HIR, 287.

76. IR, 292.

77. IR, 305.

78. Th. C. Vriezen, *An outline of Old Testament Theology*, 15.

79. Op. cit., 217.

80. Benito, *Enki*, 99, lines 248–9.

81. Based on a private communication by Professor M. C. Albrow; see also J. Middleton, 'Lineage', C., in J. Gould and W. L. Kolb (editors), *A dictionary of the Social Sciences*, 391–2, with further reference ad loc.

82. H. Winckler, KS, II, pl. 43, Cylinder-Inschrift, lines 72–3.

83. It is possible to see an explicit statement of universalism in such a personal name as *Ma-nu-ba-lu-um-A-na* 'Who is without An(n)a?' (Hirsch, *Untersuchungen*, 27). On An(n)a see ibid, n. 131.

84. At an early period it was accepted that the gods of Mesopotamia were not

territorially bounded: thus, of the third millennium ruler Naram-Sin, on campaign away from his homeland, it is said: 'Naram-Sin goes on his path; the god(s) of the land go with him' (AfO 13 (1939), 46, ii lines 2–3.

85. E.g., the Assyrians brought Elamite gods from Susa and settled them in Erech (D. J. Wiseman, CCK, 50, line 16). In Ebeling, 'Kultische Texte aus Assur', OrNS 22 (1953), 29, VAT 13717, 2. Seite, linke Kolumne, line 15, the gods of ᵐᵃᵗ*su-bar-ti* play a part in the ritual. (Subartu in some contexts may connote Assyria, but hardly here.)

86. See n. 80 above.

87. W. W. Hallo, 'The cultic setting of Sumerian poetry', RAI XVII (1970), 124, II, line 10.

88. S. N. Kramer, *Enmerkar and the Lord of Aratta*.

89. Op. cit., 16, line 171.

90. Op. cit., 6, 8, lines 28–30.

91. Op. cit., 14, lines 141–6.

92. BWL, 126, lines 23–6, 32.

93. J. A. Knudtson, *Die El-Amarna Tafeln* I, 178–80, Nr. 23, lines 13–19, 24–5.

94. TCL, III, 48, lines 314–16; VAB, 4, 112, Nebukadnezar Nr. 14, Col. I, lines 13–17. Relevant also are such divine titles as *ēpiš kullat dadmē, muballiṭ šiknat napištim, banû tēnišēt gimri, re'û gimir kalama, re'û kīnu ša tēnišēti, rā'imat kullat nišē* (K. Tallqvist, *Götterepitheta*, 31, 67–8, 70, 164, 165, 167).

95. A. Goetze, 'An inscription of Simbar-Šiḫu', JCS 19 (1965), 121, lines 1, 3–4.

96. See 219 above, n.76

97. A well-worn example of this tension is given by the opposing biblical attitudes to kingship.

98. See above, 97–8.

99. For the relevant texts see references in CAD, L, 187a.

100. See above, 19.

101. There are possible exceptions—strictly limited and temporary—to this statement in the instances of a distinction between Yahweh and El inside a pantheon, of which O. Eissfeldt has seen traces; see above, 39–40.

102. *Patterns*, 29.

103. See above, 1.

BIBLIOGRAPHY

AHLSTROEM, G. W., *Aspects of syncretism in Israelite religion.* Translated by E. J. Sharpe. (Gleerup, Lund, 1963).

AISTLEITNER, J., *Wörterbuch der ugaritischen Sprache.* (= Berichte über die Verhandlungen der sächsischen Akademie der Wissenschaften zu Leipzig, philologisch-historische Klasse, Band 106, Heft 3; Akademie-Verlag, Berlin, 1967).

ALBREKTSON, B., *History and the Gods. An essay on the idea of historical events as divine manifestations in the Ancient Near East and in Israel.* (Gleerup, Lund, 1967).

ALT, A., *Essays on Old Testament history and religion.* Translated by R. A. Wilson. (Blackwell, Oxford, 1966).

ALTMANN, A. (ed.), *Biblical motifs. Origins and transformations.* (Harvard University Press, Cambridge, Massachusetts, 1966).

BARR, J., *Old and new in interpretation: a study of the two Testaments.* (SCM Press, London, 1966).

BAUDISSIN, W. W., *Adonis und Esmun: eine Untersuchung zur Geschichte des Glaubens an Auferstehungsgötter und an Heilgötter.* (Hinrichs, Leipzig, 1911).

BEHRENS, E., *Assyrisch-babylonische Briefe kultischen Inhalts.* (= LSS II/1; Hinrichs, Leipzig, 1906).

BENITO, C., *'Enki and Ninmah' and 'Enki and the World Order'.* [Sumerian and Akkadian texts with English translations and notes.] (University of Pennsylvania unpublished Ph.D. thesis, authorized facsimile by microfilm-xerography, Xerox University Microfilms, Ann Arbor, Michigan, 1974).

BERGMAN, J., DRYNJEFF, K. and RINGGREN, H. (edd.), *Ex orbe religionum. Studia Geo Widengren.* Pars Prior. (= Numen Sup 21; Brill, Leiden, 1972).

BERNHARDT, K.-H., *Das Problem der altorientalischen Königsideologie im Alten Testament . . .* (= VTSup 8; Brill, Leiden, 1961).

BIANCHI, U., BLEEKER, C. J. and BAUSANI, A. (edd.), *Problems and methods of the history of religions.* (= Numen Sup 19; Brill, Leiden, 1972).

BIGG, C., *The Christian Platonists of Alexandria.* (Clarendon Press, Oxford, 1886).

BLEEKER, C. J. and WIDENGREN, G. (edd.), *Historia religionum: handbook for the history of religions*. Vol. I. *Religions of the past*. (Brill, Leiden, 1969).

BOISSIER, A., *Choix de textes relatifs à la divination Assyro-babylonienne*. 2 vols. (Kündig, Geneva, 1905–6).

BORGER, R., *Die Inschriften Asarhaddons Königs von Assyrien* (= *Archiv für Orientforschung*, Beiheft 9; Osnabrück, 1956, new impression 1967).

BOTTA, P.-E. and FLANDIN, E., *Monument de Ninive découvert et décrit par M. P.-E. Botta, mesuré et dessiné par M. E. Flandin*. 5 vols. (Paris, 1849–50).

BRANDON, S. G. F., *Creation legends of the Ancient Near East*. (Hodder & Stoughton, London, 1963).

—— (ed.), *The Saviour God*. (Manchester University Press, 1963).

BRIGHT, J., *A history of Israel*. (SCM Press, London, second edition, 1972).

BROWN, F., DRIVER, S. R. and BRIGGS, C. A., *A Hebrew and English Lexicon of the Old Testament* . . . (Clarendon Press, Oxford, 1906).

BRUCE, F. F. (ed.), *Promise and Fulfilment; Essays presented to Professor S. H. Hooke*. (T. & T. Clark, Edinburgh, 1963).

BUDGE, E. A. W. and KING, L. W., *Annals of the kings of Assyria*. (British Museum, 1902).

CARRINGTON, P., *The Early Christian Church*. 2 vols. (Cambridge University Press, 1957).

CHEYNE, T. K., *Founders of Old Testament criticism*. (Methuen, London, 1893).

CHWOLSOHN, D., *Die Ssabier und der Ssabismus*. 2 vols. (St. Petersburg, 1856; reprint by Oriental Press, Amsterdam, 1965).

CLARK, E. T., *The small sects in America*. (Abingdon Press, New York, Nashville, Tennessee, revised edition, 1965).

CORY, I. P., *Ancient fragments of the Phoenician, Chaldaean, Egyptian*, . . ., *and other writers* . . . (William Pickering, London, second edition, 1832).

CRAIG, J. A., *Assyrian and Babylonian religious texts, being prayers, oracles, hymns, etc.* . . . 2 vols. (Hinrichs, Leipzig, 1895, 1897).

CRENSHAW, J. L., *Prophetic conflict; its effect upon Israelite religion* (= BZAW 124; de Gruyter, Berlin, 1971).

CROSS, F. M., *Canaanite myth and Hebrew epic. Essays in the history of the religion of Israel.* (Harvard University Press, Cambridge, Massachusetts, 1973).

CULLMANN, O., *Salvation in history.* Translated by S. G. Sowers. (SCM Press, London, 1967).

DAVIDSON, A. B., *The Theology of the Old Testament.* (T. & T. Clark, Edinburgh, 1904).

DEIMEL, A., *Pantheon Babylonicum. Nomina deorum e textibus cuneiformibus excerpta* . . . (Pontifical Biblical Institute, Rome, 1914).

——, *Šumerisches Lexikon.* (Pontifical Biblical Institute, Rome; third edition, 1947).

DIJK, J. J. A. VAN, *La sagesse Suméro-accadienne.* (Brill, Leiden, 1953).

DRIEL, G. VAN, *The cult of Aššur.* (Van Gorcum, Assen, 1969).

DRIJVERS, H. J. W., *The book of the laws of countries. Dialogue on Fate of Bardaiṣan of Edessa.* (Van Gorcum, Assen, 1965).

DRIVER, G. R. and MILES, J. C. (edd.), *The Babylonian laws.* Vol. II. *Transliterated text, translation, philological notes, glossary.* (Clarendon Press, Oxford, 1955).

EBELING, E., *Keilschrifttexte aus Assur Religiösen Inhalts.* 2 vols. (Hinrichs, Leipzig, 1919–20).

——, *Neubabylonische Briefe aus Uruk.* (= *Beiträge zur Keilschriftforschung und Religionsgeschichte des Vorderen Orients* 1–4; Berlin, 1930–4).

——, *Tod und Leben nach den Vorstellungen der Babylonier.* I. Teil: *Texte.* (de Gruyter, Berlin and Leipzig, 1931).

——, *Die akkadische Gebetsserie 'Handerhebung' von neuem gesammelt und herausgegeben.* (= *Deutsche Akademie der Wissenschaften zu Berlin, Institut für Orientforschung,* Veröffentlichung Nr. 20; Akademie-Verlag, Berlin, 1953).

——, MEISSNER, B. and WEIDNER, E. F. (edd.), *Die Inschriften der altassyrischen Könige.* (Quelle & Meyer, Leipzig, 1926).

——, MEISSNER, B. et al. (edd.), *Reallexikon der Assyriologie.* 4 vols., in progress. (de Gruyter, Berlin, 1932–).

EICHRODT, W., *Theology of the Old Testament.* Translated by J. A. Baker. Vol. 1. (SCM Press, London, 1961).

EISSFELDT, O., *The Old Testament. An Introduction.* Translated by P. R. Ackroyd. (Blackwell, Oxford, 1965).

ELIADE, M., *Patterns in Comparative Religion.* Translated by R. Sheed. (Sheed & Ward, London and New York, 1958).

ELIADE M., *The Quest: history and meaning in religion.* (University of Chicago Press, London and Chicago, 1969).

—— and KITAGAWA, J. M. (edd.), *The history of religions: essays in methodology.* (University of Chicago Press, London and Chicago, 1959).

ELLERMEIER, F., *Prophetie in Mari und Israel.* (= *Theologische und Orientalistische Arbeiten*, 1; Erwin Jungfer, Herzberg, 1968).

ENGNELL, I.: *Critical essays on the Old Testament.* Translated by J. T. Willis, with the collaboration of H. Ringgren. (S.P.C.K., London 1970).

FAHD, T., *La divination arabe: études religieuses, sociologiques et folkloriques sur le milieu natif de l'Islam.* (Brill, Leiden, 1966).

FALKENSTEIN, A., *Die Haupttypen der sumerischen Beschwörung, literarisch untersucht.* (= LSS, neue Folge, Band 1; Leipzig, 1931).

—— and SODEN, W. VON, *Sumerische und Akkadische Hymnen und Gebete.* (Artemis-Verlag, Zürich and Stuttgart, 1953).

FARBER-FLÜGGE, G., *Der Mythos 'Inanna und Enki' unter besonderer Berücksichtigung der Liste der m e.* (= *Studia Pohl*, 10; Biblical Institute Press, Rome, 1973).

FERM, V. (ed.), *Forgotten religions.* (The Philosophical Library, New York, 1950).

FESTUGIÈRE, A. J., *Antioche païenne et chrétienne: Libanius, Chrysostome et les moines de Syrie.* (Éditions E. de Boccard, Paris, 1959).

FOHRER, G., *History of Israelite religion.* Translated by D. E. Green. (Abingdon Press, Nashville, New York, 1972).

FONTENROSE, J., *The ritual theory of myth.* (= University of California Publications, Folklore Studies, 18; University of California Press, Berkeley, Los Angeles, London, 1971).

FRANK, C., *Bilder und Symbole babylonisch-assyrischer Götter.* (= LSS, Band 2, Heft 2; Leipzig, 1906).

FRANK, C., *Babylonische Beschwörungsreliefs, ein Beitrag zur Erklärung der sog. Hadesreliefs.* (= LSS, Band 3, Heft 3; Leipzig, 1908).

——[or K.], *Lamastu, Pazuzu und andere Dämonen. Ein Beitrag zur babyl.-assyr. Dämonologie.* (= MAOG, Band 14, Heft 2; Leipzig, 1941).

FRAZER, SIR J. G., *Folk-lore in the Old Testament.* (Macmillan, London, abridged edition, 1923).

GAMPER, A., *Gott als Richter in Mesopotamien und im Alten Testament:*

zum Verständnis einer Gebetsbitte. (Universitätsverlag Wagner, Innsbruck, 1966).

GELLER, S., *Die sumerisch-assyrische Serie Lugal-e Ud Me-lam-bi Nir-gál.* (= *Altorientalische Texte und Untersuchungen* I/4; Brill, Leiden, 1917).

GOETZE, A., *Old Babylonian omen texts.* (= *Yale Oriental Series, Babylonian Texts,* 10; Yale University Press, New Haven and London, second printing, 1966).

GOFF, B. L., *Symbols of prehistoric Mesopotamia.* (Yale University Press, New Haven and London, 1963).

GOULD, J. and KOLB, W. L. (edd.), *A dictionary of the Social Sciences* (Tavistock Publications, London, 1964).

GRAYSON, A. K., *Assyrian royal inscriptions.* Vol. I. *From the beginning to Ashur-resha-ishi I.* (Harrassowitz, Wiesbaden, 1972).

GUILLAUME, A., *Prophecy and Divination among the Hebrew and other Semites.* (Hodder & Stoughton, London, 1938).

GUNKEL, H.: *Schöpfung und Chaos in Urzeit und Endzeit. Eine religions-geschichtliche Untersuchung über Gen 1 und Ap Joh 12.* Mit Beiträ-gen von H. Zimmern. (Vandenhoeck & Ruprecht, Göttingen, 1895).

GÜTERBOCK, H. G. and JACOBSEN, Th. (edd.), *Studies in honor of Benno Landsberger on his seventy-fifth birthday, April 21, 1965.* (University of Chicago Press, 1965).

HALLO, W. W. and DIJK, J. J. A. VAN, *The exaltation of Inanna.* (= *Yale Near Eastern Researches,* 3; Yale University Press, New Haven and London, 1968).

HARPER, R. F., *Assyrian and Babylonian letters belonging to the Kouyunjik collection of the British Museum.* 14 vols. (London and Chicago, 1892–1914).

HARRIS, J. R. and ROBINSON, A. (edd.), *The apology of Aristides.* (Cambridge University Press, 1891).

HAUSSIG, H. W. (ed.), *Wörterbuch der Mythologie.* Erste Abteilung: *Die alten Kulturvölker,* Band I, *Götter und Mythen im Vorderen Orient.* (Ernst Klett Verlag, Stuttgart, 1965).

HEIDEL, A., *The Gilgamesh Epic and Old Testament parallels.* (University of Chicago Press, second edition, 1949).

——, *The Babylonian Genesis. The story of Creation.* (Phoenix Books, University of Chicago Press, 1963).

HIRSCH, H., *Untersuchungen zur altassyrischen Religion.* (= AfO Beiheft 13/14; Graz, 1961).

JACOBSEN, Th., *The Sumerian King List.* (= *Assyriological Studies*, 11; University of Chicago Press, 1939).

——, *Towards the image of Tammuz and other essays on Mesopotamian history and culture.* Edited by W. L. Moran. (Harvard University Press, Cambridge, Massachusetts, 1970).

JENSEN, P., *Assyrisch-babylonische Mythen und Epen.* (= KB 6/1; Berlin, 1901).

——, *Texte zur assyrisch-babylonischen Religion.* (= KB 6/2; Berlin, 1915).

JEREMIAS, J., *Theophanie: die Geschichte einer Alttestamentlichen Gattung.* (Neukirchener Verlag, Neukirchen-Vluyn, 1965).

JOHNSON, A. R., *The Cultic Prophet in ancient Israel.* (University of Wales Press, Cardiff, second edition, 1962).

——, *Sacral Kingship in ancient Israel.* (University of Wales Press, Cardiff, second edition, 1967).

KING, L. W., *Babylonian magic and sorcery, being 'The prayers of the Lifting of the Hand'.* (Luzac, London, 1896).

——, *The seven tablets of Creation, or the Babylonian and Assyrian legends concerning the creation of the world and of mankind.* 2 vols. (Luzac, London, 1902).

——, *Chronicles concerning early Babylonian kings, including records of the early history of the Kassites and the Country of the Sea.* 2 vols. (Luzac, London, 1907).

KLUGER, R. S., *Satan in the Old Testament.* (Northwestern University Press, Evanston, 1967).

KNUDTZON, J. A., *Assyrische Gebete an den Sonnengott für Staat und königliches Haus aus der Zeit Asarhaddons und Asurbanipals.* 2 vols. (Eduard Pfeiffer, Leipzig, 1893).

——, *Die El-Amarna-Tafeln.* 2 vols. (= VAB, Band 2, Hefte 1, 2; Hinrichs, Leipzig, 1915).

KOCH, K., *The growth of the biblical tradition. The form-critical method.* (A. & C. Black, London, 1969).

KOSTER, W. J. W., *Le mythe de Platon, de Zarathoustra et des Chaldéens: étude critique sur les relations intellectuelles entre Platon et l'Orient.* (Brill, Leiden, 1951).

KRAMER, S. N., *Sumerian mythology. A study of spiritual and literary achievement in the third millennium B.C.* (1944; revised edition, Harper Torchbooks, Harper & Brothers, New York, 1961).

——, *Enmerkar and the Lord of Aratta: a Sumerian epic tale of Iraq and Iran.* (University Museum, University of Pennsylvania, 1952).

—— (ed.), *Mythologies of the ancient world.* (Anchor Books, Doubleday, New York, 1961).

——, *The Sumerians. Their history, culture, and character.* (University of Chicago Press, 1963).

KRAUS, F. R., *Vom mesopotamischen Menschen der altbabylonischen Zeit und seiner Welt. Eine Reihe Vorlesungen.* (= *Mededelingen der Koninklijke Nederlandse Akademie van Wetenschappen*, Afd. Letterkunde, Nieuwe Reeks, Deel 36, No. 6; Amsterdam and London, 1973).

KRISTENSEN, W. B., *The meaning of religion.* (Martinus Nijhoff, The Hague, 1960).

LABAT, R., *Le poème babylonien de la création.* (Adrien-Maisonneuve, Paris, 1935).

LAGRANGE, M.-J., *Études sur les religions sémitiques.* (Victor Lecoffre, Paris, second edition, 1905).

LAISTNER, M. L. W., *Christianity and pagan culture in the later Roman Empire,* . . . (Cornell Paperbacks, Cornell University Press, Ithaca, New York, 1967).

LAMBERT, W. G., *Babylonian Wisdom literature.* (Clarendon Press, Oxford, 1960).

——, and MILLARD, A. R., *Atra-ḫasīs: the Babylonian story of the Flood,* with *The Sumerian Flood story* by M. Civil. (Clarendon Press, Oxford, 1969).

LANDSBERGER, B., *Der kultische Kalender der Babylonier und Assyrer.* (= LSS, Band 6, Hefte 1, 2; Leipzig, 1915).

——, AND SODEN, W. VON, *Die Eigenbegrifflichkeit der babylonischen Welt* . . . [= *Islamica* 2 (1926), 355–72 and *Nachwort*, by B. Landsberger; and *Die Welt als Geschichte* 2 (1936), 411–64, 509–577 and *Nachträge*, by W. von Soden]. (Wissenschaftliche Buchgesellschaft, Darmstadt, 1965).

LANGDON, S., *Die neubabylonischen Königsinschriften.* (= VAB, Band 4; Hinrichs, Leipzig, 1912).

LEEUW, G. VAN DER, *Religion in essence and manifestation. A study in Phenomenology.* Translated by J. E. Turner. (Allen & Unwin, London, 1938).

232   BIBLIOGRAPHY

LIE, A. G., *The inscriptions of Sargon II, king of Assyria*. Part I. *The Annals.* (Geuthner, Paris, 1929).

LINDBLOM, J., *Prophecy in ancient Israel*. (Blackwell, Oxford, 1962).

LUCKENBILL, D. D., *The annals of Sennacherib*. University of Chicago Press, 1924).

——, *Ancient records of Assyria and Babylonia*. 2 vols. (University of Chicago Press, 1926, 1927).

MEIER, G., *Die assyrische Beschwörungssammlung Maqlû, neu bearbeitet.* (= AfO Beiheft 2; Berlin, 1937).

MEINERS, G., *Allgemeine kritische Geschichte der Religionen*. Erster Band. (Hannover, 1806).

MORENZ, S., *Egyptian religion*. Translated by A. E. Keep. (Methuen, London, 1973).

MORGENSTERN, J., *Some significant antecedents of Christianity*. (Brill, Leiden, 1966).

MOWINCKEL, S., *The Psalms in Israel's worship*. Translated by D. R. Ap-Thomas. 2 vols. (Blackwell, Oxford, 1962).

MUELLER, W. F. (ed.), *Aufstieg und Untergang der Grossreiche des Altertums*. (Kohlhammer, Stuttgart, 1958).

NOTH, M., *The History of Israel*. English translation revised by P. R. Ackroyd. (A. & C. Black, London, second edition, 1960).

OHLER, A., *Mythologische Elemente im Alten Testament: eine motivgeschichtliche Untersuchung*. (Patmos-Verlag, Düsseldorf, 1969).

OPPENHEIM, A. L. *et al.* (edd.), *The Assyrian Dictionary of the Oriental Institute of the University of Chicago*. In progress. (Oriental Institute, Chicago, and Augustin Verlagsbuchhandlung, Glückstadt, 1956–).

OPPENHEIM, A. L., *The interpretation of dreams in the Ancient Near East, with a translation of an Assyrian dream-book*. (= TAPS 46/3; Philadelphia, 1956).

——, *Ancient Mesopotamia: portrait of a dead civilization*. (University of Chicago Press, 1964).

PARROT, A., *Malédictions et violations de tombes*. (Geuthner, Paris, 1939).

PETTAZZONI, R., *The all-knowing God. Researches into early religion and culture*. (Methuen, London, 1956).

PETTINATO, G., *Die Ölwahrsagung bei den Babyloniern*. (Istituto di Studi del Vicino Oriente, Rome, 1966).

——, *Das altorientalische Menschenbild und die sumerischen und akkadischen*

Schöpfungmythen. (= *Abhandlungen der Heidelberger Akademie der Wissenschaft*, Philosophisch-historische Klasse, Jahrgang 1971, I. Abhandlung; Universitätsverlag, Heidelberg, 1971).

PREUSS, H. D., *Verspottung fremder Religionen im Alten Testament* (= BWANT, 5. Folge, Heft 12; 1971).

PRITCHARD, J. B. (ed.), *Ancient Near Eastern texts relating to the Old Testament.* (Princeton University Press, Princeton, New Jersey; third edition with supplement, 1969).

RAD, G. VON, *Old Testament Theology.* Translated by D. M. G. Stalker. 2 vols. (Oliver & Boyd, Edinburgh and London; vol. 1, 1962; vol. 2, 1965).

——, *Der heilige Krieg im alten Israel.* (Vandenhoeck und Ruprecht, Göttingen, fourth edition, 1965).

——, *Genesis. A commentary.* (SCM Press, London, revised edition, 1972).

REINER, E., *Šurpu. A collection of Sumerian and Akkadian incantations.* (= AfO Beiheft 11; Graz, 1958).

RENCONTRE ASSYRIOLOGIQUE INTERNATIONALE, *La divination en Mésopotamie ancienne et dans les régions voisines* (= *Comptes rendus de la XIVe Rencontre Assyriologique Internationale, Strasbourg, 2–6 juillet 1965;* Presses Universitaires de France, Paris, 1966).

RINGGREN, H., *Israelite religion.* Translated by D. [E.] Green. (S.P.C.K., London, second impression, corrected, 1969).

ROBERTS, J. J. M., *The earliest Semitic pantheon: a study of the Semitic deities attested in Mesopotamia before Ur III.* (Johns Hopkins University Press, Baltimore and London, 1972).

ROGERSON, J. W., *Myth in Old Testament interpretation.* (= BZAW 134; de Gruyter, Berlin, 1974).

ROWLEY, H. H. (ed.), *The Old Testament and modern study.* (Clarendon Press, Oxford, 1951).

SABOURIN, L., *Priesthood: a comparative study.* (= *Numen* Sup. 25; Brill, Leiden, 1973).

SAGGS, H. W. F., *The greatness that was Babylon.* (Sidgwick & Jackson, London, 1962).

SCHMIDT, W. H., *Alttestamentlicher Glaube und seine Umwelt: zur Geschichte des alttestamentlichen Gottesverständnisses.* (Neukirchener Verlag, Neukirchen-Vluyn, 1968).

SCHNABEL, P., *Berossos und die babylonisch-hellenistische Literatur.* (Teubner, Leipzig, 1923).

SEEBASS, H., *Der Erzvater Israel und die Einführung der Jahweverehrung in Kanaan.* (= BZAW 98; Töpelmann, Berlin, 1966).

SJÖBERG, A. [W.], *Der Mondgott Nanna-Suen in der sumerischen Überlieferung.* (Almqvist & Wiksell, Uppsala, Stockholm, 1960).

—— and BERGMANN, E., *The collection of the Sumerian temple hymns; and The Keš temple hymn,* by G. B. Gragg. (Augustin, Glückstadt, 1969).

SMART, N., *The phenomenon of religion.* (Macmillan, London, 1973).

SMITH, SIDNEY, *Babylonian historical texts relating to the capture and downfall of Babylon.* (Methuen, London, 1924).

SMITH, W. R., *The religion of the Semites. The fundamental institutions.* (Second edition, 1894; Meridian Library, Meridian Books, New York, 1957).

SNAITH, N. H., *The distinctive ideas of the Old Testament.* (Epworth Press, London, 1944).

SODEN, W. VON, *Grundriss der akkadischen Grammatik.* (= Analecta Orientalia, 33; Pontificium Institutum Biblicum, Rome, 1952).

——, *Akkadisches Handwörterbuch.* In progress. (Harrassowitz, Wiesbaden, 1965–).

——, *Ergänzungsheft zum Grundriss der akkadischen Grammatik.* (= Analecta Orientalia, 47; Pontificium Institutum Biblicum, Rome, 1969).

SOLLBERGER, E. and KUPPER, J.-R., *Inscriptions royales sumériennes et akkadiennes.* (Éditions du Cerf, Paris, 1971).

SOURDEL, D., *Les cultes du Hauran à l'époque romaine.* (Imprimerie Nationale, Paris, 1952).

STADELMANN, L. I. J., *The Hebrew conception of the world. A philological and literary study.* (= AnBi 39; Pontifical Biblical Institute, Rome, 1970).

STAMM, J. J., *Die akkadische Namengebung.* (= MVAG 44; Leipzig, 1939).

STRECK, M., *Assurbanipal und die letzten assyrischen Könige bis zum Untergange Niniveh's. I. Teil: Einleitung. II. Teil. Texte: III. Teil: Register.* (= VAB 7; Hinrichs, Leipzig, 1916).

TALLQVIST, K., *Akkadische Götterepitheta mit einem Götterverzeichnis und einer Liste der prädikativen Elemente der sumerischen Götternamen.*

(= *Studia Orientalia* [Societas Orientalis Fennica] VII; Helsinki, 1938).

TERTULLIAN, *The writings of Tertullian*, ed. by A. Roberts and J. Donaldson, vol. 1. (= Ante-Nicene Christian Library, vol. 11; T. & T. Clark, Edinburgh, 1869).

——, *Adversus Marcionem*, ed. by E. Evans. (Clarendon Press, Oxford, 1972).

THOMPSON, R. C., *The devils and evil spirits of Babylonia.* 2 vols. (Luzac, London, 1903, 1904).

——, *The Epic of Gilgamish. Text, transliteration, and notes.* (Clarendon Press, Oxford, 1930).

THUREAU-DANGIN, F., *Une relation de la huitième campagne de Sargon (714 av. J.-C.).* (= *Textes cunéiformes*, Musée du Louvre, 3; Geuthner, Paris, 1912).

——, *Rituels accadiens.* (Leroux, Paris, 1921).

TIELE, C. P., *Outlines of the history of religion to the spread of the universal religions.* Translated by J. E. Carpenter. (English and Foreign Philosophical Library, London, 1877).

UNNIK, W. C. VAN and WOUDE, A. S. VAN DER (edd.), *Studia Biblica et Semitica Theodoro Christiano Vriezen . . . Dedicata.* (Wageningen, 1966).

VAUX, R. DE, *Histoire ancienne d'Israël; des origines à l'installation en Canaan.* (Gabalda, Paris, 1971).

VOEGELIN, E., *Order and history.* Vol. 1: *Israel and revelation.* (Louisiana State University Press, 1956).

VOLLMER, J., *Geschichtliche Rückblicke und Motive in der Prophetie des Amos, Hosea und Jesaja.* (= BZAW 119; de Gruyter, Berlin, 1971).

VOLZ, P., *Das Dämonische in Jahwe.* (J. C. B. Mohr (Paul Siebeck), Tübingen, 1924).

VRIEZEN, T. C., *An outline of Old Testament Theology.* (Blackwell, Oxford, 1958).

——, *The religion of ancient Israel.* Translated by H. Hoskins. (Westminster Press, Philadelphia, Pennsylvania, 1967).

WAARDENBURG, J., *Classical approaches to the study of religion. Aims, methods, and theories of research.* 1: *Introduction and anthology.* (Mouton, The Hague, Paris, 1973).

WAKEMAN, M. K., *God's battle with the Monster. A study in biblical imagery.* (Brill, Leiden, 1973).

WASCHOW, H., *Babylonische Briefe aus der Kassitenzeit.* (= MAOG X/1; 1936).

WATERMAN, L., *Royal correspondence of the Assyrian empire.* 4 vols. (University of Michigan Press, Ann Arbor, 1930–6).

WEIHER, E. VON, *Der babylonische Gott Nergal.* (Butzon & Bercker Kevelaer, Neukirchen-Vluyn, 1971).

WELLHAUSEN, J., *Reste Arabischen Heidenthums gesammelt und erläutert.* (Reimer, Berlin, third edition, 1887).

WESTERMANN, C., *Creation.* Translated by J. J. Scullion. (S.P.C.K., London, 1974).

WIDENGREN, G., *The Accadian and Hebrew Psalms of lamentation as religious documents. A comparative study.* (Almsqvist & Wiksells, Uppsala, 1937).

WINCKLER, H., *Die Keilschrifttexte Sargons nach den Papierabklatschen und Originalen neu herausgegeben.* 2 vols. (Eduard Pfeiffer, Leipzig, 1889).

WISEMAN, D. J., *Chronicles of Chaldaean kings (626–556 B.C.).* (British Museum, London, 1956).

WOLFF, H. W. (ed.), *Probleme biblischer Theologie, Gerhard von Rad zum 70. Geburtstag.* (Chr. Kaiser Verlag, München, 1971).

WRIGHT, G. E., *God who acts. Biblical Theology as recital.* (SCM Press, London, 1952).

WRIGHT, G. E. and FULLER, R. H., *The book of the acts of God.* (Duckworth, London, 1960).

WRIGHT, W., *A grammar of the Arabic language.* Third edition revised by W. R. Smith and M. J. de Goeje. 2 vols. (Cambridge University Press, 1896, 1898, re-issued 1962).

YAMAUCHI, E. M., *Gnostic Ethics and Mandaean origins.* (Harvard University Press, 1970).

ZIMMERLI, W., *Man and his hope in the Old Testament.* (SCM Press, London, 1971).

ZIMMERN, H., *Beiträge zur Kenntnis der babylonischen Religion.* (Hinrichs, Leipzig, 1901).

GENERAL INDEX

INDEX OF BIBLICAL REFERENCES